The Humbugs of the World

The Humbugs of the World

An Account of the Humbugs, Delusions, Impositions,
Quackeries, Deceits and Deceivers Generally, in All Ages

P. T. Barnum

Waking Lion Press

ISBN 978-1-4341-0595-0

Published by Waking Lion Press, an imprint of the Editorium

Waking Lion Press™ and Editorium™ are trademarks of:

The Editorium, LLC
West Jordan, UT 84081-6132
www.editorium.com

Contents

Publisher's Note   xv

Introduction   xix

I   Personal Reminiscences   1

1   General view of the Subject—Humbug universal—
     In religion—In politics—In business—In science—
     In medicine—How is it to cease—The greatest
     humbug of all.   3

2   Definition of the word humbug—Warren of
     London—Genin, The hatter—Gosling's blacking.   10

3   Monsieur Mangin, the French humbug.   21

4   Old Grizzly Adams.   29

5   The golden pigeons—Grizzly Adams—German
     chemist—Happy family—French naturalist.   38

6   The whale, the angel fish, and the golden pigeon.   44

7   Pease's hoarhound candy—the Dorr rebellion—
The Philadelphia aldermen.   48

8   Brandreth's pills—Magnificent advertising—
Power of imagination.   56

II   **The Spiritualists**   **63**

9   The Davenport brothers, their rise and progress—
Spiritual rope-tying—Music playing—Cabinet
secrets—"They choose darkness rather than
light," etc.—The spiritual hand—How the thing
is done—Dr. W. F. Van Vleck.   65

10   The spirit-rapping and medium humbugs—Their
origin—How the thing is done—$500 reward.   74

11   The "ballot-test"—The old gentleman and
his "diseased" relatives—A "hungry spirit"—
"Palming" a ballot—Revelations on strips of paper. 80

12   Spiritual "letters on the arm"—How to make
them yourself—The tambourine and ring feats—
Dexter's dancing hats—Phosphorescent oil—
Some spiritual slang.   88

13   Demonstrations by "Sampson" under a table—A
medium who is handy with her feet—Exposé of
another operator in dark circles.   94

14   Spiritual photographing—Colorado Jewett and the spirit-photographs of General Jackson, Henry Clay, Daniel Webster, Stephen A. Douglas, Napoleon Bonaparte, etc—A lady of distinction seeks and finds a spiritual photograph of her deceased infant, and her dead braother who was yet alive—How it was done.   101

15   Banner of Light—Messages from the dead— Spiritual civilities—Spirit "hollering"—Hans von Vleet, the female Dutchman—Mrs. Conant's "circles"—Paine's table-tipping humbug exposed.   111

16   Spiritualist humbugs waking up—Foster heard from—S. B. Brittan heard from—The Boston artists and their spiritual portraits—The Washington medium and his spiritual hands—The Davenport brothers and the sea-captain's wheat-flour— The Davenport brothers roughly shown up by John Bull—How a shingle "stumped" the spirits.   122

17   The Davenport brothers shown up once more— Dr. Newton at Chicago—The spiritualist bogus baby—A lady brings forth a motive force— "Gum" arabic—Spiritualist hebrew—The Allen boy—Dr. Randall—Portland Evening Courier— The fools not all dead yet.   130

III   Trade and Business Impositions   143

18   Adulterations of food—Adulterations of liquor—
The colonel's whiskey—The humbugometer.   145

19   Adulterations in drinks—Riding home on your
wine-barrel—List of things to make rum—Things
to color it with—Canal-boat hash—English adulteration law—Effects of drugs used—How to use
them—Buying liquors under the customhouse
lock—A homeoopathic dose.   153

20   The Peter Funks and their functions—The rural
divine and the watch—Rise and progress of mock
auctions—Their decline and fall.   160

21   Lottery sharks—Boult and his brothers—Kenneth,
Kimball and Company—A more central loca-
tion wanted for business—Two seventeenth lies—
Strange coincidence.   168

22   Another lottery humbug—Two hundred and
fifty recipes—Vile books—"Advantage-cards"—
A package for you; Please send the money—
Peddling in western New York.   175

23   A California coal mine—A Hartford coal mine—
Mysterious subterranean canal on the isthmus.   182

IV **Money Manias**   **187**

24   The petroleum humbug—The New York and Rangoon Petroleum Company.   189

25   The Tulipomania.   198

26   John Bull's great money humbug—The south sea bubble in 1720.   208

27   Business humbugs—John Law—The Mississippi scheme—Johnny Crapaud as greedy as Johnny Bull.   215

V   **Medicine and Quacks**   **225**

28   Doctors And imagination—Firing a joke out of a cannon—The Paris eye water—Majendie on medical knowledge—Old sands of life.   227

29   The consumptive remedy—E. Andrews, M.D.— Born without birthrights—Hasheesh candy— Roback the Great—A conjurer opposed to lying. 232

30   Monsignore Cristoforo Rischio; or, Il Creso, the nostrum-vender of Florence—A model for our quack doctors.   238

VI   Hoaxes   **245**

31   The Twenty-Seventh Street ghost—Spirits on ohe
       rampage.   247

32   The moon-hoax.   255

33   The miscegenation hoax—A great literary
       sell—Political humbugging—Tricks of the wire-
       pullers—Machinery employed to render the pam-
       phlet notorious—Who were sold and how it was
       done.   269

VII   Ghosts and Witchcrafts   **281**

34   Haunted houses—A night spent alone with a
       ghost—Kirby, the actor—Colt's pistols versus
       hobgoblins—The mystery explained.   283

35   Haunted houses—Ghosts—Ghouls—Phantoms—
       Vampires—Conjurors—Divining—   Goblins—
       Fortune-telling—Magic—Witches—Sorcery—
       Obi—Dreams— Signs—Spiritual mediums—
       False prophets—Demonology—Deviltry generally. 292

36   Magical humbugs—Virgil—A pickled sorcerer—
       Cornelius Agrippa—His students and his
       black   dog—Doctor   Faustus—Humbugging
       horse-jockeys—Ziito and his large swallow—
       Salamanca—Devil take the hindmost.   300

37 Witchcraft—New York witches—The Witch
    mania—How fast they burned them—The mode
    of trial—Witches today in Europe.   307

38 Charms and incantations—How Cato cured
    sprains—The secret name of God—Secret
    names of cities—Abracadabra—Cures for cramp—
    Mr. Wright's sigil—Whiskerifusticus—Witches'
    horses—Their curses—How to raise the devil.   313

VIII **Adventurers**   **323**

39 The Princess Cariboo; or, The Queen Of The Isles. 325

40 Count Cagliostro, alias Joseph Balsamo, known
    also as "Cursed Joe."   332

41 The diamond necklace.   339

42 The Count de St. Germain, sage, prophet, and
    magician.   355

43 Riza Bey, the Persian envoy to Louis XIV. 362

IX **Religious Humbugs**   **371**

44 Diamond cut diamond; or, yankee superstitions—
    Matthias the impostor—New York follies thirty
    years ago.   373

45   A religious humbug on John Bull—Joanna
      Southcott—The second Shiloh.   383

46   The first humbug in the world—Advantages
      of studying the impositions of former ages—
      Heathen humbugs—The ancient mysteries—The
      cabiri—Eleusis—Isis.   389

47   Heathen humbugs No. 2—Heathen stated
      services—Oracles—Sibyls—Auguries.   395

48   Modern heathen humbugs—Fetishism—Obi—
      Vaudoux—Indian   powwows—Lamaism—
      Revolving prayers—Praying to death.   403

49   Ordeals—Duels—Wager of battle—Abraham
      Thornton—Red   hot   iron—Boiling   water—
      Swimming—Swearing—Corsned—Pagan ordeals. 410

50   Apollonius of Tyana.   417

"Omne Ignotum Pro Mirifico."—Wonderful, Because Mysterious."

Publisher's Note

One of Mr. Barnum's secrets of success is his unique methods of advertising, and we can readily understand how he can bear to be denounced as a "Humbug," because this popular designation though undeserved in the popular acceptation of it, "brought grist to his mill." He has constantly kept himself before the public—nay, we may say that he has *been* kept before the public constantly, by the stereotyped word in question; and what right, or what desire, could he have to discard or complain of an epithet which was one of the prospering elements of his business as "a showman?" In a narrow sense of the word he is a "Humbug:" in the larger acceptation he is *not*.

He has in several chapters of this book elaborated the distinction, and we will only say in this place, what, indeed, no one who knows him will doubt, that, aside from his qualities as a caterer to popular entertainment, he is one of the most remarkable men of the age. As a business man, of far-reaching vision and singular executive force, he has for years been the life of Bridgeport, near which city he has long resided, and last winter he achieved high rank in the Legislature of Connecticut, as both an effective speaker and a patriot, having "no axe to grind," and seeking only the public welfare. We, indeed, agree with the editor of *The New York*

Independent, who, in an article drawn out by the burning of the American Museum, says: "Mr. Barnum's rare talent as a speaker has always been exercised in behalf of good morals, and for patriotic objects. No man has done better service in the temperance cause by public lectures during the past ten years, both in America and Great Britain, and during the war he was most efficient in stimulating the spirit which resulted in the preservation of the Union, and the destruction of Slavery."

We cannot forbear quoting two or three additional paragraphs from that article, especially as they are so strongly expressive of the merits of the case:

"Mr. Barnum's whole career has been a very transparent one. He has never befooled the public to its injury, and, though his name has come to be looked upon as a synonym for humbuggery, there never was a public man who was less of one.

"The hearty good wishes of many good men, and the sympathies of the community in which he has lived, go with him, and the public he has so long amused, but never abused, will be ready to sustain him whenever he makes another appeal to them. Mr. Barnum is a very good sort of representative Yankee. When crowds of English traders and manufacturers in Liverpool, Manchester, and London, flocked to hear his lectures on the art of making money, they expected to hear from him some very smart recipes for knavery; but they were as much astonished as they were edified to learn that the only secret he had to tell them was to be honest, and not to expect something for nothing."

We could fill many pages with quotations of corresponding tenor from the leading and most influential men and journals in the land, but we will close this publisher's note with the following from the *N.Y. Sun*.

"One of the happiest impromptu oratorical efforts that we have heard for some time was that made by Barnum at the benefit performance given for his employees on Friday afternoon. If a stranger wanted to satisfy himself how the great showman had managed so to monopolize the ear and eye of the public during his long career he could not have had a better opportunity of doing so than by listening to this address. Every word, though delivered with apparent carelessness, struck a keynote in the hearts of his listeners. Simple, forcible, and touching, it showed how thoroughly this extraordinary man comprehends the character of his countrymen, and how easily he can play upon their feelings.

"Those who look upon Barnum as a mere charlatan, have really no knowledge of him. It would be easy to demonstrate that the qualities that have placed him in his present position of notoriety and affluence would, in another pursuit, have raised him to far greater eminence. In his breadth of views, his profound knowledge of mankind, his courage under reverses, his indomitable perseverance, his ready eloquence, and his admirable business tact, we recognise the elements that are conducive to success in most other pursuits. More than almost any other living man, Barnum may be said to be a representative type of the American mind."

Introduction

In the *Autobiography of P. T. Barnum*, published in 1855, I partly promised to write a book which should expose some of the chief humbugs of the world. The invitation of my friends Messrs. Cauldwell and Whitney of the *Weekly Mercury* caused me to furnish for that paper a series of articles in which I very naturally took up the subject in question. This book is a revision and rearrangement of a portion of those articles. If I should find that I have met a popular demand, I shall in due time put forth a second volume. There is not the least danger of a dearth of materials.

I once travelled through the Southern States in company with a magician. The first day in each town, he astonished his auditors with his deceptions. He then announced that on the following day he would show how each trick was performed, and how every man might thus become his own magician. That exposé spoiled the legerdemain market on that particular route, for several years. So, if we could have a full exposure of "the tricks of trade" of all sorts, of humbugs and deceivers of past times, religious, political, financial, scientific, quackish and so forth, we might perhaps look for a somewhat wiser generation to follow us. I shall be well satisfied if I can do something towards so good a purpose.

Part I

PERSONAL REMINISCENCES

Chapter 1

*General view of the Subject—Humbug universal—In
religion—In politics—In business—In science—In
medicine—How is it to cease—The greatest humbug of
all.*

A little reflection will show that humbug is an astonishingly
widespread phenomenon—in fact almost universal. And this
is true, although we exclude crimes and arrant swindles
from the definition of it, according to the somewhat careful
explanation which is given in the beginning of the chapter
succeeding this one.

I apprehend that there is no sort of object which men
seek to attain, whether secular, moral or religious, in which
humbug is not very often an instrumentality. Religion is and
has ever been a chief chapter of human life. False religions
are the only ones known to two thirds of the human race,
even now, after nineteen centuries of Christianity; and false
religions are perhaps the most monstrous, complicated and
thoroughgoing specimens of humbug that can be found. And
even within the pale of Christianity, how unbroken has been
the succession of impostors, hypocrites and pretenders, male
and female, of every possible variety of age, sex, doctrine
and discipline!

Politics and government are certainly among the most important of practical human interests. Now it was a diplomatist—that is, a practical manager of one kind of government matters—who invented that wonderful phrase— a whole world full of humbug in half-a-dozen words—that "Language was given to us to conceal our thoughts." It was another diplomatist, who said "An ambassador is a gentleman sent to *lie* abroad for the good of his country." But need I explain to my own beloved countrymen that there is humbug in politics? Does anybody go into a political campaign without it? are no exaggerations of *our* candidate's merits to be allowed? no depreciations of the *other* candidate? Shall we no longer prove that the success of the party opposed to us will overwhelm the land in ruin? Let me see. Leaving out the two elections of General Washington, eighteen times that very fact has been proved by the party that was beaten, and immediately we have *not* been ruined, notwithstanding that the dreadful fatal fellows on the other side got their hands on the offices and their fingers into the treasury.

Business is the ordinary means of living for nearly all of us. And in what business is there not humbug? "There's cheating in all trades but ours," is the prompt reply from the boot-maker with his brown paper soles, the grocer with his floury sugar and chicoried coffee, the butcher with his mysterious sausages and queer veal, the dry goods man with his "damaged goods wet at the great fire" and his "selling at a ruinous loss," the stockbroker with his brazen assurance that your company is bankrupt and your stock not worth a cent (if he wants to buy it,) the horse jockey with his black arts and spavined brutes, the milkman with his tin aquaria, the land agent with his nice new maps and beautiful descriptions of distant scenery, the newspaper man with his "immense circulation," the publisher with his "Great American Novel," the city auctioneer with his "Pictures by the Old Masters"— all and everyone protest each his own innocence, and warn you against the deceits of the rest. My inexperienced friend, take it for granted that they all tell the truth—about each other! and then transact your business to the best of your ability on your own judgment. Never fear but that you will get experience enough, and that you will pay well for it too; and towards the time when you shall no longer need earthly goods, you will begin to know how to buy.

Literature is one of the most interesting and significant expressions of humanity. Yet books are thickly peppered with humbug. "Travellers' stories" have been the scoff of ages, from the "True Story" of witty old Lucian the Syrian down to the gorillarities—if I may coin a word—of the Frenchman Du Chaillu. Ireland's counterfeited Shakespeare plays, Chatterton's forged manuscripts, George Psalmanazar's forged Formosan language, Jo Smith's Mormon Bible, (it should be noted that this and the Koran sounded two strings of humbug together—the literary and the religious,) the more recent counterfeits of the notorious Greek Simonides—such literary humbugs as these are equal in presumption and in ingenuity too, to any of a merely business kind, though usually destitute of that sort of impiety which makes the great religious humbugs horrible as well as impudent.

Science is another important field of human effort. Science is the pursuit of pure truth, and the systematizing of it. In such an employment as that, one might reasonably hope to find all things done in honesty and sincerity. Not at all, my ardent and inquiring friends, there is a scientific humbug just as large as any other. We have all heard of the Moon Hoax. Do none of you remember the *Hydrarchos Sillimannii*, that awful Alabama snake? It was only a little while ago that a grave account appeared in a newspaper of a whole new business of compressing ice. Perpetual motion has been the dream of scientific visionaries, and a pretended but cheating realization of it has been exhibited by scamp after scamp. I understand that one is at this moment being invented over in Jersey City. I have purchased more than one "perpetual motion" myself. Many persons will remember Mr. Paine— The Great Shot-at" as he was called, from his story that people were constantly trying to kill him—and his water-gas. There have been other water gases too, which were each going to show us how to set the North River on fire, but something or other has always broken down just at the wrong moment. Nobody seems to reflect, when these water gases come up, that if water could really be made to burn, the right conditions would surely have happened at some one of the thousands of city fires, and that the very stuff with which our stout firemen were extinguishing the flames, would have itself caught and exterminated the whole brave wet crowd!

Medicine is the means by which we poor feeble creatures try to keep from dying or aching. In a world so full of pain it would seem as if people could not be so foolish, or practitioners so knavish, as to sport with men's and women's and children's lives by their professional humbugs. Yet there are many grave M.D.'s who, if there is nobody to hear, and if they speak their minds, will tell you plainly that the whole practice of medicine is in one sense a humbug. One of its features is certainly a humbug, though so innocent and even useful that it seems difficult to think of any objection to it.

This is the practice of giving a *placebo*; that is, a bread pill or a dose of colored water, to keep the patient's mind easy while imagination helps nature to perfect a cure. As for the quacks, patent medicines and universal remedies, I need only mention their names. Prince Hohenlohe, Valentine Greatrakes, John St. John Long, Doctor Graham and his wonderful bed, Mesmer and his tub, Perkins' metallic tractors—these are half a dozen. Modern history knows of hundreds of such.

It would almost seem as if human delusions became more unreasoning and abject in proportion as their subject is of greater importance. A machine, a story, an animal skeleton, are not so very important. But the humbugs which have prevailed about that wondrous machine, the human body, its ailments and its cures, about the unspeakable mystery of human life, and still more about the far greater and more awful mysteries of the life beyond the grave, and the endless happiness and misery believed to exist there, the humbugs about these have been infinitely more absurd, more shocking, more unreasonable, more inhuman, more destructive.

I can only allude to whole sciences (falsely so called) which are unmingled humbugs from beginning to end. Such was Alchemy, such was Magic, such was and still is Astrology, and above all, Fortune-telling.

But there is a more thorough humbug than any of these enterprises or systems. The greatest humbug of all is the man who believes—or pretends to believe—that everything and everybody are humbugs. We sometimes meet a person who professes that there is no virtue; that every man has his price, and every woman hers; that any statement from anybody is just as likely to be false as true, and that the only way to decide which, is to consider whether truth or a lie was likely to have paid best in that particular case. Religion he thinks one of the smartest business dodges extant, a first rate investment, and by all odds the most respectable disguise that a lying or swindling business man can wear. Honor he thinks is a sham. Honesty he considers a plausible word to flourish in the eyes of the greener portion of our race, as you would hold out a cabbage leaf to coax a donkey. What people want, he thinks, or says he thinks, is something good to eat, something good to drink, fine clothes, luxury, laziness, wealth. If you can imagine a hog's mind in a man's body—sensual, greedy, selfish, cruel, cunning, sly, coarse, yet stupid, shortsighted, unreasoning, unable to comprehend anything except what concerns the flesh, you have your man. He thinks himself philosophic and practical, a man of the world; he thinks to show knowledge and wisdom, penetration, deep acquaintance with men and things. Poor fellow! he has exposed his own nakedness. Instead of showing that others are rotten inside, he has proved that he is. He claims that it is not safe to believe others—it is perfectly safe to disbelieve him. He claims that every man will get the better of you if possible—let him alone! Selfishness, he says, is the universal rule—leave nothing to depend on his generosity or honor; trust him just as far as you can sling an elephant by the tail. A bad world, he sneers, full of deceit and nastiness—it is his own foul breath that he smells; only a thoroughly corrupt heart could suggest such vile thoughts. He sees only what suits him, as a turkey-buzzard spies only carrion, though amid the loveliest landscape. I pronounce him who thus virtually slanders his father and dishonors his mother and defiles the sanctities of home and the glory of patriotism and the merchant's honor and the martyr's grave and the saint's crown—who does not even know that every sham shows that there is a reality, and that hypocrisy is the homage that vice pays to virtue—I pronounce him—no, I do not pronounce him a humbug, the word does not apply to him. He is a fool.

Looked at on one side, the history of humbug is truly humiliating to intellectual pride, yet the long silly story is less absurd during the later ages of history, and grows less and less so in proportion to the spread of real Christianity. This religion promotes good sense, actual knowledge, contentment with what we cannot help, and the exclusive use of intelligent means for increasing human happiness and decreasing human sorrow. And whenever the time shall come when men are kind and just and honest; when they only want what is fair and right, judge only on real and true evidence, and take nothing for granted, then there will be no place left for any humbugs, either harmless or hurtful.

Chapter 2

Definition of the word humbug—Warren of London—Genin, The hatter—Gosling's blacking.

Upon a careful consideration of my undertaking to give an account of the "Humbugs of the World," I find myself somewhat puzzled in regard to the true definition of that word. To be sure, Webster says that humbug, as a noun, is an "imposition under fair pretences;" and as a verb, it is "to deceive; to impose on." With all due deference to Doctor Webster, I submit that, according to present usage, this is not the only, nor even the generally accepted definition of that term.

We will suppose, for instance, that a man with "fair pretences" applies to a wholesale merchant for credit on a large bill of goods. His "fair pretences" comprehend an assertion that he is a moral and religious man, a member of the church, a man of wealth, etc., etc. It turns out that he is not worth a dollar, but is a base, lying wretch, an impostor and a cheat. He is arrested and imprisoned "for obtaining property under false pretences" or, as Webster says, "fair pretences." He is punished for his villainy. The public do not call him a "humbug;" they very properly term him a swindler.

A man, bearing the appearance of a gentleman in dress

and manners, purchases property from you, and with "fair pretences" obtains your confidence. You find, when he has left, that he paid you with counterfeit banknotes, or a forged draft. This man is justly called a "forger," or "counterfeiter;" and if arrested, he is punished as such; but nobody thinks of calling him a "humbug."

A respectable-looking man sits by your side in an omnibus or rail-car. He converses fluently, and is evidently a man of intelligence and reading. He attracts your attention by his "fair pretences." Arriving at your journey's end, you miss your watch and your pocketbook. Your fellow passenger proves to be the thief. Everybody calls him a "pickpocket," and not withstanding his "fair pretences," not a person in the community calls him a "humbug."

Two actors appear as stars at two rival theatres. They are equally talented, equally pleasing. One advertises himself simply as a tragedian, under his proper name—the other boasts that he is a prince, and wears decorations presented by all the potentates of the world, including the "King of the Cannibal Islands." He is correctly set down as a "humbug," while this term is never applied to the other actor. But if the man who boasts of having received a foreign title is a miserable actor, and he gets up gift-enterprises and bogus entertainments, or pretends to devote the proceeds of his tragic efforts to some charitable object, without, in fact, doing so—he is then a humbug in Dr. Webster's sense of that word, for he is an "impostor under fair pretences."

Two physicians reside in one of our fashionable avenues. They were both educated in the best medical colleges; each has passed an examination, received his diploma, and been dubbed an M.D. They are equally skilled in the healing art.

One rides quietly about the city in his gig or brougham, visiting his patients without noise or clamor—the other sallies out in his coach and four, preceded by a band of music, and his carriage and horses are covered with handbills and placards, announcing his "wonderful cures." This man is properly called a quack and a humbug. Why? Not because he cheats or imposes upon the public, for he does not, but because, as generally understood, "humbug" consists in putting on glittering appearances—outside show—novel expedients, by which to suddenly arrest public attention, and attract the public eye and ear.

Clergymen, lawyers, or physicians, who should resort to such methods of attracting the public, would not, for obvious reasons, be apt to succeed. Bankers, insurance-agents, and others, who aspire to become the custodians of the money of their fellow-men, would require a different species of advertising from this; but there are various trades and occupations which need only notoriety to insure success, always provided that when customers are once attracted, they never fail to get their money's worth. An honest man who thus arrests public attention will be called a "humbug," but he is not a swindler or an impostor. If, however, after attracting crowds of customers by his unique displays, a man foolishly fails to give them a full equivalent for their money, they never patronize him a second time, but they very properly denounce him as a swindler, a cheat, an impostor; they do not, however, call him a "humbug." He fails, not because he advertises his wares in an outré manner, but because, after attracting crowds of patrons, he stupidly and wickedly cheats them.

When the great blacking-maker of London dispatched his agent to Egypt to write on the pyramids of Ghiza, in huge letters, "Buy Warren's Blacking, 30 Strand, London," he was not "cheating" travelers upon the Nile. His blacking was really a superior article, and well worth the price charged for it, but he was "humbugging" the public by this queer way of arresting attention. It turned out just as he anticipated, that English travelers in that part of Egypt were indignant at this desecration, and they wrote back to the *London Times* (every Englishman writes or threatens to "write to the *Times*," if anything goes wrong,) denouncing the "Goth" who had thus disfigured these ancient pyramids by writing on them in monstrous letters: "Buy Warren's Blacking, 30 Strand, London." The *Times* published these letters, and backed them up by several of those awful, grand and dictatorial editorials peculiar to the great "Thunderer," in which the blacking-maker, "Warren, 30 Strand," was stigmatized as a man who had no respect for the ancient patriarchs, and it was hinted that he would probably not hesitate to sell his blacking on the sarcophagus of Pharaoh, "or any other"—mummy, if he could only make money by it. In fact, to cap the climax, Warren was denounced as a "humbug." These indignant articles were copied into all the Provincial journals, and very soon, in this manner, the columns of every newspaper in Great Britain were teeming with this advice: "Try Warren's Blacking, 30 Strand, London." The curiosity of the public was thus aroused, and they did "try" it, and finding it a superior article, they continued to purchase it and recommend it to their friends, and Warren made a fortune by it. He always attributed his success to his having "humbugged" the public by this unique method of advertising his blacking in Egypt! But Warren did not cheat his customers, nor practice "an imposition under fair pretences." He was a humbug, but he was an honest upright man, and no one called him an impostor or a cheat.

When the tickets for Jenny Lind's first concert in America were sold at auction, several businessmen, aspiring to notoriety, "bid high" for the first ticket. It was finally knocked down to "Genin, the hatter," for $225. The journals in Portland (Maine) and Houston (Texas), and all other journals throughout the United States, between these two cities, which were connected with the telegraph, announced the fact in their columns the next morning. Probably two millions of readers read the announcement, and asked, "Who is Genin, the hatter?" Genin became famous in a day. Every man involuntarily examined his hat, to see if it was made by Genin; and an Iowa editor declared that one of his neighbors discovered the name of Genin in his old hat and immediately announced the fact to his neighbors in front of the Post Office. It was suggested that the old hat should be sold at auction. It was done then and there, and the Genin hat sold for fourteen dollars! Gentlemen from city and country rushed to Genin's store to buy their hats, many of them willing to pay even an extra dollar, if necessary, provided they could get a glimpse of Genin himself. This singular freak put thousands of dollars into the pocket of "Genin, the hatter," and yet I never heard it charged that he made poor hats, or that he would be guilty of an "imposition under fair pretences." On the contrary, he is a gentleman of probity, and of the first respectability.

When the laying of the Atlantic Telegraph was nearly completed, I was in Liverpool. I offered the company one thousand pounds sterling ($5,000) for the privilege of sending the first twenty words over the cable to my Museum in New York—not that there was any intrinsic merit in the words, but that I fancied there was more than $5,000 worth of notoriety in the operation. But Queen Victoria and "Old Buck" were ahead of me. Their messages had the preference, and I was compelled to "take a back seat."

By thus illustrating what I believe the public will concede to be the sense in which the word "humbug" is generally used and understood at the present time, in this country as well as in England, I do not propose that my letters on this subject shall be narrowed down to that definition of the word. On the contrary, I expect to treat of various fallacies, delusions, and deceptions in ancient and modern times, which, according to Webster's definition, may be called "humbugs," inasmuch as they were "impositions under fair pretences."

In writing of modern humbugs, however, I shall sometimes have occasion to give the names of honest and respectable parties now living, and I felt it but just that the public should fully comprehend my doctrine, that a man may, by common usage, be termed a "humbug," without by any means impeaching his integrity.

Speaking of "blacking-makers," reminds me that one of the first sensationists in advertising whom I remember to have seen, was Mr. Leonard Gosling, known as "Monsieur Gosling, the great French blacking-maker." He appeared in New York in 1830. He flashed like a meteor across the horizon; and before he had been in the city three months, nearly everybody had heard of "Gosling's Blacking." I well remember his magnificent "four in hand." A splendid team of blood bays, with long black tails, was managed with such dexterity by Gosling himself, who was a great "whip," that they almost seemed to fly. The carriage was emblazoned with the words "Gosling's Blacking," in large gold letters, and the whole turnout was so elaborately ornamented and bedizened that everybody stopped and gazed with wondering admiration. A bugle-player or a band of music always accompanied the great Gosling, and, of course, helped to attract the public attention to his establishment. At the turning of every street-corner your eyes rested upon "Gosling's Blacking." From every show-window gilded placards discoursed eloquently of the merits of "Gosling's Blacking." The newspapers teemed with poems written in its praise, and showers of pictorial handbills, illustrated almanacs, and tinseled souvenirs, all lauding the virtues of "Gosling's Blacking," smothered you at every point.

The celebrated originator of delineations, "Jim Crow Rice," made his first appearance at Hamblin's Bowery Theatre at about this time. The crowds which thronged there were so great that hundreds from the audience were frequently ad-mitted upon the stage. In one of his scenes, Rice introduced a negro boot-blacking establishment. Gosling was too "wide awake" to let such an opportunity pass unimproved, and Rice was paid for singing an original black Gosling ditty, while a score of placards bearing the inscription, "Use Gosling's Blacking," were suspended at different points in this negro boot polishing hall. Everybody tried "Gosling's Blacking;" and as it was a really good article, his sales in city and country soon became immense; Gosling made a fortune in seven years, and retired but, as with thousands before him, it was "easy come easy go." He engaged in a lead-mining speculation, and it was generally understood that his fortune was, in a great measure, lost as rapidly as it was made.

Here let me digress, in order to observe that one of the most difficult things in life is for men to bear discreetly sudden prosperity. Unless considerable time and labor are devoted to earning money, it is not appreciated by its possessor; and, having no practical knowledge of the value of money, he generally gets rid of it with the same ease that marked its accumulation. Mr. Astor gave the experience of thousands when he said that he found more difficulty in earning and saving his first thousand dollars than in accumulating all the subsequent millions which finally made up his fortune. The very economy, perseverance, and discipline which he was obliged to practice, as he gained his money dollar by dollar, gave him a just appreciation of its value, and thus led him into those habits of industry, prudence, temperance, and untiring diligence so conducive and necessary to his future success.

Mr. Gosling, however, was not a man to be put down by a single financial reverse. He opened a store in Canajoharie, N.Y., which was burned, and on which there was no insurance. He came again to New York in 1839, and established a restaurant, where, by devoting the services of himself and several members of his family assiduously to the business, he soon reveled in his former prosperity, and snapped his fingers in glee at what unreflecting persons term "the freaks of Dame Fortune." He is still living in New York, hale and hearty at the age of seventy. Although called a "French" blacking-maker, Mr. Gosling is in reality a Dutchman, having been born in the city of Amsterdam, Holland. He is the father of twenty-four children, twelve of whom are still living, to cheer him in his declining years, and to repay him in grateful attentions for the valuable lessons of prudence, integrity, and industry through the adoption of which they are honored as respectable and worthy members of society.

I cannot however permit this chapter to close without recording a protest in principle against that method of advertising of which Warren's on the Pyramid is an instance. Not that it is a crime or even an immorality in the usual sense of the words; but it is a violent offense against good taste, and a selfish and inexcusable destruction of other people's enjoyments. No man ought to advertise in the midst of landscapes or scenery, in such a way as to destroy or injure their beauty by introducing totally incongruous and relatively vulgar associations. Too many transactions of the sort have been perpetrated in our own country. The principle on which the thing is done is, to seek out the most attractive spot possible—the wildest, the most lovely, and there, in the most staring and brazen manner to paint up advertisements of quack medicines, rum, or as the case may be, in letters of monstrous size, in the most obtrusive colors, in such a prominent place, and in such a lasting way as to destroy the beauty of the scene both thoroughly and permanently.

Any man with a beautiful wife or daughter would probably feel disagreeably, if he should find branded indelibly across her smooth white forehead, or on her snowy shoulder in blue and red letters such a phrase as this: "Try the Jigamaree Bitters!" Very much like this is the sort of advertising I am speaking of. It is not likely that I shall be charged with squeamishness on this question. I can readily enough see the selfishness and vulgarity of this particular sort of advertising, however.

It is outrageously selfish to destroy the pleasure of thousands, for the sake of a chance of additional gain. And it is an atrocious piece of vulgarity to flaunt the names of quack nostrums, and of the coarse stimulants of sots, among the beautiful scenes of nature. The pleasure of such places depends upon their freedom from the associations of every-day concerns and troubles and weaknesses. A lovely nook of forest scenery, or a grand rock, like a beautiful woman, depends for much of its attractiveness upon the attendant sense of freedom from whatever is low; upon a sense of purity and of romance. And it is about as nauseous to find "Bitters" or "Worm Syrup" daubed upon the landscape, as it would be upon the lady's brow.

Since writing this I observe that two legislatures—those of New Hampshire and New York—have passed laws to prevent this dirty misdemeanor. It is greatly to their credit, and it is in good season. For it is matter of wonder that some more colossal vulgarian has not stuck up a sign a mile long on the Palisades. But it is matter of thankfulness too. At the White Mountains, many grand and beautiful views have been spoiled by these nostrum and bedbug souled fellows.

It is worth noticing that the chief haunts of the city of New York, the Central Park, has thus far remained unvio-lated by the dirty hands of these vulgar advertisers. Without knowing anything about it, I have no doubt whatever that the commissioners have been approached often by parties desiring the privilege of advertising within its limits. Among the advertising fraternity it would be thought a gigantic op-portunity to be able to flaunt the name of some bug-poison, fly-killer, bowel-rectifier, or disguised rum, along the walls of the Reservoir; upon the delicate stonework of the Terrace, or the graceful lines of the Bow Bridge; to nail up a tin sign on every other tree, to stick one up right in front of every seat; to keep a gang of young wretches thrusting pamphlet or handbill into every person's palm that enters the gate, to paint a vulgar sign across every gray rock; to cut quack words in ditch-work in the smooth green turf of the mall or ball-ground. I have no doubt that it is the peremptory decision and clear good taste of the Commissioners alone, which have kept this last retreat of nature within our crowded city from being long ago plastered and daubed with placards, hand-bills, signboards and paint, from side to side and from end to end, over turf, tree, rock, wall, bridge, archway, building and all.

Chapter 3

Monsieur Mangin, the French humbug.

One of the most original, unique, and successful humbugs of the present day was the late Monsieur Mangin, the blacklead pencil maker of Paris. Few persons who have visited the French capital within the last ten or twelve years can have failed to have seen him, and once seen he was not to be forgotten. While passing through the public streets, there was nothing in his personal appearance to distinguish him from any ordinary gentlemen. He drove a pair of bay horses, attached to an open carriage with two seats, the back one always occupied by his valet. Sometimes he would take up his stand in the Champs Élysées; at other times, near the column in the Place Vendôme; but usually he was seen in the afternoon in the Place de la Bastille, or the Place de la Madeleine. On Sundays, his favorite locality was the Place de la Bourse. Mangin was a well-formed, stately-looking individual, with a most self-satisfied countenance, which seemed to say: "I am master here; and all that my auditors have to do is, to listen and obey." Arriving at his destined stopping-place, his carriage halted. His servant handed him a case from which he took several large portraits of himself, which he hung prominently upon the sides of his carriage, and also placed in front of him a vase filled with medals bearing his likeness on one side and a description of his pencils on the other. He then leisurely commenced a change of costume. His round hat was displaced by a magnificent burnished helmet, mounted with rich plumes of various brilliant colors. His overcoat was laid aside, and he donned in its stead a costly velvet tunic with gold fringes. He then drew a pair of polished steel gauntlets upon his hands, covered his breast with a brilliant cuirass, and placed a richly-mounted sword at his side. His servant watched him closely, and upon receiving a sign from his master, he too put on his official costume, which consisted of a velvet robe and a helmet. The servant then struck up a tune on the richly-toned organ which always formed a part of Mangin's outfit. The grotesque appearance of these individuals, and the music, soon drew together an admiring crowd.

Then the great charlatan stood upon his feet. His manner was calm, dignified, imposing, indeed almost solemn, for his face was as serious as that of the chief mourner at a funeral. His sharp, intelligent eye scrutinized the throng which was pressing around his carriage, until it rested apparently upon some particular individual, when he gave a start; then, with a dark, angry expression, as if the sight was repulsive, he abruptly dropped the visor of his helmet and thus covered his face from the gaze of the anxious crowd. This bit of coquetry produced the desired effect in whetting the appetite of the multitude, who were impatiently waiting to hear him speak. When he had carried this kind of byplay as far as he thought the audience would bear it, he raised his hand, and his servant understanding the sign, stopped the organ. Mangin then rang a small bell, stepped forward to the front of the carriage, gave a slight cough indicative of a preparation to speak, opened his mouth, but instantly giving a more fearful start and assuming a more sudden frown than before, he took his seat as if quite overcome by some unpleasant object which his eyes had rested upon. Thus far he had not spoken a word. At last the prelude ended, and the comedy commenced. Stepping forward again to the front of his carriage where all the gaping crowd could catch every word, he exclaimed:

"Gentlemen, you look astonished! You seem to wonder and ask yourselves who is this modern Quixote. What mean this costume of bygone centuries—this golden chariot—these richly caparisoned steeds? What is the name and purpose of this curious knight-errant? Gentlemen, I will condescend to answer your queries. I am Monsieur Mangin, the great charlatan of France! Yes, gentlemen, I am a charlatan—a mountebank; it is my profession, not from choice, but from necessity. You, gentlemen, created that necessity! You would not patronize true, unpretending, honest merit, but you are attracted by my glittering casque, my sweeping crest, my waving plumes. You are captivated by din and glitter, and therein lies my strength. Years ago, I hired a modest shop in the Rue Rivoli, but I could not sell pencils enough to pay my rent, whereas, by assuming this disguise—it is nothing else—I have succeeded in attracting general attention, and in selling literally millions of my pencils; and I assure you there is at this moment scarcely an artist in France or in Great Britain who don't know that I manufacture by far the best blacklead pencils ever seen."

And this assertion was indeed true. His pencils were everywhere acknowledged to be superior to any other.

While he was thus addressing his audience, he would take

a blank card, and with one of his pencils would pretend to be drawing the portrait of some man standing near him; then showing his picture to the crowd, it proved to be the head of a donkey, which, of course, produced roars of laughter.

"There, do you see what wonderful pencils these are? Did you ever behold a more striking likeness?"

A hearty laugh would be sure to follow, and then he would exclaim: "Now who will have the first pencil—only five sous." One would buy, and then another; a third and a fourth would follow; and with the delivery of each pencil he would rattle off a string of witticisms which kept his patrons in capital good-humor; and frequently he would sell from two hundred to five hundred pencils in immediate succession. Then he would drop down in his carriage for a few minutes and wipe the perspiration from his face, while his servant played another overture on the organ. This gave his purchasers a chance to withdraw, and afforded a good opportunity for a fresh audience to congregate. Then would follow a repetition of his previous sales, and in this way he would continue for hours. To those disposed to have a *souvenir* of the great humbug he would sell six pencils, a medal and a photograph of himself for a franc (twenty cents.) After taking a rest he would commence a new speech.

"When I was modestly dressed, like any of my hearers, I was half starved. Punch and his bells would attract crowds, but my good pencils attracted nobody. I imitated Punch and his bells, and now I have two hundred depots in Paris. I dine at the best cafés, drink the best wine, live on the best of every-thing, while my defamers get poor and lank, as they deserve to be. Who are my defamers? Envious swindlers! Men who try to ape me, but are too stupid and too dishonest to succeed.

They endeavor to attract notice as mountebanks, and then foist upon the public worthless trash, and hope thus to succeed. Ah! defamers of mine, you are fools as well as knaves. Fools, to think that any man can succeed by systematically and persistently cheating the public. Knaves, for desiring the public's money without giving them an equivalent. I am an honest man. I have no bad habits; and I now declare, if any trader, inventor, manufacturer, or philanthropist will show me better pencils than mine, I will give him 1,000f.—no, not to him, for I abhor betting—but to the poor of the Thirty-first Arrondissement, where I live."

Mangin's harangues were always accompanied by a peculiar play of feature and of voice, and with unique and original gestures, which seemed to excite and captivate his audience.

About seven years ago, I met him in one of the principal restaurants in the Palais Royale. A mutual friend introduced me.

"Ah!" said he, "Monsieur Barnum, I am delighted to see you. I have read your book with infinite satisfaction. It has been published here in numerous editions. I see you have the right idea of things. Your motto is a good one—we study to please.' I have much wanted to visit America; but I cannot speak English, so I must remain in my dear belle France."

I remarked that I had often seen him in public, and bought his pencils.

"Aha! you never saw better pencils. You know I could never maintain my reputation if I sold poor pencils. But sacre bleu, my miserable would-be imitators do not know our grand secret. First, attract the public by din and tinsel, by brilliant skyrockets and Bengola lights, then give them as much as possible for their money."

"You are very happy," I replied, "in your manner of attracting the public. Your costume is elegant, your chariot is superb, and your valet and music are sure to draw."

"Thank you for your compliment, Mr. B., but I have not forgotten your Buffalo-hunt, your Mermaid, nor your Woolly Horse. They were a good offset to my rich helmet and sword, my burnished gauntlets and gaudy cuirass. Both are intended as advertisements of something genuine, and both answer the purpose."

After comparing notes in this way for an hour, we parted, and his last words were:

"Mr. B., I have got a grand humbug in my head, which I shall put in practice within a year, and it shall double the sale of my pencils. Don't ask me what it is, but within one year you shall see it for yourself, and you shall acknowledge Monsieur Mangin knows something of human nature. My idea is *magnifique*, but it is one grand secret."

I confess my curiosity was somewhat excited, and I hoped that Monsieur Mangin would "add another wrinkle to my horns." But, poor fellow! within four months after I bade him adieu, the Paris newspapers announced his sudden death. They added that he had left two hundred thousand francs, which he had given in his will to charitable objects. The announcement was copied into nearly all the papers on the Continent and in Great Britain, for almost everybody had seen or heard of the eccentric pencil maker.

His death caused many an honest sigh, and his absence seemed to cast a gloom over several of his favorite halting-places. The Parisians really loved him, and were proud of his genius.

"Well," people in Paris would remark, "Mangin was a clever

fellow. He was shrewd, and possessed a thorough knowledge of the world. He was a gentleman and a man of intelligence, extremely agreeable and witty. His habits were good; he was charitable. He never cheated anybody. He always sold a good article, and no person who purchased from him had cause to complain."

I confess I felt somewhat chagrined that the Monsieur had thus suddenly taken "French leave" without imparting to me the "grand secret" by which he was to double the sales of his pencils. But I had not long to mourn on that account; for after Monsieur Mangin had been for six months—as they say of John Brown—mouldering in his grave" judge of the astonishment and delight of all Paris at his reappearance in his native city in precisely the same costume and carriage as formerly, and heralded by the same servant and organ that had always attended him. It now turned out that Monsieur Mangin had lived in the most rigid seclusion for half a year, and that the extensively-circulated announcements of his sudden death had been made by himself, merely as an "advertising dodge" to bring him still more into notice, and give the public something to talk about. I met Mangin in Paris soon after this event.

"Aha, Monsieur Barnum!" he exclaimed, "did I not tell you I had a new humbug that would double the sales of my pencils? I assure you my sales are more than quadrupled, and it is sometimes impossible to have them manufactured fast enough to supply the demand. You Yankees are very clever, but by gar, none of you have discovered you should live all the better if you would die for six months. It took Mangin to teach you that."

The patronizing air with which he made this speech, slapping me at the same time familiarly upon the back, showed him in his true character of egotist. Although good-natured and social to a degree, he was really one of the most self-conceited men I ever met.

Monsieur Mangin died the present year, and it is said that his heirs received more than half a million of francs as the fruit of his eccentric labors.

Chapter 4

Old Grizzly Adams.

James C. Adams, or "Grizzly Adams," as he was generally termed, from the fact of his having captured so many grizzly bears, and encountered such fearful perils by his unexampled daring, was an extraordinary character. For many years a hunter and trapper in the Rocky and Sierra Nevada Mountains, he acquired a recklessness which, added to his natural invincible courage, rendered him truly one of the most striking men of the age. He was emphatically what the English call a man of "pluck." In 1860, he arrived in New York with his famous collection of California animals, captured by himself, consisting of twenty or thirty immense grizzly bears, at the head of which stood "Old Sampson"—now in the American Museum—wolves, half a dozen other species of bear, California lions, tigers, buffalo, elk, etc., and Old Neptune, the great sea-lion, from the Pacific.

Old Adams had trained all these monsters so that with him they were as docile as kittens, while many of the most ferocious among them would attack a stranger without hesitation, if he came within their grasp. In fact, the training of these animals was no fool's play, as Old Adams learned to his cost; for the terrific blows which he received from time to time, while teaching them "docility," finally cost him his life.

When Adams and his other wild beasts (for he was nearly as wild as any of them) arrived in New York, he called immediately at the Museum. He was dressed in his hunter's suit of buckskin, trimmed with the skins and bordered with the hanging tails of small Rocky Mountain animals; his cap consisting of the skin of a wolf's head and shoulders, from which depended several tails as natural as life, and under which appeared his stiff bushy gray hair and his long white grizzly beard. In fact, Old Adams was quite as much of a show as his bears. They had come around Cape Horn on the clipper-ship Golden Fleece, and a sea-voyage of three and a half months had probably not added much to the beauty or neat appearance of the old bear-hunter.

During our conversation, Grizzly Adams took off his cap, and showed me the top of his head. His skull was literally broken in. It had on various occasions been struck by the fearful paws of his grizzly students; and the last blow, from the bear called "General Fremont," had laid open his brain, so that its workings were plainly visible. I remarked that I thought that was a dangerous wound, and might possibly prove fatal.

"Yes," replied Adams, "that will fix me out. It had nearly healed; but old Fremont opened it for me, for the third or fourth time, before I left California, and he did his business so thoroughly, I'm a used-up man. However, I reckon I may live six months or a year yet."

This was spoken as coolly as if he had been talking about the life of a dog.

The immediate object of "Old Adams" in calling upon me

was this. I had purchased one-half interest in his California menagerie from a man who had come by way of the Isthmus from California, and who claimed to own an equal interest with Adams in the show. Adams declared that the man had only advanced him some money, and did not possess the right to sell half of the concern. However, the man held a bill of sale for one-half of the "California Menagerie," and Old Adams finally consented to accept me as an equal partner in the speculation, saying that he guessed I could do the managing part, and he would show up the animals. I obtained a canvas tent, and erecting it on the present site of Wallack's Theatre, Adams there opened his novel California Menagerie. On the morning of opening, a band of music preceded a procession of animal-cages, down Broadway and up the Bowery; Old Adams dressed in his hunting costume, heading the line, with a platform-wagon on which were placed three immense grizzly bears, two of which he held by chains, while he was mounted on the back of the largest grizzly, which stood in the center, and was not secured in any manner whatever. This was the bear known as "General Fremont;" and so docile had he become that Adams said he had used him as a packbear to carry his cooking and hunting apparatus through the mountains for six months, and had ridden him hundreds of miles. But apparently docile as were many of these animals, there was not one among them that would not occasionally give even Adams a sly blow or a sly bite when a good chance offered; hence Old Adams was but a wreck of his former self, and expressed pretty nearly the truth when he said:

"Mr. Barnum, I am not the man I was five years ago. Then I felt able to stand the hug of any grizzly living, and was always glad to encounter, single-handed, any sort of an animal that dared present himself. But I have been beaten to a jelly, torn almost limb from limb, and nearly chawed up and spit out by these treacherous grizzly bears. However, I am good for a few months yet, and by that time I hope we shall gain enough to make my old woman comfortable, for I have been absent from her some years."

His wife came from Massachusetts to New York, and nursed him. Dr. Johns dressed his wounds every day, and not only told Adams he could never recover, but assured his friends that probably a very few weeks would lay him in his grave.

But Adams was as firm as adamant and as resolute as a lion. Among the thousands who saw him dressed in his grotesque hunter's suit, and witnessed the apparent vigor with which he "performed" the savage monsters, beating and whipping them into apparently the most perfect docility, probably not one suspected that this rough, fierce-looking, powerful demi-savage, as he appeared to be, was suffering intense pain from his broken skull and fevered system, and that nothing kept him from stretching himself on his deathbed but that most indomitable and extraordinary will of his.

After the exhibition had been open six weeks, the Doctor insisted that Adams should sell out his share in the animals and settle up all his worldly affairs; for he assured him that he was growing weaker every day, and his earthly existence must soon terminate.

"I shall live a good deal longer than you doctors think for," replied Adams, doggedly; and then, seeming after all to realize the truth of the Doctor's assertion, he turned to me and said: "Well, Mr. B., you must buy me out." He named his price for his half of the "show," and I accepted his offer. We had arranged to exhibit the bears in Connecticut and Massachusetts during the summer, in connection with a circus, and Adams insisted that I should hire him to travel for the summer, and exhibit the bears in their curious performances. He offered to go for $60 per week and traveling expenses of himself and wife.

I replied that I would gladly engage him as long as he could stand it, but I advised him to give up business and go to his home in Massachusetts; "for," I remarked, "you are growing weaker every day, and at best cannot stand it more than a fortnight."

"What will you give me extra if I will travel and exhibit the bears every day for ten weeks?" asked old Adams, eagerly.

"Five hundred dollars," I replied, with a laugh.

"Done!" exclaimed Adams. "I will do it; so draw up an agreement to that effect at once. But mind you, draw it payable to my wife, for I may be too weak to attend to business after the ten weeks are up, and if I perform my part of the contract, I want her to get the $500 without any trouble."

I drew up a contract to pay him $60 per week for his services, and if he continued to exhibit the bears for ten consecutive weeks I was then to hand him, or his wife $500 extra.

"You have lost your $500!" exclaimed Adams on taking the contract; "for I am bound to live and earn it."

"I hope you may, with all my heart, and a hundred years more if you desire it," I replied.

"Call me a fool if I don't earn the $500!" exclaimed Adams, with a triumphant laugh.

The "show" started off in a few days, and at the end of a fortnight I met it at Hartford, Connecticut.

"Well," says I, "Adams, you seem to stand it pretty well. I hope you and your wife are comfortable?"

"Yes," he replied, with a laugh; "and you may as well try to be comfortable too, for your $500 is a goner."

"All right," I replied; "I hope you will grow better every day."

But I saw by his pale face, and other indications, that he was rapidly failing.

In three weeks more, I met him again at New Bedford, MA. It seemed to me, then, that he could not live a week, for his eyes were glassy and his hands trembled, but his pluck was great as ever.

"This hot weather is pretty bad for me," he said, "but my ten weeks are half expired, and I am good for your $500, and, probably, a month or two longer."

This was said with as much bravado as if he was offering to bet upon a horse-race. I offered to pay him half of the $500 if he would give up and go home; but he peremptorily declined making any compromise whatever.

I met him the ninth week in Boston. He had failed considerably since I last saw him, but he still continued to exhibit the bears and chuckled over his almost certain triumph. I laughed in return, and sincerely congratulated him on his nerve and probable success. I remained with him until the tenth week was finished, and handed him his $500. He took it with a leer of satisfaction, and remarked, that he was sorry I was a teetotaller, for he would like to stand treat!

Just before the menagerie left New York, I had paid $150 for a new hunting-suit, made of beaver-skins similar to the one which Adams had worn. This I intended for Herr Driesbach, the animal-tamer, who was engaged by me to take the place of Adams whenever he should be compelled to give up.

Adams, on starting from New York, asked me to loan this new dress to him to perform in once in a while in a fair day when we had a large audience, for his own costume was considerably soiled. I did so, and now when I handed him his $500 he remarked:

"Mr. B., I suppose you are going to give me this new hunting-dress."

"Oh no," I replied. "I got that for your successor, who will exhibit the bears tomorrow; besides, you have no possible use for it."

"Now, don't be mean, but *lend* me the dress, if you won't *give* it to me, for I want to wear it home to my native village."

I could not refuse the poor old man anything, and I therefore replied:

"Well, Adams, I will lend you the dress; but you will send it back to me."

"Yes, when I have done with it," he replied, with an evident chuckle of triumph.

I thought to myself, he will soon be done with it, and replied:

"That's all right."

A new idea evidently seized him, for, with a brightening look of satisfaction, he said:

"Now, Barnum, you have made a good thing out of the California menagerie, and so have I; but you will make a heap more. So, if you won't give me this new hunter's dress, just draw a little writing, and sign it, saying that I may wear it until I have done with it."

Of course, I knew that in a few days at longest he would be "done" with this world altogether, and, to gratify him, I cheerfully drew and signed the paper.

"Come, old Yankee, I've got you this time—see if I hain't!" exclaimed Adams, with a broad grin, as he took the paper.

I smiled, and said:

"All right, my dear fellow; the longer you live, the better I shall like it."

We parted, and he went to Neponset, a small town near Boston, where his wife and daughter lived. He took at once to his bed, and never rose from it again. The excitement had passed away, and his vital energies could accomplish no more.

The fifth day after arriving home, the physician told him he could not live until the next morning. He received the announcement in perfect calmness, and with the most apparent indifference; then, turning to his wife, with a smile, he requested her to have him buried in the new hunting suit.

"For," said he, "Barnum agreed to let me have it until I have done with it, and I was determined to fix his flint this time. He shall never see that dress again."

His wife assured him that his request should be complied with. He then sent for the clergyman, and they spent several hours in communing together.

Adams told the clergyman he had told some pretty big stories about his bears, but he had always endeavored to do the straight thing between man and man. "I have attended preaching every day, Sundays and all," said he, "for the last six years. Sometimes an old grizzly gave me the sermon, sometimes it was a panther; often it was the thunder and lightning, the tempest, or the hurricane on the peaks of the

Sierra Nevada, or in the gorges of the Rocky Mountains; but whatever preached to me, it always taught me the majesty of the Creator, and revealed to me the undying and unchanging love of our kind Father in heaven. Although I am a pretty rough customer," continued the dying man, "I fancy my heart is in about the right place, and look with confidence to the blessed Saviour for that rest which I so much need, and which I have never enjoyed upon Earth." He then desired the clergyman to pray with him, after which he grasped him by the hand, thanked him for his kindness, and bade him farewell.

In another hour his spirit had taken its flight; and it was said by those present that his face lighted up into a smile as the last breath escaped him, and that smile he carried into his grave. Almost his last words were: "Won't Barnum open his eyes when he finds I have humbugged him by being buried in his new hunting-dress?" That dress was indeed the shroud in which he was entombed.

And that was the last on Earth of "Old Grizzly Adams."

Chapter 5

The golden pigeons—Grizzly Adams—German chemist—Happy family—French naturalist.

"Old Grizzly Adams" was quite candid when, in his last hours, he confessed to the clergyman that he had "told some pretty large stories about his bears." In fact, these "large stories" were Adam's "besetting sin." To hear him talk, one would suppose that he had seen and handled everything ever read or heard of. In fact, according to his story, California contained specimens of all things, animate and inanimate, to be found in any part of the globe. He talked glibly about California lions, California tigers, California leopards, California hyenas, California camels, and California hippopotami. He furthermore declared he had, on one occasion, seen a California elephant, "at a great distance," but it was "very shy," and he would not permit himself to doubt that California giraffes existed somewhere in the neighborhood of the "tall trees."

I was anxious to get a chance of exposing to Adams his weak point, and of showing him the absurdity of telling such ridiculous stories. A fit occasion soon presented itself. One day, while engaged in my office at the Museum, a man with marked Teutonic features and accent approached the door and asked if I would like to buy a pair of living golden pigeons.

"Yes," I replied, "I would like a *flock* of 'golden pigeons,' if I could buy them for their weight in *silver*; for there are no '*golden*' pigeons in existence, unless they are made from the pure metal."

"You shall see some golden pigeons alive," he replied, at the same time entering my office and closing the door after him. He then removed the lid from a small basket which he carried in his hand, and sure enough there were snugly ensconced a pair of beautiful living ruff-necked pigeons, as yellow as saffron and as bright as a double eagle fresh from the mint.

I confess I was somewhat staggered at this sight, and quickly asked the man where those birds came from.

A dull, lazy smile crawled over the sober face of my German visitor, as he replied in a slow, guttural tone of voice:

"What you think yourself?"

Catching his meaning, I quickly answered:

"I think it is a humbug?"

"Of course, I know you will say so; because you 'forstha' such things better as any man living, so I shall not try to humbug you. I have color them myself."

On further inquiry, I learned that this German was a chemist, and that he possessed the art of coloring birds any hue desired, and yet retain a natural gloss on the feathers, which gave every shade the appearance of reality.

"I can paint a green pigeon or a blue pigeon, a gray pigeon or a black pigeon, a brown pigeon or a pigeon half blue and half green," said the German; "and if you prefer it, I can paint them pink or purple, or give you a little of each color, and make you a rainbow pigeon."

The "rainbow pigeon" did not strike me as particularly desirable; but, thinking here was a good chance to catch "Grizzly Adams," I bought the pair of golden pigeons for ten dollars, and sent them up to the "Happy Family," marked "Golden Pigeons from California." Mr. Taylor the great pacificator, who has charge of the Happy Family, soon came down in a state of perspiration.

"Really, Mr. Barnum," said he, "I could not think of putting those elegant golden pigeons into the Happy Family—they are too valuable a bird—they might get injured—they are by far the most beautiful pigeons I ever saw; and as they are so rare, I would not jeopardize their lives for anything."

"Well," I replied, "you may put them in a separate cage, properly labeled."

Monsieur Guillaudeu, the naturalist and taxidermist of the Museum, has been attached to that establishment since the year it was founded, 1810. He is a Frenchman, and has read everything upon Natural History that was ever published in his own or in the English language. He is now seventy-five years old, but is lively as a cricket, and takes as much interest in Natural History as he ever did. When he saw the "golden pigeons from California," he was considerably astonished! He examined them with great delight for half an hour, expatiating upon their beautiful color, and the near resemblance which every feature bore to the American ruff-neck pigeon. He soon came to my office and said:

"Mr. B., these golden pigeons are superb, but they cannot be from California. Audubon mentions no such bird in his work upon American Ornithology."

I told him he had better take Audubon home with him that night, and perhaps by studying him attentively he would see occasion to change his mind.

The next day, the old naturalist called at my office and remarked:

"Mr. B., those pigeons are a more rare bird than you imagine. They are not mentioned by Linnaeus, Cuvier, Goldsmith, or any other writer on Natural History, so far as I have been able to discover. I expect they must have come from some unexplored portion of Australia."

"Never mind," I replied, "we may get more light on the subject, perhaps, before long. We will continue to label them 'California Pigeons' until we can fix their nativity elsewhere."

The next, morning, "Old Grizzly Adams," whose exhibition of bears was then open in Fourteenth street, happened to be passing through the Museum, when his eyes fell on the "Golden California Pigeons." He looked a moment and doubtless admired. He soon after came to my office.

"Mr. B.," said he, "you must let me have those California pigeons."

"I can't spare them," I replied.

"But you *must* spare them. All the birds and animals from California ought to be together. You own half of my California menagerie, and you must lend me those pigeons."

"Mr. Adams, they are too rare and valuable a bird to be hawked about in that manner; besides, I expect they will attract considerable attention here."

"Oh, don't be a fool," replied Adams. "Rare bird, indeed! Why, they are just as common in California as any other pigeon! I could have brought a hundred of them from San Francisco, if I had thought of it."

"But why did you not think of it?" I asked, with a suppressed smile.

"Because they are *so common* there," said Adams. "I did not think they would be any curiosity here. I have eaten them in pigeon-pies hundreds of times, and shot them by the thousand!"

I was ready to burst with laughter to see how readily Adams swallowed the bait, but maintaining the most rigid gravity, I replied:

"Oh well, Mr. Adams, if they are really so common in California, you had probably better take them, and you may write over and have half a dozen pairs sent to me for the Museum."

"All right," said Adams; "I will send over to a friend in San Francisco, and you shall have them here in a couple of months."

I told Adams that, for certain reasons, I would prefer to change the label so as to have it read: "Golden Pigeons from Australia."

"Well, call them what you like," replied Adams; "I suppose they are probably about as plenty in Australia as they are in California."

I fancied I could discover a sly smile lurking in the eye of the old bear-hunter as he made this reply.

The pigeons were labeled as I suggested, and this is how it happened that the Bridgeport non-believing lady, mentioned in the next chapter, was so much attracted as to solicit some of their eggs in order to perpetuate the species in old Connecticut.

Six or eight weeks after this incident, I was in the California Menagerie, and noticed that the "Golden Pigeons" had assumed a frightfully mottled appearance. Their feathers had grown out, and they were half white. Adams had been so busy with his bears that he had not noticed the change. I called him up to the pigeon cage, and remarked:

"Mr. Adams, I fear you will lose your Golden Pigeons; they must be very sick; I observe they are turning quite pale!"

Adams looked at them a moment with astonishment; then turning to me, and seeing that I could not suppress a smile, he indignantly exclaimed:

"Blast the Golden Pigeons! You had better take them back to the Museum. You can't humbug me with your painted pigeons!"

This was too much, and "I laughed till I cried" to witness the mixed look of astonishment and vexation which marked the "grizzly" features of old Adams.

"These Golden Pigeons," I remarked, "are very common in California, I think I heard you say? When do you expect my half-dozen pairs will arrive?"

"You go to thunder, you old humbug!" replied Adams, as he marched off indignantly, and soon disappeared behind the cages of his grizzly bears.

From that time, Adams seemed to be more careful about telling his large stories. Perhaps he was not cured altogether of his habit, but he took particular pains when making marvelous statements to have them of such a nature that they could not be disproved so easily as was that regarding the "Golden California Pigeons."

Chapter 6

The whale, the angel fish, and the golden pigeon.

If the fact could be definitely determined, I think it would be discovered that in this "wide awake" country there are more persons humbugged by believing too little than too much. Many persons have such a horror of being taken in, or such an elevated opinion of their own acuteness, that they believe everything to be a sham, and in this way are continually humbugging themselves.

Several years since, I purchased a living white whale, captured near Labrador, and succeeded in placing it, "in good condition," in a large tank, fifty feet long, and supplied with salt water, in the basement of the American Museum. I was obliged to light the basement with gas, and that frightened the sea-monster to such an extent that he kept at the bottom of the tank, except when he was compelled to stick his nose above the surface in order to breathe or "blow," and then down he would go again as quick as possible. Visitors would sometimes stand for half an hour, watching in vain to get a look at the whale; for, although he could remain under water only about two minutes at a time, he would happen to appear in some unlooked for quarter of the huge tank, and before they could all get a chance to see him, he would be out of sight again. Some impatient and incredulous persons after waiting ten minutes, which seemed to them an hour, would sometimes exclaim:

"Oh, humbug! I don't believe there is a whale here at all!"

This incredulity often put me out of patience, and I would say:

"Ladies and gentlemen, there is a living whale in the tank. He is frightened by the gaslight and by visitors; but he is obliged to come to the surface every two minutes, and if you will watch sharply, you will see him. I am sorry we can't make him dance a hornpipe and do all sorts of wonderful things at the word of command; but if you will exercise your patience a few minutes longer, I assure you the whale will be seen at considerably less trouble than it would be to go to Labrador expressly for that purpose."

This would usually put my patrons in good humor; but I was myself often vexed at the persistent stubbornness of the whale in not calmly floating on the surface for the gratification of my visitors.

One day, a sharp Yankee lady and her daughter, from Connecticut, called at the Museum. I knew them well; and in answer to their inquiry for the locality of the whale, I directed them to the basement. Half an hour afterward, they called at my office, and the acute mother, in a half-confidential, seriocomic whisper, said:

"Mr. B., it's astonishing to what a number of purposes the ingenuity of us Yankees has applied India-rubber."

I asked her meaning, and was soon informed that she was perfectly convinced that it was an India-rubber whale, worked by steam and machinery, by means of which he was made to rise to the surface at short intervals, and puff with the regularity of a pair of bellows. From her earnest, confident manner, I saw it would be useless to attempt to disabuse her mind on the subject. I therefore very candidly acknowledged that she was quite too sharp for me, and I must plead guilty to the imposition; but I begged her not to expose me, for I assured her that she was the only person who had discovered the trick.

It was worth more than a dollar to see with what a smile of satisfaction she received the assurance that nobody else was as shrewd as herself; and the patronizing manner in which she bade me be perfectly tranquil, for the secret should be considered by her as "strictly confidential," was decidedly rich. She evidently received double her money's worth in the happy reflection that she could not be humbugged, and that I was terribly humiliated in being detected through her marvelous powers of discrimination! I occasionally meet the good lady, and always try to look a little sheepish, but she invariably assures me that she has never divulged my secret and never will!

On another occasion, a lady equally shrewd, who lives neighbor to me in Connecticut, after regarding for a few minutes the "Golden Angel Fish" swimming in one of the Aquaria, abruptly addressed me with:

"You can't humbug me, Mr. Barnum; that fish is painted!"

"Nonsense!" said I, with a laugh; "the thing is impossible!"

"I don't care, I know it is painted; it is as plain as can be."

"But, my dear Mrs. H., paint would not adhere to a fish while in the water; and if it would, it would kill him. Besides," I added, with an extra serious air, "we never allow humbugging here!"

"Oh, here is just the place to look for such things," she

replied with a smile; "and I must say I more than half believe that Angel Fish is painted."

She was finally nearly convinced of her error, and left. In the afternoon of the same day, I met her in Old Adams' California Menagerie. She knew that I was part-proprietor of that establishment, and seeing me in conversation with "Grizzly Adams," she came up to me in some haste, and with her eyes glistening with excitement, she said:

"O, Mr. B., I never saw anything so beautiful as those elegant 'Golden Pigeons' from Australia. I want you to secure some of their eggs for me, and let my pigeons hatch them at home. I should prize them beyond all measure."

"Oh, you don't want 'Golden Australian Pigeons,'" I replied; "they are painted."

"No, they are not painted," said she, with a laugh, "but I half think the Angel Fish is."

I could not control myself at the curious coincidence, and I roared with laughter while I replied:

"Now, Mrs. H., I never let a good joke be spoiled, even if it serves to expose my own secrets. I assure you, upon honor, that the Golden Australian Pigeons, as they are labeled, are really painted; and that in their natural state they are nothing more nor less than the common ruff-necked white American pigeons!"

And it was a fact. How they happened to be exhibited under that auriferous disguise was owing to an amusing circumstance, explained in another chapter.

Suffice it at present to say, that Mrs. H. to this day "blushes to her eyebrows" whenever an allusion is made to "Angel Fish" or "Golden Pigeons."

Chapter 7

Pease's hoarhound candy—the Dorr rebellion—The Philadelphia aldermen.

In the year 1842, a new style of advertising appeared in the newspapers and in handbills which arrested public attention at once on account of its novelty. The thing advertised was an article called "Pease's Hoarhound Candy;" a very good specific for coughs and colds. It was put up in twenty-five cent packages, and was eventually sold wholesale and retail in enormous quantities. Mr. Pease's system of advertising was one which, I believe, originated with him in this country, although many have practiced it since, but of course, with less success—for imitations seldom succeed. Mr. Pease's plan was to seize upon the most prominent topic of interest and general conversation, and discourse eloquently upon that topic in fifty to a hundred lines of a newspaper-column, then glide off gradually into a panegyric of "Pease's Hoarhound Candy." The consequence was, every reader was misled by the caption and commencement of his article, and thousands of persons had "Pease's Hoarhound Candy" in their mouths long before they had seen it! In fact, it was next to impossible to take up a newspaper and attempt to read the legitimate news of the day without stumbling upon a package of "Pease's Hoarhound Candy." The reader would often feel vexed to find that, after reading a quarter of a column of interesting news upon the subject uppermost in his mind, he was trapped into the perusal of one of Pease's hoarhound candy advertisements. Although inclined sometimes to throw down the newspaper in disgust, he would generally laugh at the talent displayed by Mr. Pease in thus captivating and capturing the reader. The result of all this would generally be, a trial of the candy on the first premonitory symptoms of a cough or influenza. The degree to which this system of advertising has since been carried has rendered it a bore and a nuisance. The usual result of almost any great and original achievement is, the production of a shoal of brainless imitators, who are "neither useful nor ornamental."

In the same year that Pease's hoarhound candy appeared upon the commercial and newspaper horizon, the "Governor Dorr Rebellion" occurred in Rhode Island. As many will re-member, this rebellion caused a great excitement throughout the country. Citizens of Rhode Island took up arms against each other, and it was feared by some that a bloody civil war would ensue.

At about this time a municipal election was to come off in the city of Philadelphia. The two political parties were pretty equally divided there, and there were some special causes why this was regarded as an unusually important election. Its near approach caused more excitement in the "Quaker City" than had been witnessed there since the preceding Presidential election. The party-leaders began to lay their plans early, and the wire-pullers on both sides were unusually busy in their vocation. At the head of the rabble upon which one of the parties depended for many votes, was a drunken and profane fellow, whom we will call Tom Simmons. Tom was great at electioneering and stump-spouting in barrooms and rum-caucuses, and his party always looked to him, at each election, to stir up the subterraneans "with a long pole"— and a whiskey-jug at the end of it.

The exciting election which was now to come off for Mayor and Aldermen of the good city of Brotherly Love soon brought several of the "ring" to Tom.

"Now, Tom," said the head wire-puller, "this is going to be a close election, and we want you to spare neither talent nor liquor in arousing up and bringing to the polls every voter within your influence."

"Well, Squire," replied Tom carelessly, "I've concluded I won't bother myself with this 'lection—it don't pay!"

"Don't pay!" exclaimed the frightened politician. "Why, Tom, are you not a true friend to your party? Haven't you always been on hand at the primary meetings, knocked down interlopers, and squelched every man who talked about conscience, or who refused to support regular nominations, and vote the entire clean ticket straight through? And as for 'pay,' haven't you always been supplied with money enough to treat all doubtful voters, and in fact to float them up to the polls in an ocean of whiskey? I confess Tom, I am almost petrified with astonishment at witnessing your present indifference to the alarming crisis in which our country and our party are involved, and which nothing on Earth can avert, except our success at the coming election."

"Oh, tell that to the marines," said Tom. "We never yet had an election that there wasn't a 'crisis,' and yet, whichever party gained, we somehow managed to live through it, crisis or no crisis. In fact, my curiosity has got a little excited, and I would like to see this 'crisis' that is such a bugaboo at every election; so trot out your crisis—let us see how it looks. Besides, talking of pay, I acknowledge the whiskey, and that is all. While I and my companions lifted you and your companions into fat offices that enabled you to roll in your carriages, and live on the fat of the land, we got nothing—or, at least, next to nothing—all we got was—well—we got drunk! Now, Squire, I will go for the other party this 'lection if you don't give me an office."

"Give you an office!" exclaimed the "Squire," raising his hands and rolling his eyes in utter amazement; "why, Tom, what office do you want?"

"I want to be Alderman!" replied Tom, "and I can control votes enough to turn the 'lection either way; and if our party don't gratefully remember my past services and give me my reward, t'other party will be glad to run me on their ticket, and over I go."

The gentleman of the "ring" saw by Tom's firmness and clenched teeth that he was immovable; that his principles, like those of too many others, consisted of "loaves and fishes;" they therefore consented to put Tom's name on the municipal ticket; and the worst part of the story is, he was elected.

In a very short time, Tom was duly installed into the Aldermanic chair, and, opening his office on a prominent corner, he was soon doing a thriving business. He was generally occupied throughout the day in sitting as a judge in cases of book debt and promissory notes which were brought before him, for various small sums ranging from two to five, six, eight, and ten dollars. He would frequently dispose of thirty or forty of these cases in a day, and as imprisonment for debt was permitted at that time, the poor defendants would "shin" around and make any sacrifice almost, rather than go to jail. The enormous "costs" went into the capacious pocket of the Alderman; and this dignitary, as a natural sequence, "waxed fat" and saucy, exemplifying the truth of the adage "Put a beggar on horseback," etc.

As the Alderman grew rich, he became overbearing, head-strong, and dictatorial. He began to fancy that he monopolized the concentrated wisdom of his party, and that his word should be law. Not a party-caucus or a political meeting could be held without witnessing the vulgar and profane harangues of the self-conceited Alderman, Tom Simmons. As he was one of the "ring," his fingers were in all the "pickings and stealings;" he kept his family-coach, and in his general swagger exhibited all the peculiarities of "high life below stairs."

But after Tom had disgraced his office for two years, a State election took place and the other party were successful. Among the first laws which they passed after the convening of the Legislature, was one declaring that from that date imprisonment for debt should not be permitted in the State of Pennsylvania for any sum less than ten dollars.

This enactment, of course, knocked away the chief prop which sustained the Alderman, and when the news of its passage reached Philadelphia, Tom was the most indignant man that had been seen there for some years.

Standing in front of his office the next morning, surrounded by several of his political chums, Tom exclaimed:

"Do you see what them infernal tories have done down there at Harrisburg? They have been and passed an outrageous, oppressive, barbarous, and unconstitutional law! A pretty idea, indeed, if a man can't put a debtor in jail for a less sum than ten dollars! How am I going to support my family, I should like to know, if this law is allowed to stand? I tell you, gentlemen, this law is unconstitutional, and you will see blood running in our streets, if them tory scoundrels try to carry it out!"

His friends laughed, for they saw that Tom was reasoning from his pocket instead of his head; and, as he almost foamed at the mouth in his impotent wrath they could not suppress a smile.

"Oh, you may laugh, gentlemen—you may laugh; but you will see it. Our party will never disgrace itself a permitting the tories to rob them of their rights by passing unconstitutional laws; and I say, the sooner we come to blood, the better!"

At this moment, a gentleman stepped up, and addressing the Alderman, said:

"Alderman, I want to bring a case of book debt before you this morning."

"How much is your claim?" asked Tom.

"Four dollars," replied the rumseller—for such he proved to be—and his debt was for drinks chalked up against one of his "customers."

"You can't have your four dollars, Sir," replied the excited Alderman. "You are robbed of your four dollars, Sir. Them legislative tories at Harrisburg, Sir, have cheated you out of your four dollars, Sir. I undertake to say, Sir, that fifty thousand honest men in Philadelphia have been robbed of their four dollars by these bloody tories and their cursed unconstitutional law! Ah, gentlemen, you will see blood running in our streets before you are a month older. (A laugh.) Oh, you may laugh; but you will see it—see if you don't!"

A newsboy was just passing by.

"Here, boy, give me the *Morning Ledger*," said the Alderman, at the same time taking the paper and handing the boy a penny. "Let us see what them blasted cowboys are doing down at Harrisburg now. Ah!—what is this?" (Reading:) " 'Blood, blood, blood!' Aha! laugh, will you, gentlemen? Here it is." Reads:

"'Blood, blood, blood! The Dorrites have got possession of Providence. The military are called out. Father is arrayed against father, and son against son. Blood is already running in our streets.'

"Now laugh, will you, gentlemen? Blood is running in the streets of Providence; blood will be running in the streets of Philadelphia before you are a fortnight older! The tories of Providence and the tories of Harrisburg must answer for this blood, for they and their unconstitutional proceedings are the cause of its flowing! Let us see the rest of this tragic scene." Reads:

"'Is there any remedy for this dreadful state of things?'"

Alderman.—Of course not, except to hang every rascal of them for trampling on our g-l-orious Constitution." Reads:

"'Is there any remedy for this dreadful state of things? Yes, there is.'"

Alderman.—Oh, there is, is there? What is it? Let me see." Reads:

"'Buy two packages of Pease's hoarhound candy.'"

"Blast the infernal *Ledger*!" exclaimed the now doubly incensed and indignant Alderman, throwing the paper upon the pavement with the most ineffable disgust, amid the shouts and hurrahs of a score of men who by this time had gathered around the excited Alderman Tom Simmons.

As I before remarked, the "candy" was a very good article for the purposes for which it was made; and as Pease was an indefatigable man, as well as a good advertiser, he soon acquired a fortune. Mr. Pease, Junior, is now living in affluence in Brooklyn, and is bringing up a "happy family" to enjoy the fruits of his industry, probity, good habits, and genius.

The "humbug" in this transaction, of course consisted solely in the manner of advertising. There was no humbug or deception about the article manufactured.

Chapter 8

Brandreth's pills—Magnificent advertising—Power of imagination.

In the year 1834, Dr. Benjamin Brandreth commenced advertising in the city of New York, "Brandreth's Pills specially recommended to purify the blood." His office consisted of a room about ten feet square, located in what was then known as the *Sun* building, an edifice ten by forty feet, situated at the corner of Spruce and Nassau Streets, where the *Tribune* is now published. His "factory" was at his residence in Hudson Street. He put up a large gilt sign over the *Sun* office, five or six feet wide by the length of the building, which attracted much attention, as at that time it was probably the largest sign in New York. Dr. Brandreth had great faith in his pills, and I believe not without reason; for multitudes of persons soon became convinced of the truth of his assertions, that "all diseases arise from impurity or imperfect circulation of the blood, and by purgation with Brandreth's Pills all disease may be cured."

But great and reasonable as might have been the faith of Dr. Brandreth in the efficacy of his pills, his faith in the potency of advertising them was equally strong. Hence he commenced advertising largely in the *Sun* newspaper—paying at least $5,000 to that paper alone, for his first year's advertisements. That may not seem a large sum in these days, when parties have been known to pay more than five thousand dollar for a single day's advertising in the leading journals; but, at the time Brandreth started, his was considered the most liberal newspaper-advertising of the day.

Advertising is to a genuine article what manure is to land—it largely increases the product. Thousands of persons may be reading your advertisement while you are eating, or sleeping, or attending to your business; hence public attention is attracted, new customers come to you, and, if you render them a satisfactory equivalent for their money, they continue to patronize you and recommend you to their friends.

At the commencement of his career, Dr. Brandreth was indebted to Mr. Moses Y. Beach, proprietor of the *New York Sun*, for encouragement and means of advertising. But this very advertising soon caused his receipts to be enormous. Although the pills were but twenty-five cents per box, they were soon sold to such a great extent, that tons of huge cases filled with the "purely vegetable pill" were sent from the new and extensive manufactory every week. As his business increased, so in the same ratio did he extend his advertising. The doctor engaged at one time a literary gentleman to attend, under the supervision of himself, solely to the advertising department. Column upon column of advertisements appeared in the newspapers, in the shape of learned and scientific pathological dissertations, the very reading of which would tempt a poor mortal to rush for a box of Brandreth's Pills; so evident was it (according to the advertisement) that nobody ever had or ever would have "pure blood," until from one to a dozen boxes of the pills had been taken as "purifiers." The ingenuity displayed in concocting these advertisements was superb, and was probably hardly equaled by that required to concoct the pills.

No pain, ache, twinge, or other sensation, good, bad, or indifferent, ever experienced by a member of the human family, but was a most irrefragable evidence of the impurity of the blood; and it would have been blasphemy to have denied the "self-evident" theory, that "all diseases arise from impurity or imperfect circulation of the blood, and that by purgation with Brandreth's Pills all disease may be cured."

The doctor claims that his grandfather first manufactured the pills in 1751. I suppose this may be true; at all events, no *living* man will be apt to testify to the contrary. Here is an extract from one of Dr. Brandreth's early advertisements, which will give an idea of his style:

> "'What has been longest known has been most considered, and what has been most considered is best understood.
>
> "'The life of the flesh is in the blood.' —*Leviticus 22:2*
>
> "Bleeding reduces the vital powers; Brandreth's Pills increase them. So in sickness never be bled, especially in Dizziness and Apoplexy, but always use Brandreth's Pills.
>
> "The laws of life are written upon the face of Nature. The Tempest, Whirlwind, and Thunderstorm bring health from the Solitudes of God. The Tides are the daily agitators and purifiers of the Mighty World of Waters.
>
> "What these Providential means are as purifiers of the Atmosphere or Air, Brandreth's Pills are to man."

This splendid system of advertising, and the almost reckless outlay which was required to keep it up, challenged the admiration of the business community. In the course of a few years, his office was enlarged; and still being too small, he took the store 241 Broadway, and also opened a branch at 187 Hudson Street. The doctor continued to let his advertising keep pace with his patronage; and he was finally, in the year 1836, compelled to remove his manufactory to Sing Sing, where such perfectly incredible quantities of Brandreth's Pills have been manufactured and sold that it would hardly be safe to give the statistics. Suffice it to say, that the only "humbug" which I suspect in connection with the pills was, the very harmless and unobjectionable yet novel method of advertising them; and as the doctor amassed a great fortune by their manufacture, this very fact is prima facie evidence that the pill was a valuable purgative.

A funny incident occurred to me in connection with this great pill. In the year 1836, while I was travelling through the States of Alabama, Mississippi, and Louisiana, I became convinced by reading Doctor Brandreth's advertisements that I needed his pills. Indeed, I there read the proof that every symptom that I experienced, either in imagination or in reality, rendered their extensive consumption absolutely necessary to preserve my life. I purchased a box of Brandreth's Pills in Columbus, MS The effect was miraculous! Of course, it was just what the advertisement told me it would be. In Tuscaloosa, Alabama, I purchased half a dozen boxes. They were all used up before my perambulating show reached Vicksburg, MS, and I was a confirmed disciple of the blood theory. There I laid in a dozen boxes. In Natchez, I made a similar purchase. In New Orleans, where I remained several months, I was a profitable customer, and had become thoroughly convinced that the only real "greenhorns" in the world were those who preferred meat or bread to Brandreth's Pills. I took them morning, noon, and night. In fact, the advertisements announced that one could not take too many; for if one box was sufficient to purify the blood, eleven extra boxes would have no injurious effect.

I arrived in New York in June 1838, and by that time I had become such a firm believer in the efficacy of Brandreth's Pills, that I hardly stopped long enough to speak with my family, before I hastened to the "principal office" of Doctor Brandreth to congratulate him on being the greatest public benefactor of the age.

I found the doctor "at home," and introduced myself without ceremony. I told him my experiences. He was delighted. I next heartily endorsed every word stated in his advertisements. He was not surprised, for he knew the effects of his pills were such as I described. Still he was elated in having another witness whose extensive experiments with his pills were so eminently satisfactory. The doctor and myself were both happy—he in being able to do so much good to mankind; I in being the recipient of such untold benefits through his valuable discovery.

At last, the doctor chanced to say that he wondered how I happened to get his pills in Natchez, "for," said he, "I have no agent there as yet."

"Oh!" I replied, "I always bought my pills at the drug stores."

"Good Heavens!" exclaimed the doctor, "then they are were all counterfeits! vile impositions! poisonous compounds! I never sell a pill to a druggist—I never permit an apothecary to handle one of my pills. But they counterfeit them by the bushel; the unprincipled, heartless, murderous impostors!"

I need not say I was surprised. Was it possible, then, that my imagination had done all this business, and that I had been cured by poisons which I supposed were Brandreth's Pill? I confess I laughed heartily; and told the doctor that, after all, it seemed the counterfeits were as good as the real pills, provided the patient had sufficient faith.

The doctor was puzzled as well as vexed, but an idea struck him that soon enabled him to recover his usual equanimity.

"I'll tell you what it is," said he, "those Southern druggists have undoubtedly obtained the pills from me under false pretences. They have pretended to be planters, and have purchased pills from me in large quantities for use on the plantations, and then they have retailed the pills from their drug-shops."

I laughed at this shrewd suggestion, and remarked: "This may be so, but I guess my imagination did the business!"

The doctor was uneasy, but he asked me as a favor to bring him one of the empty pill boxes which I had brought from the South. The next day, I complied with his request, and I will do the doctor justice to say that, on comparison, it proved as he had suspected; the pills were genuine, and although he had advertised that no druggist should sell them, they were so popular that druggists found it necessary to get them "by hook or by crook;" and the consequence was, I had the pleasure of a glorious laugh, and Doctor Brandreth experienced "a great scare."

The doctor "made his pile" long ago, although he still

devotes his personal attention to the "entirely vegetable and innocent pills, whose life-giving power no pen can describe."

In 1849, the doctor was elected President of the Village of Sing Sing, N.Y. (where he still resides,) and was reelected to the same office for seven consecutive years. In the same year, he was elected to the New York State Senate, and in 1859 was again elected.

Dr. Brandreth is a liberal man and a pleasant, entertaining, and edifying companion. He deserves all the success he has ever received. "Long may he wave!"

Part II

THE SPIRITUALISTS

The Davenport brothers, their rise and progress—Spiritual rope-tying—Music playing—Cabinet secrets—"They choose darkness rather than light," etc.—The spiritual hand—How the thing is done—Dr. W. F. Van Vleck.

The Davenport Brothers are natives of Buffalo, N.Y., and in that city commenced their career as "mediums" about twelve years ago. They were then mere lads. For some time, their operations were confined to their own place, where, having obtained considerable notoriety through the press, they were visited by people from all parts of the country. But, in 1855, they were induced by John F. Coles, a very worthy spiritualist of New York City, to visit that metropolis, and there exhibit their powers. Under the management of Mr. Coles, they held "circles" afternoon and evening, for several days, in a small hall at 195 Bowery. The audience were seated next the walls, the principal space being required for the use of "the spirits." The "manifestations" mostly consisted in the thrumming and seemingly rapid movement about the hall of several stringed instruments, the room having been made entirely dark, while the boys were supposed or asserted to be quietly seated at the table in the center. Two guitars, with sometimes a banjo, were the instruments used, and the noise made by "the spirits" was about equal to the united honking of a large flock of wild geese. The manifestations were stunning as well as astonishing; for not only was the sense of hearing smitten by the dreadful sounds, but, sometimes, a member of the circle would get a "striking demonstration" over his head!

At the request of the "controlling spirit," made through a horn, the hall was lighted at intervals during the entertainment, at which times the mediums could be seen seated at the table, looking very innocent and demure, as if they had never once thought of deceiving anybody. On one of these occasions, however, a policeman suddenly lighted the hall by means of a dark lantern, without having been specially called upon to do so; and the boys were clearly seen with instruments in their hands. They dropped them as soon as they could, and resumed their seats at the table. Satisfied that the thing was a humbug, the audience left in disgust; and the policeman was about to march the boys to the station-house on the charge of swindling, when he was prevailed upon to remain and farther test the matter. Left alone with them, and the three seated together at the table on which the instruments had been placed, he laid, at their request, a hand on each medium's head; they then clasped both his arms with their hands. While they remained thus situated (as he supposed,) the room being dark, one of the instruments, with an infernal twanging of its strings, rose from the table and hit the policeman several times on the head; then a strange voice through the trumpet advised him not to interfere with the work of the spirits by persecuting the mediums! Considerably astonished, if not positively scared, he took his hat and left, fully persuaded that there was "something in it!"

The boys produced the manifestations by grasping the neck of the instrument, swinging it around, and thrusting it into different parts of the open space of the room, at the same time vibrating the strings with the forefinger. The faster the finger passed over the strings, the more rapidly the instrument seemed to move. Two hands could thus use as many instruments.

When sitting with a person at the table, as they did with the policeman, one hand could be taken off the investigator's arm without his knowing it, by gently increasing, at the same time, the pressure of the other hand. It was an easy matter then to raise and thrum the instrument or talk through the horn.

About a dozen gentlemen—several of whom were members of the press—had a private séance with the boys one afternoon, on which occasion "the spirits" ventured upon an extra "manifestation." All took seats at one side of a long, high table—the position of the mediums being midway of the row. This time, a little, dim, ghostly gaslight was allowed in the room. What seemed to be a hand soon appeared, partly above the edge of the vacant side of the table, and opposite the "mediums." One excited spiritualist present said he could see the fingernails.

John F. Coles—who had for several days, suspected the innocence of the boys—sprang from his seat, turned up the gaslight, and pounced on the elder boy, who was found to have a nicely stuffed glove drawn partly on to the toe of his boot. That, then, was the spirit-hand! The nails that the imaginative spiritualist thought he saw were not on the fingers. The boy alleged that the spirits made him attempt the deception.

The father of these boys, who had accompanied them to New York, took them home immediately after that exposure. In Buffalo, they continued to hold "circles," hoping to retrieve their lost reputation as good mediums—by being, not more honest, but more cautious. To prevent anyone getting hold of them while operating, they hit upon the plan of passing a rope through a buttonhole of each gentleman's coat, the ends to be held by a trusty person—assigning, as a reason for that arrangement, that it would then be known no one in the circle could assist in producing the manifestations. The plan did not always work well, however; for a skeptic would sometimes cut the rope, and then pounce upon "the spirit"—that is, if he didn't happen to miss that individual, on account of the darkness and while trying to avoid a collision with the instruments.

To secure greater immunity from detection, and to enable them to exhibit in large halls which could not easily be darkened, the boys finally fixed upon a "cabinet" as the best thing in which to work. They had, some time before, made the "rope-test" a feature of their exhibitions; and in their cabinet-show they depended for success in deceiving entirely upon the presumption of the audience that their hands were so secured with ropes as to prevent their playing upon the musical instruments, or doing whatever else the spirits were assumed to do.

Their cabinet is about six feet high, six feet long, and two and a half feet deep, the front consisting of three doors, opening outward. In each end is a seat, with holes through which the ropes can be passed in securing the mediums. In the upper part of the middle door is a lozenge-shaped aperture, curtained on the inside with black muslin or oilcloth. The bolts are on the inside of the doors.

The mediums are generally first tied by a committee of two gentlemen appointed from the audience. The doors of the cabinet are then closed, those at the ends first, and then the middle one, the bolt of which is reached by the manager through the aperture.

By the time the end doors are closed and bolted, the Davenports, in many instances, have succeeded in loosening the knots next their wrists, and in slipping their hands out, the latter being then exhibited at the aperture. Lest the hands should be recognized as belonging to the mediums, they are kept in a constant shaking motion while in view; and to make the hands look large or small, they spread or press together the fingers. With that peculiar rapid motion imparted to them, four hands in the aperture will appear to be half-a-dozen. A lady's flesh colored kid glove, nicely stuffed with cotton, is sometimes exhibited as a female hand—a critical observation of it never being allowed. It does not take the medium long to draw the knots close to their wrists again. They are then ready to be inspected by the Committee, who report them tied as they were left. Supposing them to have been securely bound all the while, those who witness the show are very naturally astonished.

Sometimes, after being tied by a committee, the mediums cannot readily extricate their hands and get them back as they were; in which case they release themselves entirely from the ropes before the doors are again opened, concluding to wait till after "the spirits" have bound them, before showing hands or making music.

It is a common thing for these impostors to give the rope

between their hands a twist while those limbs are being bound; and that movement, if dexterously made, while the attention of the committeemen is momentarily diverted, is not likely to be detected. Reversing that movement will let the hand out.

The great point with the Davenports in tying themselves is, to have a knot next their wrists that looks solid, "fair and square," at the same time that they can slip it and get their hands out in a moment. There are several ways of forming such a knot, one of which I will attempt to describe. In the middle of a rope a square knot is tied, loosely at first, so that the ends of the rope can be tucked through, in opposite directions, below the knot, and the latter is then drawn tight. There are then two loops—which should be made small—through which the hands are to pass after the rest of the tying is done. Just sufficient slack is left to admit of the hands passing through the loops, which, lastly, are drawn close to the wrists, the knot coming between the latter. No one, from the appearance of such a knot, would suspect it could be slipped. The mediums thus tied can, immediately after the committee have inspected the knots, and closed the doors, show hands or play upon musical instruments, and in a few seconds be, to all appearance, firmly tied again.

If flour has been placed in their hands, it makes no difference as to their getting those members out of or into the ropes; but, to show hands at the aperture, or to make a noise on the musical instruments, it is necessary that they should get the flour out of one hand into the other. The moisture of the hand and squeezing, packs the flour into a lump, which can be laid into the other hand and returned without losing any. The little flour that adheres to the empty hand can be wiped off in the pantaloons pocket. The mediums seldom if ever take flour in their hands while they are in the bonds put upon them by the committee. The principal part of the show is after the tying has been done in their own way. Wm. Fay, who accompanies the Davenports, is thus fixed when the hypothetical spirits take the coat off his back.

As I before remarked, there are several ways in which the mediums tie themselves. They always do it, however, in such a manner that, though the tying looks secure, they can immediately get one or both hands out. Let committees insist upon untying the knots of the spirits, whether the mediums are willing or not. A little critical observation will enable them to learn the trick.

To make this subject of tying clearer, I will repeat that the Davenports always untie themselves by using their hands; as they are able in ninety-nine cases out of a hundred, however impossible it may seem, to release their hands by loosening the knots next their wrists. Sometimes they do this by twisting the rope between their wrists; sometimes it is by keeping their muscles as tense as possible during the tying, so that when relaxed there shall be some slack. Most "committees" know so little about tying, that anybody, by a little pulling, slipping, and wriggling, could slip his hands out of their knots.

A violin, bell, and tambourine, with perhaps a guitar and drum, are the instruments used by the Davenports in the cabinet. The one who plays the violin holds the bell in his hand with the bow. The other chap beats the tambourine on his knee, and has a hand for something else.

The "mediums" frequently allow a person to remain with them, providing he will let his hands be tied to their knees, the operators having previously been tied by "the spirits." The party who ventures upon that experiment is apt to be considerably "mussed up," as "the spirits" are not very gentle in their manipulations.

To expose all the tricks of these impostors would require more space than I can afford at present. They have exhibited throughout the Northern States and the Canadas; but never succeeded very well pecuniarily until about two years ago, when they employed an agent, who advertised them in such a way as to attract public attention. In September last, they went to England, where they have since created considerable excitement.

If the hands of these boys were tied close against the side of their cabinet, the ropes passing through holes and fastened on the outside, I think "the spirits" would always fail to work.

Dr. W. F. Van Vleck, of Ohio, to whom I am indebted for some of the facts contained in this chapter, can beat the Davenport brothers at their own game. In order that he might the better learn the various methods pursued by the professed "mediums" in deceiving the public, Dr. Van Vleck entered into the medium-business himself, and by establishing confidential relations with those of the profession whose acquaintance he made, he became duly qualified to expose them.

He was accepted and endorsed by leading spiritualists in different parts of the country, as a good medium, who performed the most remarkable spiritual wonders. As the worthy doctor practiced this innocent deception on the professed mediums solely in order that he might thus be able to expose their blasphemous impositions, the public will scarcely dispute that in this case the end justified the means. I suppose it is not possible for any professed medium to puzzle or deceive the doctor. He is up to all their "dodges," because he has learned in their school. Mediums always insist upon certain conditions, and those conditions are just such as will best enable them to deceive the senses and pervert the judgment.

Anderson "the Wizard of the North," and other conjurers in England, gave the Davenports battle, but the "prestidigitators" did not reap many laurels. Conjurers are no more likely to understand the tricks of the mediums than any other person is. Before a trick can be exposed it must be learned. Dr. Van Vleck, having learned "the ropes," is competent to expose them; and he is doing it in many interesting public lectures and illustrations.

If the Davenports were exhibiting simply as jugglers, I might admire their dexterity, and have nothing to say against them; but when they presumptuously pretend to deal in "things spiritual," I consider it my duty, while treating of humbugs, to do this much at least in exposing them.

Chapter 10

The spirit-rapping and medium humbugs—Their origin—How the thing is done—$500 reward.

The "spirit-rapping" humbug was started in Hydesville, New York, about seventeen years ago, by several daughters of a Mr. Fox, living in that place. These girls discovered that certain exercises of their anatomy would produce mysterious sounds—mysterious to those who heard them, simply because the means of their production were not apparent. Reports of this wonder soon went abroad, and the Fox family were daily visited by people from different sections of the country—all having a greed for the marvelous. Not long after the strange sounds were first heard, someone suggested that they were, perhaps, produced by spirits; and a request was made for a certain number of raps, if that suggestion was correct. The specified number were immediately heard. A plan was then proposed by means of which communications might be received from "the spirits." An investigator would repeat the alphabet, writing down whatever letters were designated by the "raps." Sentences were thus formed—the orthography, however, being decidedly bad.

What purported to be the spirit of a murdered peddler, gave an account of his "taking off." He said that his body was buried beneath that very house, in a corner of the cellar; that he had been killed by a former occupant of the premises. A peddler really had disappeared, somewhat mysteriously, from that part of the country some time before; and ready credence was given the statements thus spelled out through the "raps." Digging to the depth of eight feet in the cellar did not disclose any "dead corpus," or even the remains of one. Soon after that, the missing peddler reappeared in Hydesville, still "clothed with mortality," and having a new assortment of wares to sell.

That the "raps" were produced by disembodied spirits many firmly believed. False communications were attributed to evil spirits. The answers to questions were as often wrong as right; and only right when the answer could be easily guessed, or inferred from the nature of the question itself.

The Fox family moved to Rochester, New York, soon after the rapping-humbug was started; and it was there that their first public effort was made. A committee was appointed to investigate the matter, most of whom reported adversely to the claims of the "mediums;" though all of them were puzzled to know how the thing was done. In Buffalo, where the Foxes subsequently let their spirits flow, a committee of doctors reported that these loosely-constructed girls produced the "raps" by snapping their toe and knee joints. That theory, though very much ridiculed by the spiritualists then and since, was correct, as further developments proved.

Mrs. Culver, a relative of the Fox girls, made a solemn deposition before a magistrate, to the effect that one of the girls had instructed her how to produce the "raps," on condition that she (Mrs. C.) should not communicate a knowledge of the matter to anyone. Mrs. Culver was a good Christian woman, and she felt it her duty—as the deception had been carried so far—to expose the matter. She actually produced the "raps," in presence of the magistrate, and explained the manner of making them.

Doctor Von Vleck—to whom I referred in connection with my exposition of the Davenport imposture—produces very loud "raps" before his audiences, and so modulates them that they will seem to be at any desired point in his vicinity; yet not a movement of his body betrays the fact that the sounds are caused by him.

The Fox family found that the rapping business would be made to pay; and so they continued it, with varying success, for a number of years, making New York city their place of residence and principal field of operation. I believe that none of them are now in the "spiritual line." Margaret Fox, the youngest of the rappers, has for some time been a member of the Roman Catholic Church.

From the very commencement of spiritualism, there has been a constantly increasing demand for "spiritual" wonders, to meet which numerous "mediums" have been "developed."

Many, who otherwise would not be in the least distinguished, have become "mediums" in order to obtain notoriety, if nothing more.

Communicating by "raps" was a slow process; so some of the mediums took to writing spasmodically; others talked in a "trance"—all under the influence of spirits!

Mediumship has come to be a profession steadily pursued by quite a number of persons, who get their living by it.

There are various classes of "mediums," the operations of each class being confined to a particular department of "spiritual" humbuggery.

Some call themselves "test mediums;" and, by insisting upon certain formulas, they succeed in astonishing, if they don't convince most of them who visit them. It is by this class that the public is most likely to be deceived.

There is a person by the name of J. V. Mansfield, who has been called by spiritualists the "Great Spirit Postmaster," his specialty being the answering of sealed letters addressed to spirits. The letters are returned—some of them at least— to the writers without appearing to have been opened, accompanied by answers purporting to be written through Mansfield by the spirits addressed. Such of these letters as are sealed with gum-arabic merely, can be steamed open, and the envelopes resealed and reglazed as they were before. If sealing-wax has been used, a sharp, thin blade will enable the medium to nicely cut off the seal by splitting the paper under it; and then, after a knowledge of the contents of the letter is arrived at, the seal can be replaced in its original position, and made fast with gum-arabic. Not more than one out of a hundred would be likely to observe that the seal had ever been tampered with. The investigator opens the envelope, when returned to him, at the end, preserving the sealed part intact, in order to show his friends that the letter was answered without being opened!

Another method of the medium is, to slit open the envelope at the end with a sharp knife, and afterward stick it together again with gum, rubbing the edge slightly as soon as the gum is dry. If the job is nicely done, a close observer would hardly perceive it.

Mr. Mansfield does not engage to answer all letters; those unanswered being too securely sealed for him to open without detection. To secure the services of the "Great Spirit-

Postmaster," a fee of five dollars must accompany your letter to the spirits; and the money is retained whether an answer is returned or not.

Rather high postage that!

Several years since, a gentleman living in Buffalo, N.Y., addressed some questions to one of his spirit-friends, and enclosed them, together with a single hair and a grain of sand, in an envelope, which he sealed so closely that no part of the contents could escape while being transmitted by mail. The questions were sent to Mr. Mansfield and answers requested through his "mediumship." The envelope containing the questions was soon returned, with answers to the letter. The former did not appear to have been opened. Spreading a large sheet of blank paper on a table before him, the gentleman opened the envelope and placed its contents on the table. The hair and grain of sand were not there.

Time and again has Mansfield been convicted of imposture, yet he still prosecutes his nefarious business.

The "Spirit-Postmaster" fails to get answers to such questions as these:

"Where did you die?"

"When?"

"Who attended you in your last illness?"

"What were your last words?"

"How many were present at your death?"

But if the questions are of such a nature as the following, answers are generally obtained:

"Are you happy?"

"Are you often near me?"

"And can you influence me?"

"Have you changed your religious notions since entering the spirit-world?"

It is to be observed that the questions which the "Spirit-Postmaster" can answer *require no knowledge of facts about the applicant*, while those which he cannot answer, do require it.

Address, for instance, your spirit-father without mentioning his name, and the name will not be given in connection with the reply purporting to come from him—unless the medium knows your family.

I will write a series of questions addressed to one of my spirit-friends, enclose them in an envelope, and if Mr. Mansfield or any other professed medium will answer those questions pertinently in my presence, and without touching the envelope, I will give to such party five hundred dollars, and think I have got the worth of my money.

Chapter 11

*The "ballot-test"—The old gentleman and his "diseased"
relatives—A "hungry spirit"—"Palming" a
ballot—Revelations on strips of paper.*

An aptitude for deception is all the capital that a person requires in order to become a "spirit-medium;" or, at least, to gain the reputation of being one. Backing up the pretence to mediumship with a show of something mysterious, is all-sufficient to enlist attention, and insure the making of converts.

One of the most noted of the mediumistic fraternity— whose name I do not choose to give at present—steadily pursued his business, for several years, in a room in Broadway, in this city, and succeeded not only in humbugging a good many people, but in what was more important to him— acquiring quite an amount of money. His mode of operating was "the ballot-test," and was as follows:

Medium and investigator being seated opposite each other at a table, the latter was handed several slips of blank paper, with the request that he write the first (or Christian) names— one on each paper—of several of his deceased relatives, which being done, he was desired to touch the folded papers, one after the other, till one should be designated, by three tips of the table, as containing the name of the spirit who would communicate. The selected paper was laid aside, and the others thrown upon the floor, the investigator being further requested to write on as many different pieces of paper as contained the names, and the relation (to himself) of the spirits bearing them. Supposing the names written were Mary, Joseph, and Samuel, being, respectively, the investigator's mother, father, and brother. The last-named class would be secondly written, and one of them designated by three tips of the table, as in the first instance. The respective ages of the deceased parties, at the time of their decease, would also be written, and one of them selected. The first "test" consisted in having the selected name, relationship, and age correspond—that is, refer to the same party; to ascertain which the investigator was desired to look at them, and state if it was the case. If the correspondence was affirmed, a communication was soon given, with the selected name, relationship, and age appended. Questions, written in the presence of the medium, were answered relevantly, if not pertinently. Investigators generally did their part of the writing in a guarded manner, interposing their left hand between the paper on which they wrote and the medium's eyes; and they were very much astonished when they received a communication, couched in affectionate terms, with the names of their spirit-friends attached.

By long practice, the medium was enabled to determine what the investigator wrote, by the motion of his hand in writing. Nine out of ten wrote the relationship first that corresponded with the first name they had written. Therefore, if the medium selected the first that was written of each class, they in most cases referred to the same spirit. He waited till the investigator had affirmed the coincidence, before proceeding; for he did not like to write a communication, appending to it, for instance, "Your Uncle John," when it ought to be "Your Father John." The reason he did not desire inquirers to write the surnames of their spirit-friends, was this: almost all Christian names are common, and he was familiar with the motions which the hand must make in writing them; but there are comparatively few people who have the same surnames, and to determine them would have been more difficult. No fact was communicated that had not been surreptitiously gleaned from the investigator.

An old gentleman, apparently from the country, one day entered the room of this medium and expressed a desire for a "sperit communication."

He was told to take a seat at the table, and to write the names of his deceased relatives. The medium, like many others, incorrectly pronounced the term "deceased," the same as "diseased"—sounding the *s* like *z*.

The old gentleman carefully adjusted his "specs" and did what was required of him. A name and relationship having been selected from those written, the investigator was desired to examine and state if they referred to one party.

"Wal, I declare they do!" said he. "But I say Mister, what has them papers to do with a sperit communication?"

"You will see, directly," replied the medium.

Whereupon the latter spasmodically wrote a "communication," which read somewhat as follows:

"My Dear Husband:—I am very glad to be able to address you through this channel. Keep on investigating, and you will soon be convinced of the great fact of spirit-intercourse. I am happy in my spirit-home; patiently awaiting the time when you will join me here, etc. Your loving wife, Betsey."

"Good gracious! But my old woman can't be dead," said the investigator, "for I left her tu hum!"

"Not dead!" exclaimed the medium. "Did I not tell you to write the names of deceazed relatives?"

"Diseased!" returned the old man; "Wal, she ain't anything else, for she's had the rumatiz orfully for six months!"

Saying which, he took his hat and left, concluding that it was not worth while to "keep on investigating" any longer at that time.

This same medium, not long since, visited Great Britain for the purpose of practicing his profession there.

In one of the cities of Scotland, some shrewd investigator divined that he was able to nearly guess from the motion of the hand what questions were written.

"Are you happy?" being a question commonly asked the "spirits," one of these gentlemen varied it by asking:

"Are you hungry?"

The reply was, an emphatic affirmative.

They tricked the trickster in other ways; one of which was to write the names of mortals instead of spirits. It made no difference, however, as to getting a "communication."

To tip the table without apparent muscular exertion, this impostor placed his hands on it in such a way that the "pisi-form bone" (which may be felt projecting at the lower corner of the palm, opposite the thumb) pressed against the edge. By pushing, the table tipped from him, it being prevented from sliding by little spikes in the legs of the side opposite the operator.

There are other "ballot-test mediums," as they are called, who have a somewhat different method of cheating. They, too, require investigators to write the names—in full, however—of their spirit-friends; the slips of paper containing the names, to be folded and placed on a table. The medium then seizes one of the "ballots," and asks:

"Is the spirit present whose name is on this?"

Dropping that and taking another:

"On this?"

So he handles all the papers without getting a response. During this time, however, he has dexterously "palmed" one of the ballots, which—while telling the investigator to be patient, as the spirits would doubtless soon come—he opens with his left hand, on his knee, under the edge of the table.

A mere glance enables him to read the name. Refolding the paper, and retaining it in his hand, he remarks:

"I will touch the ballots again, and perhaps one of them will be designated this time."

Dropping among the rest the one he had "palmed," he soon picks it up again, whereat three loud "raps" are heard.

"That paper," says he to the investigator, "probably contains the name of the spirit who rapped; please hold it in your hand."

Then seizing a pencil, he writes a name, which the investigator finds to be the one contained in the selected paper.

If the ballots are few in number, a blank is put with the pile, when the medium "palms" one, else the latter might be missed.

It seems the spirits can never give their names without

being reminded of them by the investigator, and then they are so doubtful of their own identity that they have but little to say for themselves.

One medium to whom I have already alluded, after a sojourn of several years in California—whither he went from Boston, seeking whom he might humbug—has now returned to the East, and is operating in this city. Besides answering sealed letters, he furnishes written "communications" to parties visiting him at his rooms—a "sitting," however, being granted to but one person at a time. His terms are only five dollars an hour.

Seated at a table in a part of the room where is the most light, he hands the investigator a strip of blank, white paper, rather thin and light of texture, about a yard long and six inches wide, requesting him to write across one end of it a single question, addressed to a spirit-friend, then to sign his own name, and fold the paper once or twice over what he has written. For instance:

"Brother Samuel:—Will you communicate with me through this medium? William Franklin."

To learn what has been written, the medium lays the paper down on the table, and repeatedly rubs the fingers of his right hand over the folds made by the inquirer. If that does not render the writing visible through the one thickness of paper that covers it, he slightly raises the edge of the folds with his left hand while he continues to rub with his right; and that admits of the light shining through, so that the writing can be read. The other party is so situated that the writing is not visible to him through the paper, and he is not likely to presume that it is visible to the medium; the latter having assigned as a reason for his manipulations that spirits were able to read the questions only by means of the odylic, magnetic, or some other emanation from the ends of his fingers!

Having learned the question, of course the medium can reply to it, giving the name of the spirit addressed; but before doing so, he doubles the two folds made by the inquirer, and, for a show of consistency, again rubs his fingers over the paper. Then more folds and more rubbing—all the folding, additional to the inquirer's, being done to keep the latter from observing, when he comes to read the answer, that it was possible for the medium to read the question through the two folds of paper. The answer is written upon the same strip of paper that accompanies the question.

The medium requires the investigator to write his questions each on a different strip of paper; and before answering, he every time manipulates the paper in the way I have described. When rubbing his fingers over the question, he often shuts the eye which is toward the inquirer—which prevents suspicion; but the other eye is open wide enough to enable him to read the question through the paper.

Should a person write a test-question, the medium could not answer it correctly even if he did see it. In his "communications" he uses many terms of endearment, and if possible flatters the recipient out of his commonsense, and into the belief that "after all there may be something in it!"

Should the inquirer "smell a rat," and take measures to prevent the medium from learning, in the way I have stated, what question is written, he (the medium) gets nervous and discontinues the "sitting," alleging that conditions are unfavorable for spirit-communication.

Chapter 12

Spiritual "letters on the arm"—How to make them
yourself—The tambourine and ring feats—Dexter's
dancing hats—Phosphorescent oil—Some spiritual slang.

The mediums produce "bloodred letters on the arm" in a very simple way. It is done with a pencil, or some blunt-pointed instrument, it being necessary to bear on hard while the movement of writing is being executed. The pressure, though not sufficient to abrade the skin, forces the blood from the capillary vessels over which the pencil passes, and where, when the reaction takes place, an unusual quantity of blood gathers and becomes plainly visible through the cuticle. Gradually, as an equilibrium of the circulation is restored, the letters pass away.

This "manipulation" is generally produced by the medium in connection with the ballot-test. Having learned the name of an investigator's spirit-friend, in the manner stated in a previous article, the investigator is set to writing some other names. While he is thus occupied, the medium quickly slips up his sleeve under the table, and writes on his arm the name he has learned.

Try the experiment yourself, reader. Hold out your left arm; clench the fist so as to harden the muscle a little, and write your name on the skin with a blunt pencil or any similar point, in letters say three-quarters of an inch long, pressing firmly enough to feel a little pain. Rub the place briskly a dozen times; this brings out the letters quickly, in tolerably-distinct red lines.

On thick, tough skins it is difficult to produce letters in this way. They might also be outlined more deeply by sharply pricking in dots along the lines of the desired letters.

Among others who seek to gain money and notoriety by the exercise of their talents for "spiritual" humbuggery, is a certain woman, whom I will not further designate, but whose name is at the service of any proper person, and who exhibited not long since in Brooklyn and New York. This woman is accompanied by her husband, who is a confederate in the playing of her "little game."

She seats herself at a table, which has been placed against the wall of the room. The audience is so seated as to form a semicircle, at one end of which, and near enough to the medium to be able to shake hands with her, or nearly so, sits her husband, with perhaps an accommodating spiritualist next to him. Then the medium, in an assumed voice, engages in a miscellaneous talk, ending with a request that someone sit by her and hold her hand.

A skeptic is permitted to do that. When thus placed, skeptic is directly between the medium and her husband, and with his back to the latter. The husband plays spirit, and with his right hand—which is free, the other only being held by the accommodating spiritualist—pats the investigator on the head, thumps him with a guitar and other instruments, and maybe pulls his hair.

The medium assumes all this to be done by a spirit, because her hands are held and she could not do it! Profound reasoning! If anyone suggests that the husband had better sit somewhere else, the medium will not hear to it—he is a part of the battery," and the necessary conditions must not be interfered with. Sure enough! Accommodating spiritualist also says he holds husband fast.

A tambourine-frame, without the head, and an iron ring, large enough to pass over one's arm, are exhibited to the audience. Medium says the spirits have such power over matter as to be able to put one or both those things on to her arm while someone holds her hands.

The party who is privileged to hold her hands on such occasion, has to grope his way to her in the dark. Having reached her, she seizes his hands, and passes one of them down her neck and along her arm, saying:

"Now you know there is no ring already there!"

Soon after he feels the tambourine-frame or ring slide over his hand and on to his arm. A light is produced in order that he may see it is there.

When he took her hands he felt the frame or ring—or at any rate, a frame or ring—under his elbow on the table, from which place it was pulled by some power just before it went on to his arm. Such is his report to the audience. But in fact, the medium has two frames, or else a tambourine, and a tambourine-frame. She allows the investigator to feel one of these.

She has, however, previous to his taking her hands, put one arm and head through the frame she uses; so that of course he does not feel it when she passes his hand down one side of her neck and over one of her arms, as it is under that arm. Her husband pulls the tambourine from under the investigator's elbow; then the medium gets her head back through the frame, leaving it on her arm, or sliding it on to his, and the work is done!

She has also two iron rings. One of them she puts over her arm and the point of her shoulder, where it snugly remains, covered with a cape which she persists in wearing on these occasions, till the investigator takes her hands (in the dark) and feels the other ring under his elbows; then the husband disposes of the ring on the table, and the medium works the other one down on to her arm. The audience saw but one ring, and the person sitting with the medium thought he had that under his elbow till it was pulled away and put on the arm!

Some years ago, a man by the name of Dexter, who kept an oyster and liquor saloon on Bleecker street, devised a somewhat novel exhibition for the purpose of attracting custom. A number of hats, placed on the floor of his saloon, danced (or bobbed up and down) in time to music. His place was visited by a number of the leading spiritualists of New York, several of whom were heard to express a belief that the hats were moved by spirits! Dexter, however, did not claim to be a medium, though he talked vaguely of "the power of electricity," when questioned with regard to his exhibition. Besides making the hats dance, he would (apparently) cause a violin placed in a box on the floor to sound, by waving his hands over it.

The hats were moved by a somewhat complicated arrangement of wires, worked by a confederate, out of sight. These wires were attached to levers, and finally came up through the floor, through small holes hidden from observation by the sawdust strewn there, as is common in such places.

The violin in the box did not sound at all. It was another violin, under the floor, that was heard. It is not easy for a person to exactly locate a sound when the cause is not apparent. In short, Mr. Dexter's operations may be described as only consisting of a little well-managed Dexterity!

A young man "out West," claiming to be influenced by spirits, astonished people by reading names, telling time by watches, etc., in a dark room. He sat at a center-table, which was covered with a cloth, in the middle of the room. Investigators sat next the walls. The name of a spirit, for instance, would be written and laid on a table, when in a short time he pronounced it. To tell the time by a watch, he required it to be placed on the table, or in his hand. With the tablecloth over his head, a bottle of phosphorated oil enabled him to see, when not the least glimmer of light was visible to others in the room.

If any of the "spiritualist" philosophers were to be asked what is the philosophy of these proceedings, he would probably reply with a mess of balderdash pretty much like the following:

"There is an infinitesimal influence of sympathy between mind and matter, which permeates all beings, and pervades all the delicate niches and interstices of human intelligence. This sympathetic influence working upon the affined intelligence of an affinity, coagulates itself into a corporiety, approximating closely to the adumbration of mortality in its highest admensuration, at last accuminating in an accumination."

On these great philosophic principles it will not be difficult to comprehend the following actual quotation from the Spiritual Telegraph:

"In the twelfth hour, the holy procedure shall crown the Triune Creator with the most perfect disclosive illumination. Then shall the creation in the effulgence above the divine seraphemal, arise into the dome of the disclosure in one comprehensive revolving galaxy of supreme created beatitudes."

That those not surcharged with the divine afflatus may be able to get at the meaning of the above paragraph, it is translated thus:

"Then shall all the blockheads in the nincompoopdome of disclosive procedure above the all-fired leather-fungus of Peter Nephninnygo, the gooseberry grinder, rise into the dome of the disclosure until coequaled and coexistensive and conglomerate lumuxes in one comprehensive mux shall assimilate into nothing, and revolve like a bobtailed pussy cat after the space where the tail was."

What power there is in spiritualism!

I shall be glad to receive, for publication, authentic information, from all parts of the world in regard tothe doings of pretended spiritualists, especially those who perform for money. It is high time that the credulous portion of our community should be saved from the deceptions, delusions, and swindles of these blasphemous mountebanks and impostors.

Chapter 13

Demonstrations by "Sampson" under a table—A medium who is handy with her feet—Exposé of another operator in dark circles.

Considerable excitement has been created in various parts of the West by a young woman, whose name need not here be given, who pretends to be a "medium for physical manifestations." She is rather tall and quite muscular, her general manner and expression indicating innocence and simplicity.

The "manifestations" exhibited by her purport to be produced by Samson, the Hebrew champion and anti-philistine.

In preparing for her exhibition, she has a table placed sideways against the wall of the room, and covered with a thick blanket that reaches to the floor. A large tin dishpan, with handles (or ears,) a German accordion, and a tea-bell are placed under the table, at the end of which she seats herself in such a way that her body is against the top, and her lower limbs underneath, her skirts being so adjusted as to fill the space between the end legs of the table, and at the same time allow free play for her pedal extremities. The blanket, at the end where she sits, comes to her waist and hangs down to the floor on each side of her chair. The space under the table is thus made dark—a necessary condition, it is claimed—and all therein concealed from view. The "medium" then folds her arms, looks careless, and the "manifestations" commence. The accordion is sounded, no music being executed upon it, and the bell rung at the same time. Then the dishpan receives such treatment that it makes a terrible noise. Someone is requested to go to the end of the table opposite the "medium," put his hand under the blanket, take hold of the dishpan, and pull. He does so, and finds that some power is opposing him, holding the dishpan to one place. Not being rude, he forbears to jerk with all his force, but retires to his seat. The table rises several inches and comes down "kerslap," then it tips forward a number of times; then one end jumps up and down in time to music, if there is anyone present to play; loud raps are heard upon it, and the hypothetical Samson has quite a lively time generally. Some of the mortals present, one at a time, put their fingers, by request, against the blankets, through which those members are gingerly squeezed by what might be a hand, if there was one under the table. A person being told to take hold of the top of the table at the ends, he does so, and finds it so heavy that he can barely lift it. Setting it down, he is told to raise it again several inches; and at the second lifting it is no heavier than one would naturally judge such a piece of furniture to be. Another person is asked to lift the end furthest from the medium; having done so, it suddenly becomes quite weighty, and, relaxing his hold, it comes down with much force upon the floor. Thus, by the power—exercised beneath the table—of an assumed spirit, that piece of cabinet-ware becomes heavy or light, and is moved in various ways, the medium not appearing to do it.

In addition to her other "fixins," this medium has a spirit-dial, so called, on which are letters of the alphabet, the numerals, and such words as "Yes," "No," and "Don't know." The whole thing is so arranged that the pulling of a string makes an index hand go the circuit of the dial-face, and it can be made to stop at any of the characters or words thereon. This "spirit-dial" is placed on the table, near the end furthest from the medium, the string passing through a hole and hanging beneath. In the end of the string there is a knot. While the medium remains in the same position in which she sat when the other "manifestations" were produced, communications are spelled out through the dial, the index being moved by some power under the table that pulls the string. A coil-spring makes the index fly back to the starting-point, when the power is relaxed at each indication of a character or word. The orthography of these "spirits" is "bad if not worse."

Now for an explanation of the various "manifestations" that I have enumerated.

The medium is simply handy with her feet. To sound the accordion and ring the bell at the same time, she has to take off one of her shoes or slippers, the latter being generally worn by her on these occasions. That done, she gets the handle of the tea-bell between the toes of her right foot, through a hole in the stocking, then putting the heel of the same foot on the keys of the accordion, and the other foot into the strap on the bellows part of that instrument, she easily sounds it, the motion necessary to do this also causing the bell to ring. She can readily pass her heels over the keys to produce different notes. She is thus able to make sounds on the accordion that approximate to the very simple tune of "Bounding Billows," and that is the extent of her musical ability when only using her "pedals."

To get a congress-gaiter off the foot without using the hands is quite easy; but how to get one on again, those members not being employed to do it, would puzzle most people. It is not difficult to do, however, if a cord has been attached to the strap of the gaiter and tied to the leg above the calf. The cord should be slack, and that will admit of the gaiter coming off. To get it on, the toe has to be worked into the top of it, and then pulling on the cord with the toe of the other foot will accomplish the rest.

The racket with the dishpan is made by putting the toe of the foot into one of the handles or ears, and beating the pan about. By keeping the toe in this handle and putting the other foot into the pan, the operator can "stand a pull" from an investigator, who reaches under the blanket and takes hold of the other handle.

To raise the table, the "medium" puts her knees under and against the frame of it, then lifts her heels, pressing the toes against the floor, at the same time bearing with her arms on the end. To make the table tip forward, one knee only is pressed against the frame at the back side. The raps are made with the toe of the medium's shoe against the leg, frame, or top of the table.

What feels like a hand pressing the investigator's fingers when he puts them against the blanket, is nothing more than the medium's feet, the big toe of one foot doing duty for a thumb, and all the toes of the other foot being used to imitate fingers. The pressure of these, through a thick blanket, cannot well be distinguished from that of a hand.

When this experiment is to be made, the medium wears slippers that she can readily get off her feet.

To make the table heavy, the operator presses her knees outwardly against the legs of the table, and then presses down in opposition to the party who is lifting, or she presses her knees against that surface of the legs of the table that is toward her, while her feet are hooked around the lower part of the legs; that gives her a leverage, by means of which she can make the whole table or the end furthest from her seem quite heavy, and if the person lifting it suddenly relaxes his hold, it will come down with a forcible bang to the floor.

To work the "spirit-dial," the medium has only to press the string with the toe of her foot against the top of the table, and slide it (the string) along till the index points at the letter or word she wishes to indicate. The frame of the dial is beveled, the face declining toward the medium, so that she has no difficulty in observing where the index points.

After concluding her performances under the table, this medium sometimes moves her chair about two feet back and sits with her side toward the end of the table, with one leg of which, however, the skirt of her dress comes in contact. Under cover of the skirt she then hooks her foot around the leg of the table and draws it toward her. This is done without apparent muscular exertion, while she is engaged in conversation; and parties present are humbugged into the belief that the table was moved without "mortal contact"— so they report to outsiders.

This medium has a "manager," and he does his best in managing the matter, to prevent "Samson being caught" in the act of cheating. The medium, too, is vigilant, notwithstanding her appearance of carelessness and innocent simplicity. A sudden rising of the blanket once exposed to view her pedal extremities in active operation.

Another of the "Dark Circle" mediums gets a good deal of sympathy on account of her "delicate health." Her health is not so delicate, however, as to prevent her from laboring hard to humbug people with "physical demonstrations." She operates only in private, in presence of a limited number of people.

A circle being formed, the hands of all the members are joined except at one place where a table intervenes. Those sitting next to this table place a hand upon it, the other hand of each of these parties being joined with the circle. The medium takes a position close by the table, and during the manifestations is supposed to momentarily touch with her two hands the hands of those parties sitting next to the table. Of course, she could accomplish little or nothing if she allowed her hands to be constantly held by investigators; so she hit upon the plan mentioned above, to make the people present believe that the musical instruments are not sounded by her. These instruments are within her reach; and instead of touching the hands of those next the table with both her hands, as supposed, she touches, alternately, their hands with but one of hers, the other she expertly uses in sounding the instruments.

Several years ago, at one of the circles of this medium, in St. John's, Mich., a light was suddenly introduced, and she was seen in the act of doing what she had asserted to be done by the "spirits." She has also been exposed as an impostor in other places.

As I have said before, the mediums always insist on having

such "conditions" as will best enable them to deceive the senses and mislead the judgment.

If there were a few more "detectives" like Doctor Von Vleck, the whole mediumistic fraternity would soon "come to grief."

Chapter 14

Spiritual photographing—Colorado Jewett and the spirit-photographs of General Jackson, Henry Clay, Daniel Webster, Stephen A. Douglas, Napoleon Bonaparte, etc—A lady of distinction seeks and finds a spiritual photograph of her deceased infant, and her dead braother who was yet alive—How it was done.

In answer to numerous inquiries and several threats of prosecution for libel in consequence of what I have written in regard to impostors who (for money) perform tricks of legerdemain and attribute them to the spirits of deceased persons, I have only to say, I have no malice or antipathies to gratify in these expositions. In undertaking to show up the "Ancient and Modern Humbugs of the World," I am determined so far as in me lies, to publish nothing but the truth. This I shall do, "with good motives and for justifiable ends," and I shall do it fearlessly and conscientiously. No threats will intimidate, no fawnings will flatter me from publishing everything that is true which I think will contribute to the information or to the amusement of my readers.

Some correspondents ask me if I believe that all pretensions to intercourse with departed spirits are impositions. I reply, that if people declare that they privately communicate with or are influenced to write or speak by invisible spirits, I cannot prove that they are deceived or are attempting to deceive me—although I believe that one or the other of these propositions is true. But when they pretend to give me communications from departed spirits, to tie or untie ropes—to read sealed letters, or to answer test-questions through spiritual agencies, I pronounce all such pretensions ridiculous impositions, and I stand ready at any time to prove them so, or to forfeit five hundred dollars, whenever these pretended mediums will succeed in producing their "wonderful manifestations" in a room of my selecting, and with apparatus of my providing; they not being permitted to handle the sealed letters or folded ballots which they are to answer, nor to make conditions in regard to the manner of rope tying, etc. If they can answer my test-questions relevantly and truly, without touching the envelopes in which they are sealed—or even when given to them by my word of mouth, I will hand over the $500. If they can cause invisible agencies to perform in open daylight many of the things which they pretend to accomplish by spirits in the dark, I will promptly pay $500 for the sight. In the meantime, I think I can reasonably account for and explain all pretended spiritual gymnastic performances—throwings of hairbrushes—dancing pianos—spirit-rapping—table-tipping—playing of musical instruments, and flying through the air (in the dark,) and a thousand other "wonderful manifestations" which, like most of the performances of modern "magicians," are "passing strange" until explained, and then they are as flat as dishwater. Dr. Von Vleck publicly produces all of these pretended "manifestations" in open daylight, without claiming spiritual aid.

Among the number of humbugs that owe their existence to various combinations of circumstances and the extreme gullibility of the human race, the following was related to me by a gentleman whose position and character warrant me in announcing that it may be implicitly relied upon as correct in every particular.

Some time before the Presidential election, a photographer residing in one of our cities (an ingenious man and a scientific chemist,) was engaged in making experiments with his camera, hoping to discover some new combination whereby to increase the facility of "picturing the human form divine," etc. One morning, his apparatus being in excellent order, he determined to photograph himself. No sooner thought of, than he set about making his arrangements. All being ready, he placed himself in a position, remained a second or two, and then instantly closing his camera, surveyed the result of his operation. On bringing the picture out upon the plate, he was surprised to find a shadowy representation of a human being, so remarkably ghostlike and supernatural, that he became amused at the discovery he had made. The operation was repeated, until he could produce similar pictures by a suitable arrangement of his lenses and reflectors known to no other than himself. About this time he became acquainted with one of the most famous spiritualist-writers, and in conversation with him, showed him confidentially one of those photographs, with also the shadow of another person, with the remark, mysteriously whispered:

"I assure you, Sir, upon my word as a gentleman, and by all my hopes of a hereafter, that this picture was produced upon the plate as you see it, at a time when I had locked myself in my gallery, and no other person was in the room.

It appeared instantly, as you see it there; and I have long wished to obtain the opinion of some man, like yourself, who has investigated these mysteries."

The spiritualist listened attentively, looked upon the picture, heard other explanations, examined other pictures, and sagely gave it as his opinion that the inhabitants of the unknown sphere had taken this mode of reappearing to the view of mortal eyes, that this operator must be a "medium" of especial power. The *New York Herald of Progress*, a spiritualist paper, printed the first article upon this man's spiritual photograph.

The acquaintance thus begun was continued, and the photographer found it very profitable to oblige his spiritual friend, by the reproduction of ghostlike pictures, *ad infinitum*, at the rate of five dollars each. Mothers came to the room of the artist, and gratefully retired with ghostly representations of departed little ones. Widows came to purchase the shades of their departed husbands. Husbands visited the photographer and procured the spectral pictures of their dead wives. Parents wanted the phantom-portraits of their deceased children. Friends wished to look upon what they believed to be the lineaments of those who had long since gone to the spirit-land. All who sought to look on those pictures were satisfied with what had been shown them, and, by conversation on the subject, increased the number of visitors. In short, every person who heard about this mystery determined to verify the wonderful tales related, by looking upon the ghostly lineaments of some person, who, they believed, inhabited another sphere. And here I may as well mention that one of the faithful obtained a "spirit" picture of a deceased brother who had been dead more than five years, and said that he recognized also the very pattern of his cravat as the same that he wore in life. Can human credulity go further than to suppose that the departed still appear in the old clo' of their earthly wardrobe? and the fact that the appearance of "the shade" of a young lady in one of the fashionable cut Zouave jackets of the hour did not disturb the faith of the believers, fills us indeed with wonder.

The fame of the photographer spread throughout the "spiritual circles," and pilgrims to this spiritual Mecca came from remote parts of the land, and before many months, caused no little excitement among some persons, inclined to believe that the demonstrations were entirely produced by human agency.

The demand for "spirit" pictures consequently increased, until the operator was forced to raise his price to ten dollars, whenever successful in obtaining a true "spirit-picture," or to be overwhelmed with business that now interfered with his regular labors.

About this time the famous "Peace Conference" had been concluded by the issue of Mr. Lincoln's celebrated letter, "To whom it may concern," and William Cornell Jewett (with his head full of projects for restoring peace to a suffering country) heard about the mysterious photographer, and visited the operator.

"Sir," said he, "I must consult with the spirits of distinguished statesmen. We need their counsel. This cruel war must stop. Brethren slaying brethren, it is horrible, Sir. Can you show me John Adams? Can you show me Daniel Webster? Let me look upon the features of Andrew Jackson. I must see that noble, glorious, wise old statesman, Henry Clay, whom I knew. Could you reproduce Stephen A. Douglas, with whom to counsel at this crisis in our national affairs! I should like to meet the great Napoleon. Such, here obtained, would increase my influence in the political work that I have in hand."

In his own nervous, impetuous, excited way, Colorado Jewett continued to urge upon the photographer the great importance of receiving such communications, or some evidence that the spirits of our deceased statesmen were watching over and counseling those who desire to reunite the two opposing forces, fighting against each other on the soil of a common country.

With much caution, the photographer answered the questions presented. Arranging the camera, he produced some indistinct figures, and then concluded that the "conditions" were not sufficiently favorable to attempt anything more before the next day. On the following morning, Jewett appeared—nervous, garrulous, and excited at the prospect of being in the presence of those great men, whose spirits he desired to invoke. The apparatus was prepared; utter silence imposed, and for some time the heart of the peace-seeker could almost be heard thumping within the breast of him who sought supernatural aid, in his efforts to end our cruel civil war. Then, overcome by his own thoughts, Jewett disturbed the "conditions" by changing his position, and muttering short invocations, addressed to the shades of those he wished to behold. The operator finally declared he could not proceed, and postponed his performance for that day. So, excuses were made, until the mental condition of Mr. Jewett had reached that state which permitted the photographer to expect the most complete success. Everything being prepared, Jewett breathlessly awaited the expected presence. Quietly the operator produced the spectral representation of the elder Adams. Jewett scrutinized the plate, and expressed a silent wonder, accompanied, no doubt, with some mental appeals addressed to the ancient statesman. Then, writing the name of Webster upon a slip of paper, he passed it over to the photographer, who gravely placed the scrap of writing upon the camera, and presently drew therefrom the "ghostlike" but well remembered features of the "Sage of Marshfield." Colorado Jewett was now thoroughly impressed with the spiritual power producing these images; and in ecstasy breathed a prayer that Andrew Jackson might appear to lend his countenance to the conference he wished to hold with the mighty dead. Jackson's well known features came out upon call, after due manipulation of the proper instrument. "Glorious trio of departed statesmen!" thought Jewett, "help us by your counsels in this the day of our nation's great distress." Next Henry Clay's outline was faintly shown from the tomb, and here the sitter remarked that he expected him. After him came Stephen A. Douglas, and the whole affair was so entirely satisfactory to Jewett, that, after paying fifty dollars for what he had witnessed, he, the next day, implored the presence of George Washington, offering fifty dollars more for a "spiritual" sight of the "Father of our Country." This request smote upon the ear of the photographer like an invitation to commit sacrilege. His reverence for the memory of Washington was not to be disturbed by the tempting offer of so many greenbacks. He could not allow the features of that great man to be used in connection with an imposture perpetrated upon so deluded a fanatic as Colorado Jewett. In short, the "conditions" were unfavorable for the apparition of "General Washington;" and his visitor must remain satisfied with the council of great men that had been called from the spirit world to instill wisdom into the noddle of a foolish man on this terrestrial planet. Having failed to obtain, by the agency of the operator, a glimpse of Washington, Jewett clasped his hands together, and sinking upon his knees, said, looking toward Heaven: "O spirit of the immortal Washington! look down upon the warring elements that convulse our country, and kindly let thy form appear, to lend its influence toward reuniting a nation convulsed with civil war!"

It is needless to say that this prayer was not answered. The spirit would not come forth; and, although quieted by the explanations and half promises of the photographer, the peace-messenger departed, convinced that he had been in the presence of five great statesmen, and saddened by the reflection that the shade of the immortal Washington had turned away its face from those who had refused to follow the counsels he gave while living.

Soon after this, Jewett ordered duplicates of these photographs to the value of $20 more. I now have on exhibition in my Museum several of the veritable portraits taken at this time, in which the well-known form and face of Mr. Jewett are plainly depicted, and on one of which appears the shade of Henry Clay, on another that of Napoleon the First, and on others ladies supposed to represent deceased feminines of great celebrity. It is said that Jewett sent one of the Napoleonic pictures to the Emperor Louis Napoleon.

Not long after Colorado Jewett had beheld these wonderful pictures, and worked himself up into the belief that he was surrounded by the great and good statesmen of a former generation, a lady, without making herself known, called upon the photographer. I am informed that she is the wife of a distinguished official. She had heard of the success of others, and came to verify their experience under her own bereavement. Completely satisfied by the apparition exhibited, she asked for and obtained a spectral photograph resembling her son, who, some months previously, had gone to the spirit-land. It is said that the same lady asked for and obtained a spiritual photograph of her brother, whom she had recently heard was slain in battle; and when she returned home she found him alive, and as well as could be expected under the circumstances. But this did not shake her faith in the least. She simply remarked that some evil spirit had assumed her brother's form in order to deceive her. This is a very common method of spiritualists "digging out" when the impositions of the "money-operators" are detected. This same lady has recently given her personal influence in favor of the "medium" Colchester, in Washington. One of these impressions bearing the likeness of this distinguished lady was accidentally recognized by a visitor. This capped the climax of the imposture and satisfied the photographer that he was committing a grave injury upon society by continuing to produce "spiritual pictures," and subsequently he refused to lend himself to any more "manifestations" of this kind. He had exhausted the fun.

I need only explain the modus operandi of effecting this illusion, to make apparent to the most ignorant that no super-natural agency was required to produce photographs bearing a resemblance to the persons whose "apparition" was desired. The photographer always took the precaution of inquiring about the deceased, his appearance and ordinary mode of wearing the hair. Then, selecting from countless old "negatives" the nearest resemblance, it was produced for the visitor, in dim, ghostlike outline differing so much from anything of the kind ever produced, that his customers seldom failed to recognize some lineament the dead person possessed when living, especially if such relative had deceased long since. The spectral illusions of Adams, Webster, Jackson, Clay, and Douglas were readily obtained from excellent portraits of the deceased statesmen, from which the scientific operator had prepared his illusions for Colorado Jewett.

In placing before my readers this incident of "Spiritual Photography," I can assure them that the facts are substantially as related; and I am now in correspondence with gentlemen of wealth and position who have signified their willingness to support this statement by affidavits and other documents prepared for the purpose of opening the eyes of the people to the delusions daily practised upon the ignorant and superstitious.

Chapter 15

Banner of Light—Messages from the dead—Spiritual civilities—Spirit "hollering"—Hans von Vleet, the female Dutchman—Mrs. Conant's "circles"—Paine's table-tipping humbug exposed.

The Banner of Light, a weekly journal of romance, literature, and general intelligence, published in Boston, is the principal organ of spiritualism in this country. Its "general intelligence" is rather questionable, though there is no doubt about its being a "journal of romance," strongly tinctured with humbug and imposture. It has a "Message Department," the proprietors of the paper claiming that "each message in this department of the 'Banner' was spoken by the spirit whose name it bears, through the instrumentality of Mrs. J. H. Conant, while in an abnormal condition called the trance."

I give a few specimens of these "messages." Thus, for instance, discourseth the Ghost of Lolley:

"How do? Don't know me, do you? Know George Lolley? [Yes. How do you do?] I'm first rate. I'm dead; ain't you afraid of me? You know I was familiar with those sort of things, so I wasn't frightened to go.

"Well, won't you say to the folks that I'm all right, and

happy? that I didn't suffer a great deal, had a pretty severe wound, got over that all right; went out from Petersburg. I was in the battle before Petersburg; got my discharge from there. Remember me kindly to Mr. Lord.

"Well, tell 'em as soon as I get the wheels a little greased up and in running order I'll come back with the good things, as I said I would, George W. Lolley. Goodbye."

Immediately after a "message" from the spirit of John Morgan, the guerrilla, came one from Charles Talbot, who began as follows with a curious apostrophe to his predecessor:

"Hi-yah! old grisly. It's lucky for you I didn't get in ahead of you.

"I am Charlie Talbot, of Chambersburg, Pa. Was wounded in action, captured by the Rebels, and 'died on their hands' as they say of the horse."

It seems a little rude for one "spirit" to term another "Old Grisly;" but such may be the style of compliment prevailing in the spirit-world.

Here is what Brother Klink said:

"John Klink, of the Twenty-fifth South Carolina. I want to open communication with Thomas Lefar, Charleston, S.C. I am deucedly ignorant about this coming back—dead railroad—business. It's new business to me, as I suppose it will be to some of you when you travel this way. Say I will do the best I can to communicate with my friends, if they will give me an opportunity. I desire Mr. Lefar to send my letter to my family when he receives it—he knows where they are—and then report to this office.

"Good night, afternoon or morning, I don't know which. I walked out at Petersburg."

Here is a message from George W. Gage, with some of the questions which he answered:

"[How do you like your new home?] First rate. I likes—heigho!—I likes to come here, for they clears all the truck away before you get round, and fix up so you can talk right off. [Wasn't you a medium?] No, Sir; I wasn't afraid, though; nor my mother ain't, either. Oh, I knew about it; I knew before I come to die, about it. My mother told me about it. I knew I'd be a woman when I come here, too. [Did you?] Yes, sir; my mother told me, and said I musn't be afraid. Oh, I don't likes that, but I likes to come.

"I forgot, Sir; my mother's deaf, and always had to holler. That gentleman says folks ain't deaf here."

The observable points are first that he seems to have excused his "hollering" by the habits consequent upon his mother's deafness. The "hollering" consisted of unusually heavy thumping, I suppose. But the second point is of far greater interest. George intimates that he has changed his "sect," and become a woman! For this important alteration his good mother had prepared his mind. This style of thing will not seem so strange if we consider that some men become old women before they die!

Here is another case of feminification and restitution combined. Hans Von Vleet has become a vrow—what you may call a female Dutchman! It has always been claimed that women are purer and better than men; and accordingly we see that as soon as Hans became a woman he insisted on his widow's returning to a Jew two thousand dollars that naughty Hans had "Christianed" the poor Hebrew out of. But let Hans tell his own story:

"I was Hans Von Vleet ven I vas here. I vas Von Vleet here; I is one vrow now. I is one vrow ven I comes back; I vas no vrow ven I vas here (alluding to the fact that he was temporarily occupying the form of our medium.) I wish you to know that I first live in Harlem, State of New York. Ven I vos here, I take something I had no right to take, something that no belongs to me. I takes something; I takes two thousand dollars that was no my own; that's what I come back to say about. I first have some dealings with one Jew; that's what you call him. He likes to Jew me, and I likes to Christian him. I belongs to the Dutch Reform Church. (Do you think you were a good member?) Vell, I vas. I believes in the creed; I takes the sacrament; I lives up to it outside. I no lives up to it inside, I suppose. (How do you find yourself now, Hans?) Vell, I finds myself—vell, I don't know; I not feel very happy. Ven I comes to the spirit-land, I first meet that Jew's brother, and he tells me, 'Hans, you mus go back and makes some right with my brother.' So I comes here.

"I vants my vrow, what I left in Harlem, to takes that two tousand dollars and gives it back to that Jew's vrow.

That's what I came for today, Sir. (Has your vrow got it?) Vell, my vrow has got it in a tin box. Ven I first go, I takes the money, I gives it to my vrow, and she takes care of it. Now I vants my vrow to give that two tousand dollars to that Jew's vrow.

"(How do you spell your name?) The vrow knows how to spell. (Hans Von Vleet.) There's a something you cross in it. The vrow spells the rest. Ah, that's wrong; you makes a blunder. It's V. not F. That's like all vrows. (Do all vrows make blunders?) Vell, I don't know; all do sometimes, I suppose. (Didn't you like vrows here?) Oh, vell, I likes 'em sometimes. I likes mine own vrow. I not likes to be a vrow myself. (Don't the clothes fit?) Ah, vell, I suppose they fits, but I not likes to wear what not becomes me."

It is scarcely necessary to make comments on such horrible nonsense as this. I may recur to the subject in future, should it appear expedient. At present I must drop the subject of female men.

At the head of the "Message Department" is a standing advertisement, which reads as follows:

"Our free circles are held at No. 158 Washington Street, Room No. 4 (upstairs,) on Monday, Tuesday and Thursday afternoons. The circle-room will be open for visitors at two o'clock; services commence at precisely three o'clock, after which time no one will be admitted. Donations solicited."

On the days and at the hour mentioned in the above advertisement, quite an audience assembles to hear the messages Mrs. C. may have to deliver. If a stranger present should request a message from one of his spirit-friends, he would be told that a large number ofspirits were seeking to communicate through that "instrument," and each must await his turn! Having read obituary notices in the files of old newspapers, and the published list of those recently killed in battle, the medium has data for any number of "messages." She talks in the style that she imagines the person whom she attempts to personate would use, being one of the doctrines of spiritualism that a person's character and feelings are not changed by death. To make the humbug more complete, she narrates imaginary incidents, asserting them to have occurred in the Earth-experience of the spirit who purports to have possession of her at the same time she is speaking. Mediums in various parts of the country furnish her with the names of and facts relative to different deceased people of their acquaintance, and those names and facts are used by her in supplying the "Message Department" of the *Banner of Light*.

If the assumed "mediumship" of this woman was not an imposture, some of the many people who have visited her for the purpose of getting communications from their spirit-friends would have been gratified. In most of the "messages" published in the *Banner*, the spirits purporting to give them, express a great desire to have their mortal friends receive them; but those mortals who seek to obtain through Mrs. Conant satisfactory messages from their spirit-friends, are not gratified—the medium not being posted. The mediums are as much opposed to "new tests" as a noncommittal politician.

Time and again have leading spiritualists, in various parts of the country, endorsed as "spiritual manifestations," what was subsequently proved to be an imposture.

Several years ago, a man by the name of Paine created a great sensation in Worcester, MA, by causing a table to move "without contact," he claiming that it was done by spirits through his "mediumship." He subsequently came to New York, and exhibited the "manifestation" at the house of a spiritualist—where he boarded—in the upper part of the city. A great many spiritualists and not a few "skeptics" went to see his performance. Paine was a very soft-spoken, "good sort of a fellow," and appeared to be quite sincere in his claims to "mediumship." He received no fee from those who witnessed his exhibition; and that fact, in connection with others, tended to disarm people of suspicion. His séances were held in the evening, and each visitor was received by him at the door, and immediately conducted to a seat next the wall of the room.

The visitors all in and seated, Mr. Paine took a seat with the rest in the "circle." In the middle of the room a small table had previously been placed, and the gas had been turned partly off, leaving just enough light to make objects look ghostly.

In order to get "harmonized," singing was indulged in for a short time by members of the "circle." Soon a number of raps would be heard in the direction of the table, and one side of that piece of furniture would be seen to rise about an inch from the floor. Some very naturally wanted to rush to the table and investigate the matter more closely, but Paine forbade that—the necessary "conditions" must be observed, he said, or there would be no further manifestation of spirit-power. As there was no one nearer to the table than six or eight feet, the fact of its moving, very naturally astonished the skeptics present. Several "seeing mediums" who attended Mr. Paine's séances, were able to see the spirits—so they declared—who moved the table. One was described as a "big Injun," who cut various capers, and appeared to be much delighted with the turn of affairs. Believers were wonderfully well-pleased to know that at last a medium was "developed" through whom the inhabitants of another world could manifest their presence to mortals in such a way that no one could gainsay the fact. The "invisibles" freely responded, by raps on the table, to various questions asked by those in the "circle." They thumped time to lively tunes, and seemed to have a decidedly good time of it in their particular way. When the séance was concluded, Mr. Paine freely permitted an examination of his table.

In the Sunday Spiritual Conferences, then held in Clinton Hall, leading spiritualists gave an account of the "manifestations of the spirits" through Mr. Paine, and, as believers, congratulated themselves upon the existence of such "indubitable facts." The spiritualist in whose house this exhibition of table-moving "without contact" took place, was well known as a man of strict honesty; and it was reasonably presumed that no mechanical contrivance could be used without his cognizance, in thus moving a piece of his furniture—for the table belonged to him—and that he would countenance a deception was out of the question.

There were in the city three gentlemen who had, for some time, been known as spiritualists; but they were, at the period of Paine's debut as a medium in New York, very skeptical with regard to "physical manifestations." They had, a short time before, detected the Davenports and other professed mediums in the practice of imposture; and they determined not to accept, as true, Paine's pretence to mediumship, till after a thorough investigation of his "manifestations," they should fail to find a material cause for them. After attending several of his séances, these gentlemen concluded that Paine moved the table by means of a mechanical contrivance fixed under the floor. One of this trio of investigators was a mechanic, and he had conceived a way—and it seemed to him the only way—in which the "manifestation" could be produced under the circumstances that apparently attended it. Paine was a mechanic, and these parties were aware of that fact. They made an appointment with him for a private séance. The evening fixed upon, having arrived, they met with him at his room. The table was raised and raps were made upon it, as had been done on previous occasions. One of the three investigators stepped to the door of the room, locked it, put the key in his pocket, took off his coat, and told Mr. Paine that he was determined to search his (Paine's) person, and that if he did not find about him a small short iron rod, by means of which, through a hole in the floor, a lever underneath was worked in moving the table, he (the speaker) would beg his (Mr. Paine's) pardon, and be forever after a firm believer in the power of disembodied spirits to move ponderable bodies. This impressive little speech had a decided and instant effect upon the "medium." "Gentlemen," said the latter, "I might as well own up. Please to be quietly seated, and I will tell you all about it." And he did tell them all about it; subsequently repeating his confession before quite a number of disgusted and cheaply sold spiritualists at the "New York Spiritual Lyceum." The theory formed by one of the three investigators referred to, as to Paine's method of moving the table, was singularly correct.

Whilst the family with whom Paine boarded was away, one day, in attendance at a funeral, he took up several of the floor boards of the back parlor, and on the under side of them affixed a lever, with a crosspiece at one end of it; and, in the ends of the crosspiece, bits of wire were inserted, the wire being just as far apart as the legs of the table to be moved. Small holes were made in the floorboards for the wire to come through to reach the table-legs. The other end of the lever came within an inch or two of the wall. When all the arrangements were completed, and the table being properly placed in order to move it, Mr. Paine had only to insert one end of a short iron rod in a hole in the heel of his boot, put the other end of the rod through a hole in the floor, just under the edge of the carpet near the wall, and then press the rod down upon the end of the lever.

The movements necessary in fixing the iron rod to its place were executed while he was picking up his handkerchief, that he had purposely dropped.

The middle of the lever was attached to the floor, and the end with the crosspiece, being the heavier, brought the other end close up against the floor, the wires in the crosspiece having their points just within the bottom of the holes in the floor. The room was carpeted, and there were little marks on the carpet, known only to Paine, that enabled him to know just where to place the table. Pressing down the end of the lever nearest the wall, an inch would bring the wires in the crosspiece on the other end of the lever against the legs of the table, and slightly raise the latter. One of the wires would strike the table-leg a very little before the other did, and that enabled the "medium" to very nicely rap time to the tunes that were sung or played. Of course, no holes that anyone could observe would be made in the carpet by the passage of the wires through it.

For appearance' sake, Paine, before his detection, visited, by invitation, the houses of several different spiritualists, for the purpose of holding séances; but he never got a table to move "without contact" in any other than the place where he had properly prepared the conditions.

Chapter 16

Spiritualist humbugs waking up—Foster heard from—S. B. Brittan heard from—The Boston artists and their spiritual portraits—The Washington medium and his spiritual hands—The Davenport brothers and the sea-captain's wheat-flour—The Davenport brothers roughly shown up by John Bull—How a shingle "stumped" the spirits.

I hear from spiritualists sometimes. These gentry are much exercised in their minds by my letters about them, and some of them fly out at me very much as bumblebees do at one who stirs up their nest. For instance, I received, not long ago, from my good friends, Messrs. Cauldwell & Whitney, an anonymous letter to them, dated at Washington, and suggesting that if I would attend what the latter calls "a séance of that celebrated humbug, Foster," I should see something that I could not explain. Now, this anonymous letter, as I know by a spiritual communication, (or otherwise,) is in a handwriting very wonderfully like that of Mr. Foster himself. And as for the substance of it, it is very likely that Foster has now gotten up some new tricks. He needs them. The exhibiting mediums must, of course, contrive new tricks as fast as Dr. Von Vleck and men like him show up their old ones. It is the universal method of all sorts of impostors to adopt new means of fooling people when their old ones are exposed. And Mr. Foster shall have all the attention he wants if I ever find the leisure to bestow on him, though my time is fully occupied with worthier objects.

I have also been complimented with a buzz and an attempt to sting from my old friend S. B. Brittan, the ex-Universalist minister—the very surprisingly efficient "man Friday" of Andrew Jackson Davis, in the production of the "Revelations" of the said Davis, and also ghost-fancier in general; who has gently aired part of his vocabulary in a communication to the *Banner of Light*, with the heading "Exposed for Two Shillings." I can afford very well to expose friend Brittan and his spiritualist humbugs for two shillings. The honester the cheaper. It evidently vexes the spiritualists to have their ghosts put with the monkeys in the Museum. They can't help it, though; and it is my deliberate opinion that the monkeys are much the most respectable. I have no wish to displease any honest person; but the more the spiritualists squirm, and snarl, and scold, and call names, the more they show that I am hurting them. Or—does my friend Brittan himself want an engagement at the Museum? Will he produce some "manifestations" there, and get that $500?—the money is ready!

A valued friend of mine has furnished me a pleasant and true narrative of a fine "spiritual" humbug which took place in a respectable Massachusetts village not very long ago. I give the story in his own graphic words:

"Two artists of Boston, tired of the atmosphere of their studios, resolved themselves, in joint session, into spiritual mediums, as a means of raising the wind—or the devil—and of getting a little fresh air in the rural districts. One of them had learned Mansfield's trick of answering communications and that of writing on the arms. They had large handbills printed, announcing that 'Mr. W. Howard, the celebrated test-medium, would visit the town of , and would remain at the Hotel during three days.' One of the artists preceded the other by a few hours, engaged rooms, and attended to sundry preliminaries. "Mr. Howard" donned a white choker, put his hair behind his ears, and mounted a pair of plain glass spectacles; and such was his profoundly spiritual appearance on entering his apartments at the hotel, that he had to lock the door and give his partner opportunity to explode, and absolutely roll about on the floor with laughter.

"Well, they rigged a clotheshorse for a screen; and to heighten the effect, the assistant, who was expert in portraiture, covered this screen, and, indeed, the walls of the room, with scraggy outlines of the human countenance upon large sheets of paper. These, they said, were executed by the draftsman, whose right hand, when under spiritual influence, uncontrollably jerked off these likenesses. They added, that the spirits had given information that, before the mediums left town, the people would recognize these pictures as likenesses of persons there deceased within twenty years or so. Price, two dollars each! They absolutely sold quite a large number of these portraits, as they were from time to time recognized by surviving friends! The operation of drawing portraits was also illustrated at certain hours, admission, fifty cents; if not satisfactory, the money returned.

"Other tricks of various kinds were performed with pleasure to all parties and profit to the performers. The artists stood it as long as they could, and then departed. But there was every indication that the townspeople would have stood it until this day."

Thus far my friend's curious and truthful account.

A little while ago, there was exhibiting, at Washington, a "test-medium" whose name I would print, were it not that I do not want to advertise him. One of his most impressive feats was, to cause spiritual hands and other parts of the human frame to appear in the air à la Davenport Brothers. A gentleman, whose name I also know very well indeed, but have particular reasons for not mentioning, went one day to see this "test-medium," along with a friend, and asked to see a hand. "Certainly," the medium said; and the room was darkened, and the "circle" made round the table in the usual manner. After about five minutes, my friend, who had contrived to place himself pretty near the medium, saw, sure enough, a dim glimmering blue light in the air, a foot or so before and above the head of the medium. In a minute, he could see, dimly outlined in this blue light, the form of a hand, back toward him, fingers together, and no thumb.

"Why is no thumb visible?" asked my friend of the medium in a solemn manner.

"The reason is," said the medium, still more solemnly, "that the spirits have not power enough to produce a whole hand and so they exhibit as much as they can."

"And do they always show hands without thumbs?"

"Yes."

Here my friend, with a sudden jump, grabbed for the place where the wrist of the mysterious hand ought to be. Strange to relate, he caught it, and held it stoutly, to. A light was quickly had, when, still stranger, the spirit-hand was clearly seen to be the fleshy paw of the medium—and a fat paw it was too. Mr. Medium took the matter with the coolness of a thorough rascal, and, lighting a cigar, merely observed:

"Well gentlemen, you needn't trouble yourselves to come here any more!"

He also insisted on his usual fee of five dollars, until threatened with a prosecution for swindling.

The secret of this worthy gentleman is simple and soon told. Holding one hand up in the air, he held up with the other, between the thumb and finger, a little pinch of phosphorus and bi-sulphide of carbon, which gave the blue light. If inconvenient to hold up the other hand, he had a reserve pinch of blue-light under that invisible thumb. It is a curious instance of the thorough credulity of genuine spiritualists that a believer in this wretched rogue, on being circumstantially told this whole story, not only steadily and firmly refused to credit it, and continued his faith in the fellow, but absolutely would not go to see the application of any other test. That's the sort of follower that is worth having!

Another case was witnessed as follows, by the very same person on whose authority I give the spirit-hand story. He was present—also, this time in Washington, as it happened, at an exhibition by a certain pair of spiritual brothers, since well known as the "Davenport Brothers."

These chaps, after the fashion of their kind, caused themselves to be tied up in a rope, an old sea-captain tying them. This done, their "shop" or cabinet, was shut upon them as usual, and the bangs, throwing of sticks, etc., through a window, and the like, took place. Well, this sly and inconvenient old sea-captain now slipped out of the hall a few minutes, and came back with some wheat flour. Having tied up the "brothers" again, he remarked:

"Now, gentlemen, please to take, each, your two hands full of wheat flour."

The "brothers" got mad and flatly refused. Then they cooled down and argued, saying it wouldn't make any difference, and was of no use.

"Well," said the ancient mariner, "if it won't make any difference you can just as well do it, can't you?"

The audience, seeing the point, were so evidently pleased with the old sailor, that the grumbling "brothers" though with a very bad grace, took their fists full of flour, and were shut up.

There was not the least sign of a "manifestation"—no more than if the wheat-flour had shot the "brothers" dead in their tracks. The audience were immensely delighted. The "brothers," since that time, have learned to perform some tricks with flour in their fists, but only when tied by their own friends.

Since these facts came to my knowledge, the Davenport Brothers have suffered an unpleasant exposure in Liverpool, in England, the details of which have been kindly forwarded to me by attentive friends there. The circumstances in question occurred on the evenings of Tuesday and Wednesday, February 14 and 15, 1865. On the first of these evenings, a gentleman named Cummins, selected by the audience as one of the Tying Committee, tied one of the Brothers, and a Mr. Hulley, the other committeeman, the other. But the Brothers saw instantly that they could not wriggle out of these knots. They, therefore, refused to let the tying be finished, saying that it was "brutal" although a surgeon present said it was not; one tied brother was untied by Ferguson, the agent; and then the Brothers went to work and performed their various tricks without the supervision of any committee, but amid a constant fire of derision, laughter, groans, shouts, and epithets from the audience. On the next evening, the audience insisted on having the same committee; the Brothers were very reluctant to allow it, but had to do so after a long time. Ira Davenport refused again, however, instantly to be tied, as soon as he saw what knot Mr. Cummins was going to use. Cummins, however, though Ira squirmed most industriously, got him tied fast, and then Ira called to Ferguson to cut the knot! Ferguson did so, and cut Ira's hand. Ira now showed the blood to the audience, and the Brothers, with an immense pretense of indignation, went off the stage. Cummins at once explained; the audience became disgusted, and, enraged at the impudence of the imposture, broke over the footlights, knocked Ferguson backward into the "cabinet;" and when the discomfited agent had scrambled out and run away, smashed the thing fairly into kindling-wood, and carried it off, all distributed into splinters and chips. Early next morning, the terrified Davenports ran away out of Liverpool; and a number of the audience were, at last accounts, intending to go to law to get back the money paid for an exhibition which they did not see.

The very thorough exposure of the Davenports thus made is an additional proof—if such were needed—of the truth of what I have alleged about the impostures perpetrated by them and their "mysterious" brethren of the exhibiting sort.

Once the "spirits" were "stumped" with a shingle—a very proper yankee jawbone of an ass to route such disembodied Philistines. One day a certain person was present where some tables were rambling about, and other revolutions taking place in the furniture-business, when he stepped boldly forth like a herald bearing defiance, and cast down a common white pine shingle upon the floor. "There," said he, coolly, "if you can trot those tables about in that style, do it with that shingle. Make it go about the room. Make it move an inch!" And lo, and behold! the shingle lay perfectly still.

Chapter 17

The Davenport brothers shown up once more—Dr. Newton at Chicago—The spiritualist bogus baby—A lady brings forth a motive force—"Gum" arabic—Spiritualist hebrew—The Allen boy—Dr. Randall—Portland Evening Courier—The fools not all dead yet.

Other "spiritual" facts have come to my hand, some of them furnishing additional details about persons to whom I have already alluded, and others being important to illustrate some general tendencies of spiritualism.

And first, about the Davenport Brothers; they have met with another "awful exposure," at the hands of a merciless Mr. Addison. This gentleman is a London stockbroker, and his cool, sharp business habits seem to have stood him in good stead in taking some fun out of the fools who follow the Davenports. Mr. Addison, it seems, went to work, and, just to amuse his friends, executed all the Davenport tricks. Upon this the spiritualist newspapers in England, which, like the *Boston Herald of Progress*, claim to believe in the "Brothers," came out and said that Addison was a very wonderful medium indeed. On this the cold-blooded Addison at once printed a letter, in which he not only said he had done all their tricks without spiritual aid, but he moreover explained exactly how he caught the Davenports in their impositions. He and a long-legged friend went to one of the "dark séances" of the Davenports, during which musical instruments were to fly about over the heads of the audience, bang their pates, thrum, twang, etc. Addison and his friend took a front seat; as soon as the lights were put out they put out their legs too; stretching as far as possible; and, to use the unfeeling language of Mr. Addison, they "soon had the satisfaction of feeling someone falling over them." They then caught hold of an arm, from which a guitar was forthwith let drop on the floor. In order to be certain who the guitar-carrier was, they waited until the next time the lights were put out, took each a mouthful of dry flour, and blew it out right among the "manifestations." When the lamps were lighted, lo and behold! there was Fay, the agent and manager of the Davenports, with his back all powdered with flour. Addison showed this to an acquaintance, who said, "Yes, he saw the flour; but he could not understand what made Addison and his friend laugh so excessively at it."

The spiritualist newspapers don't think Addison is so great a medium as they did!

Great accounts have recently come eastward from Chicago, of a certain Doctor Newton, who is said to be working miracles by the hundred in the way of healing diseases. This man operates with exactly the weapons all the miracle-workers, quacks, and impostors, ancient and modern use. All of them have appealed to the imaginations of their patients, and no person acquainted with mental philosophy is ignorant that many a sickman has been cured either by medicine and imagination together, or by imagination alone. Therefore, even if this Newton should really be the cause of the recovery of some persons from their ailments, it would be no more a miracle than if Dr. Mott should do it; nor would Newton be any the less a quack and a humbug.

Newton has operated at the East already. He had a career at New Haven and Hartford, and in other places, before he steered westward in the wake of the "Star of Empire." What he does is simply to ask what is the matter, and where it hurts. Then he sticks his thumb into the seat of the difficulty, or he pokes or strokes or pats it, as the case may be. Then he says, "There—you're cured! God bless you!—Take yourself off!"

Chicago must be a credulous place, for we are informed of immense crowds besieging this man, and undergoing his manipulations. One of the Chicago papers, having little faith and a good deal of fun—which in such cases is much better—published some burlesque stories and certificates about "Doctor" Newton, some of them humorous enough. There is a certificate from a woman with fourteen children, all having the measles at once. She says that no sooner had Doctor Newton received one lock of hair of one of them, than the measles left them all, and she now has said measles corked up in a bottle! Another case was that of a merchant who had lost his strength, but went and was stroked by Newton, and the very next day was able to lift a note in bank, which had before been altogether too heavy for him. There was also an old lady, whose story I fear was imitated from Hood's funny conceit of the deaf woman who bought an ear-trumpet, which was so effective that

"The very next day
She heard from her husband in Botany Bay!"

The Chicago old lady in like manner, after having had Doctor Newton's thumbs "jobbed" into her ears, certifies that she heard next morning from her son in California.

One would think that this ridicule would put the learned Dr. Newton to flight; but it will not until he is through with the fools.

I have already given an account of some of the messages from the other world in the "Banner of Light," in which some of the spirits explain that they have turned into women since they died. This is by no means the first remarkable trick that the spirits have performed upon the human organization. Here is what they did at High Rock, in Massachusetts, a number of years ago. It beats Joanna Southcott in funny absurdity, if not in blasphemy.

At High Rock, in the year 1854 or thereabouts, certain spiritualist people were building some mysterious machinery. While this was in process of erection, a female medium, of considerable eminence in those parts, was informed by certain spirits, with great solemnity and pomp, that "she would become the Mary of a new dispensation;" that is, she was going to be a mother. Well, this was all proper, no doubt, and the lady herself—so say the spiritualist accounts—had for some time experienced indications that she was pregnant. These indications continued, and became increasingly obvious, and also, it was observed, a little queer in some particulars.

After a while, one Spear—a "Reverend Mr. Spear"— who was mixed up, it appears, with the machinery-part of the business, and who was a medium himself, transmitted to the lady a request from the spirits that she would visit said Spear at High Rock on a certain day. She did so, of course; and while there was unexpectedly taken with the pains of childbirth, which the spiritualist authorities say, were "internal"—where should they be, pray?—and "of the spirit rather than of the physical nature; but were, nevertheless, quite as uncontrollable as those of the latter, and not less severe." The labor proceeded. It lasted two hours. As it went on, lo and behold! one part and another part of the machinery began to move! And when, at the end of the two hours, the parturition was safely over, all the machinery was going!

The lady had given birth to a Motive Force. Does anybody suppose I am manufacturing this story? Not a bit of it. It is all told at length in a book published by a spiritualist; and probably a good many of my readers will remember about it.

Well, the baby had to be nursed—fact! This superhumanly silly female actually went through the motions of nursing the motive force for some weeks. Though how the thing sucked—Excuse me, ladies; I would not discuss such delicate subjects did not the interests of truth require it.

If I had been the physician, at any rate, I think I should have recommended to hire a healthy female steam-engine for a wet nurse to this young motive force; say a locomotive, for instance. I feel sure the thing would have lived if it could have had a gauge-faucet or something of that sort to draw on. But the medical folks in charge chose to permit the mother to nurse the child, and she not being able to supply proper nutriment, the poor little innocent faded—if that word be appropriate for what couldn't be seen—and finally "gin eout;" and the machinery, after some abortive joggles and turns, stood hopelessly still.

This story is true—that is, it is true that the story was told, the pretences were gone through, and the birth was actually believed by a good many people. Some of them were prodigiously enthusiastic about it, and called the invisible brat the New Motive Power, the Physical Savior, Heaven's Last Best Gift to Man, the New Creation, the Great Spiritual Revelation of the Age, the Philosopher's Stone, the Act of all Acts, and so on, and so forth.

The great question of all was, Who was the daddy? I don't know of anybody's asking this question, but its importance is extreme and obvious. For if things like this are going to happen, the ladies will be afraid to sleep alone in the house if so much as a sewing-machine or apple-corer be about, and will not dare take solitary walks along any stream where there is a water power.

A couple of miscellaneous anecdotes may not inappropriately be appended to this story of monstrous delusion.

Once a "writing medium" was producing sentences in various foreign languages. One of these was Arabic. An enthusiastic youth, a half-believer, after inspecting the wondrous scroll, handed it to his seat-mate, a professor (as it happened) in one of our oldest colleges, and a man of real learning. The professor scrutinized the document. What was the youth's delight to hear him at last observe gravely, "It is a kind of Arabic, sure enough!"

"What kind?" asked the young man with intense interest.

"Gum-arabic," said the professor.

The spirit of the prophet Daniel came one night into the apartment of a medium named Fowler, and right before his eyes, he said, wrote down some marks on a piece of paper. These were shown to the Reverend George Bush, Professor of Hebrew in the New-York University, who said that they were "a few verses from the last chapter of Daniel" and were learnedly written. Bush was a spiritualist as well as a professor of Hebrew, and he ought to have known better than to endorse spirit-Hebrew; for shortly there came others, who, to use a rustic phrase, "took the rag off the Bush." These inconvenient personages were three or four persons of learning: one a Jew, who proved that the document was an attempt to copy the verses in question, by someone so ignorant of Hebrew as not to know that it is written backward, that is, from right to left.

During the last few months, a "boy medium," by the name of Henry B. Allen, thirteen years of age, has been astonishing people in various parts of the country by "Physical Manifestations in the Light." The exhibitions of this precocious youngster have been "managed" by a Dr. Randall, who also lectures upon Spiritualism, expounding its "beautiful philosophy." For a number of weeks this couple held forth in Boston, sometimes giving several séances during the day, not more than thirty being allowed to attend at one time, each of whom were required to pay an admission fee of one dollar.

The Banner of Light fully endorsed this Allen boy, and gave lengthy accounts of his manifestations. The arrangements for his exhibition were very simple. A dulcimer, guitar, bell, and small drum being placed on a sofa or several chairs set against the wall, a clotheshorse was set in front of them and covered with a blanket, which came to the floor. To obtain "manifestations," a person was required to take off his coat and sit with his back to the clotheshorse. The medium then took a seat close to, and facing the investigator's left side, and grasped the left arm of the latter on the under side, above the elbow, with his (the medium's) right hand and near the wrist with the other hand. The "manager" then covered with a coat, the arms and left shoulder of the medium including the left arm of the investigator. The medium soon commenced to wriggle and twist—the "manager" said he was always nervous under "influence"—and worked the coat away from the position in which it had been placed. Taking his right hand from the investigator's arm, he readjusted the coat, and availed himself of that opportunity to get the investigator's wrist between his (the medium's) left arm and knee. That brought his left hand in such a position that with it he could grasp the investigator's arm where he had previously grasped it with his right hand. With the latter he could then reach around the edge of the clotheshorse and make a noise on the instruments. With the drumsticks he thumped on the dulcimer. Taking the guitar by the neck, he could vibrate the strings and show the body of the instrument above the clotheshorse, without anyone seeing his hand! All persons present were so seated that they could not see behind the clotheshorse, or have a view of the medium's right shoulder. When asked why people were not allowed to occupy such a position, that they could have a fair view of the instruments when sounded, the "manager" replied that he did not exactly know, but presumed it was because the magnetic emanations from the eyes of the beholders would prevent the spirits being able to move the instruments at all! What was claimed to be a spirit-hand was often shown above the clotheshorse, where it flickered for an instant and was withdrawn; but it was invariably a right hand with the wrist toward the medium. When the person sitting with the medium was asked if the hands of the latter had constantly hold of his arm, he replied in the affirmative. Of course, he felt what he supposed to be both the medium's hands; but as I before explained, the pressure on his wrist was from the medium's left arm—the left hand of whom, by means of a very accommodating crook in the elbow, was grasping the investigator's arm where the medium's right hand was supposed to be.

From Boston the Allen boy went to Portland, Maine, where he succeeded "astonishingly," till some gentleman applied the lampblack test to his assumed mediumship, whereupon he "came to grief."

The following is copied from the *Portland Daily Press*, of March 21.

"Exposed.—The 'wonderful' spiritual manifestations of the 'boy-medium,' Master Henry B. Allen, in charge of Doctor J. H. Randall, of Boston, were brought to a sad end last evening by the impertinent curiosity and wicked doings of some of the gentlemen present at the séance at Congress Hall.

"As usual, one of the company present was selected to sit at the side of the boy, and allowed his hand and arm to be held by both hands of the boy while the manifestations were going on. The boy seized hold of the gentleman's wrist with his left hand, and his shoulder, or near it, with the right hand. The manifestations then began, and among them was one trick of pulling the gentleman's hair.

"Immediately after this trick was performed, the hand of the boy was discovered to be very black—from lampblack, of the best quality, with which the gentleman had dressed his head on purpose to detect whose was the 'spirit-hand' that pulled his hair. His shirt sleeve, upon which the boy immediately replaced his hand after pulling his hair, was also black where the hand had been placed. The gentleman stated the facts to the company present, and the séance broke up. Dr. Randall refunded the fifty cents admission fee to those present."

The spiritualists of the city were somewhat staggered by this exposé, but soon rallied as one of their number announced a new discovery in spiritual science. Here it is, as stated by himself:

"Whatever the electrical or 'spirit-hand' touches, will inevitably be transferred to the hand of the medium in every instance, unless something occurs to prevent the full operation of the law by which this result is produced. The spirit-hand being composed in part of the magnetic elements drawn from the medium, when it is dissolved again, and the magnetic fluid returns whence it came, it must of necessity carry with it whatever material substance it has touched, and leave it deposited upon the surface or material hand of the medium. This is a scientific question. How many innocent mediums have been wronged? and the invisible have permitted it, until we should discover that it was the natural result of a natural law."

What a great discovery! and how lucidly it is set forth! The author (who, by the way, is editor of the *Portland Evening Courier*) of this new discovery, was not so modest but that he hastened to announce and claim full credit for it in the columns of the *Banner of Light*— the editor of which journal congratulates him on having done so much for the cause of spiritualism! Those skeptics who were present when the lampblack was "transferred" from the gentleman's hair to the medium's hand, rashly concluded that the boy was an impostor. It remained for Mr. Hall— that is the philosopher's name—to make the "electromagnetic transfer" discovery. The Allen boy ought ever to hold him in grateful remembrance for coming to his rescue at such a critical period, when the spirits would not vouchsafe an explanation that would exculpate him from the grievous charge of imposture. Mr. Hall deserves a leather medal now, and a soapstone monument when he is dead.

A person, whose initials are the same as the gentleman's named above, once lived in Aroostook, Maine, and was in the habit of attending "spiritual circles," in which he was sometimes influenced as a "personating medium," and to represent the symptoms of the disease which caused the controlling spirit's translation to another sphere. It having been reported in Aroostook that a certain well-known individual, living further east, had died of cholera, a desire was expressed at the next "circle" to have him "manifest" himself. The medium above referred to got "under influence," and personated, with an exhibition of all the symptoms of cholera, the gentleman who was reported to have died of that disease. So faithful to the supposed facts was the representation, that the medium had to be cared for as if he was himself a veritable cholera-patient. Several days after, the man who was "personated" appeared in Aroostook, alive and well, never having been attacked with the cholera. The local papers gave a graphic account of the "manifestation" soon after it occurred.

But to return to the Allen boy. After his exposure by means of the lampblack test, and Mr. Hall, of the *Portland Evening Courier,* had announced his new discovery in spiritual science, several of the Portland spiritualists had a private "sitting" with the boy. While he sat with his hands upon the arm of one of their number, they tied a rope to his wrists, and around the person's arm, covering his hands in the way I have before described. After some wriggling and twisting (the usual amount of "nervousness,") the bell washeard to ring behind the clotheshorse. The boy's right hand was then examined, and it was found to be stained with some colored matter that had previously been put upon the handle of the bell. As the boy's wrists were still tied, and the rope remained upon the man's arm, the "transfer" theory was considered to be established as a fact, and the previous exposure shown to be not only no exposure at all, but a "stepping-stone to a grand truth in spiritual science." Again and again did these persistent and infatuated spiritualists try what they call the "transfer test," varying with each experiment the coloring-material used, and every time the bell was rung the medium's right hand was found out to be stained with what had been put upon the bell-handle. By having a little slack-rope between his wrist and the man's arm, it was not a difficult matter for the medium, while his "nervousness" was being manifested, to get hold of the bell and ring it, and to make sounds upon the strings of the dulcimer or guitar, with a drumstick that the "manager" had placed at a convenient distance from his (the boy's) hand.

The *Portland Daily Press*, in noticing a lecture against Spiritualism, recently delivered by Dr. Von Vleck, in that city, says:—He (Dr. V. V.) performed the principal feats of the Allen boy, with his hands tied to the arm of the person with whom he was in communication."

Horace Greeley says that if a man will be a consummate

jackass and fool, he is not aware of anything in the Constitution to prevent it. I believe Mr. Greeley is right; and I think no one can reasonably be expected to exercise common sense unless he is known to possess it. It is quite natural, therefore, that many of the spiritualists, lacking common sense, should pretend to have something better.

Part III

TRADE AND BUSINESS IMPOSITIONS

Chapter 18

*Adulterations of food—Adulterations of liquor—The
colonel's whiskey—The humbugometer.*

It was about eight hundred and fifty years before Christ when
the young prophet cried out to his master, Elisha, over the
pottage of wild gourds, "There is death in the pot!" It was
two thousand six hundred and seventy years afterward, in
1820, that Accum, the chemist cried out over again, "There is
death in the pot!" in the title page of a book so named, which
gave almost everybody a pain in the stomach, with its horrid
stories of the unhealthful humbugs sold for food and drink.
This excitement has been stirred up more than once since
Mr. Accum's time, with some success; yet nothing is more
certain than that a very large proportion of the food we eat,
of the liquid we drink—always excepting good well-filtered
water—and the medicines we take, not to say a word about
the clothes we wear and the miscellaneous merchandise we
use, is more or less adulterated with cheaper materials. Sometimes these are merely harmless; as flour, starch, annatto,
lard, etc.; sometimes they are vigorous, destructive poisons—
as red lead, arsenic, strychnine, oil of vitriol, potash, etc.

It is not agreeable to find ourselves so thickly beset by
humbugs; to find that we are not merely called on to see

them, to hear them, to believe them, to invest capital in them, but to eat and drink them. Yet so it is; and, if my short discussion of this kind of humbug shall make people a little more careful, and help them to preserve their health, I shall think myself fortunate.

To begin with bread. Alum is very commonly put into it by the bakers, to make it white. Flour of inferior quality, "runny" flour, and even that from wormy wheat—ground-up worms, bugs, and all—is often mixed in as much as the case will bear. Potato flour has been known to be mixed with wheat; and so, thirty years ago, were plaster-of-Paris, bone-dust, white clay, etc. But these are little used now, if at all; and the worst thing in bread, aside from bad flour, which is bad enough, is usually the alum. It is often put in ready mixed with salt, and it accomplishes two things, viz., to make the bread white, and to suck up a good deal of water, and make the bread weigh well. It has been sometimes found that the alum was put in at the mill instead of the bakery.

Milk is most commonly adulterated with cold water; and many are the jokes on the milkmen about their best cow being choked etc., by a turnip in the pump-spout—their "cow with the wooden tail" (i.e., the pump-handle,) and so on. Awful stories are told about the London milkmen, who are said to manufacture a fearful kind of medicine to be sold as milk, the cream being made of a quantity of calf's brain beaten to a slime. Stories are told around New York, too, of a mysterious powder sold by druggists, which with water makes milk; but it is milk that must be used quickly, or it turns into a curious mess. But the worst adulteration of milk is to adulterate the old cow herself; as is done in the swill-milk establishments which received such an exposure a few years ago in a city paper. This milk is still furnished; and many a poor little baby is daily suffering convulsions from its effects. So difficult is it to find real milk for babies in the city, that physicians often prescribe the use of what is called "condensed" milk instead; which, though very different from milk not evaporated, is at least made of the genuine article. A series of careful experiments to develop the milk-humbug was made by a competent physician in Boston within a few years, but he found the milk there (aside from swill-milk) adulterated with nothing worse than water, salt, and burnt sugar.

Tea is bejuggled first by John Chinaman, who is a very cunning rascal; and second, by the seller here. Green and black tea are made from the same plant, but by different processes—the green being most expensive. To meet the increased demand for green tea, Master John takes immense quantities of black tea and "paints" it, by stirring into it over a fire a fine powder of plaster Paris and Prussian-blue, at the rate of half a pound to each hundred pounds of tea. John also sometimes takes a very cheap kind, and puts on a nice gloss by stirring it in gum-water, with some stove-polish in it. We may imagine ourselves, after drinking this kind of tea, with a beautiful black gloss on our insides. John moreover, manufactures vast quantities of what he plainly calls "Lie-tea." This is dust and refuse of tea-leaves and other leaves, made up with dust and starch or gum into little lumps, and used to adulterate better tea. Seven hundred and fifty thousand pounds of this nice stuff were imported into England in one period of eighteen months. It seems to be used in New-York only for green tea.

Coffee is adulterated with chicory-root (which costs only

about one-third as much)—dandelion-root, peas, beans, mangold-wurzel, wheat, rye, acorns, carrots, parsnips, horse-chestnuts, and sometimes with livers of horses and cattle! All these things are roasted or baked to the proper color and consistency, and then mixed in. No great sympathy need be expended on those who suffer from this particular humbug, however; for when it is so easy to buy the real berry, and roast or at least grind it one's self, it is our own fault if our laziness leaves us to eat all those sorts of stuff.

Cocoa is "extended" with sugar, starch, flour, iron-rust, Venetian-red, grease, and various earths. But it is believed by pretty good authority that the American-made preparations of cocoa are nearly or quite pure. Even if they are not the whole bean can be used instead.

Butter and lard have one tenth, and sometimes even one-quarter, of water mixed up in them. It is easy to find this out by melting a sample before the fire and putting it away to cool, when the humbug appears by the grease going up, and the water, perhaps turbid with whey, settling below.

Honey is humbugged with sugar or molasses. Sugar is not often sanded as the old stories have it. Fine white sugar is sometimes floured pretty well; and brown sugar is sometimes made of a portion of good sugar with a cheaper kind mixed in. Inferior brown sugars are often full of a certain crab-like animalcule or minute bug, often visible without a microscope, in water where the sugar is dissolved. It is believed that this pleasing insect sometimes gets into the skin, and produces a kind of itch. I do not believe there is much danger of adulteration in good loaf or crushed white sugar, or good granulated or brown sugar.

Pepper is mixed with fine dust, dirt, linseed-meal, ground

rice, or mustard and wheat-flour; ginger, with wheat flour colored by turmeric and reinforced by cayenne. Cinnamon is sometimes not present at all in what is so called—the stuff being the inferior and cheaper cassia bark; sometimes it is only part cassia; sometimes the humbug part of it is flour and ochre. Cayenne-pepper is mixed with cornmeal and salt, Venetian-red, mustard, brickdust, fine sawdust, and red-lead. Mustard with flour and turmeric. Confectionery is often poisoned with Prussian-blue, Antwerp-blue, gamboge, ultramarine, chrome yellow, red-lead, white-lead, vermilion, Brunswick-green, and Scheele's green, or arsenite of copper! Never buy any confectionery that is colored or painted. Vinegar is made of whisky, or of oil of vitriol. Pickles have verdigris in them to make them a pretty green. "Pretty green" he must be who will eat bought pickles! Preserved fruits often have verdigris in them, too.

An awful list! Imagine a meal of such bewitched food, where the actual articles are named. "Take some of the alum bread." "Have a cup of pea-soup and chicory-coffee?" "I'll trouble you for the oil-of-vitriol, if you please." "Have some sawdust on your meat, or do you prefer this flour and turmeric mustard?" "A piece of this verdigris-preserve gooseberry pie, Madam?" "Won't you put a few more sugar-bugs in your ash-leaf tea?" "Do you prefer black tea, or Prussian-blue tea?" "Do you like your tea with swill-milk, or without?"

I have not left myself space to speak of the tricks played by the druggists and the liquor-dealers; but I propose to devote another chapter exclusively to the adulteration of liquors in this country. It is a subject so fearful and so important that nothing less than a chapter can do it justice. I must now end with a story or two and a suggestion or two.

Old Colonel P. sold much whisky; and his manner was to sell by sample out of a pure barrel overnight, at a marvelous cheap rate, and then to "rectify" before morning, under pretence of coopering and marking. Certain persons having a grudge against the Colonel, once made an arrangement with a carman, who executed their plan, thus:—He went to the Colonel, and asked to see whisky. The jolly old fellow took him downstairs and showed him a great cellar full. Carman samples a barrel. "Fust rate, Colonel, how d'ye sell it?" Colonel names his price on the rectified basis. "Well, Colonel, how much yer got?" "So many barrels—two or three hundred." "Colonel, here's your money. I'll take the lot." "All right," says Colonel P.; "there's some coopering to be done on it; some of the hoops and heads are a very little loose. You shall have it all in the morning." "No, colonel, we'll roll it right out this minnit! My trucks are up there, all ready." And, sure enough, he had a string of a dozen or more brigaded in the street. The Colonel was sadly dumbfounded; he turned several colors—red mostly—stammered, made excuses. It was no go, the whisky was the customer's, and the game was up. The humbugged old humbug finally "came down," and bought his man off by paying him several hundred dollars.

There is a much older and better known story about a grocer who was a deacon, and who was heard to call downstairs before breakfast, to his clerk: "John, have you watered the rum?" "Yes, Sir." "And sanded the sugar?" "Yes, Sir." "And dusted the pepper?" "Yes, Sir." "And chicoried the coffee?" "Yes, Sir." "Then come up to prayers." Let us hope that the grocers of the present day, while they adulterate less, do not pray less.

Between 1851 and 1854, Mr. Wakley of the *London Lancet*

gave an awful roasting to the adulteration-interest in London. He employed an able analyzer, who began by going about without telling what he was at; and buying a great number of samples of all kinds of food, drugs, etc., at a great number of shops. Then he analyzed them; and when he found humbug in any sample, he published the facts, and the seller's name and place of business. It may be imagined what a terrible row this kicked up. Very numerous and violent threats were made; but the *Lancet,* was never once sued by any of the aggrieved, for it had told the truth.

Perhaps some discouraged reader may ask, What can I eat? Well, I don't pretend to direct people's diet. Ask your doctor, if you can't find out. But I will suggest that there are a few things that can't be adulterated. You can't adulterate an egg, nor an oyster, nor an apple, nor a potato, nor a salt codfish; and if they are spoiled they will notify you themselves! and when good, they are all good healthy food. In short, one good safeguard is, to use, as far as you can, things with their life in them when you buy them, whether vegetable or animal. The next best rule against these adulteration-humbugs is, to buy goods crude instead of manufactured; coffee, and pepper, and spices, etc., whole instead of ground, for instance. Thus, though you give more work, you buy purity with it. And lastly, there are various chemical processes, and the microscope, to detect adulterations; and milk, in particular, may always be tested by a lactometer—a simple little instrument which the milkmen use, which costs a few shillings, and which tells the story in an instant. It is a glass bulb, with a stem above and a scale on it, and a weight below. In good average milk, at sixty degrees of heat, the lactometer floats at twenty on its scale;

and in poorer milk, at from that figure down. If it floats at fifteen, the milk is one-fourth water; if at ten, one half.

It would be a wonderful thing for mankind if some philosophic Yankee would contrive some kind of "ometer" that would measure the infusion of humbug in anything. A "Humbugometer" he might call it. I would warrant him a good sale.

Chapter 19

Adulterations in drinks—Riding home on your wine-barrel—List of things to make rum—Things to color it with—Canal-boat hash—English adulteration law—Effects of drugs used—How to use them—Buying liquors under the customhouse lock—A homeopathic dose.

As long as the people of the United States tipple down rum and other liquors at the rate of a good deal more than one hundred million gallons a year, besides what is imported and what is called imported—as long as they pay for their tippling a good deal more than fifty millions, and probably over a hundred millions of dollars a year—so long it will be a great object to manufacture false liquors, and sell them at the price of true ones. When liquor of good quality costs from four to fifteen dollars a gallon, and an imitation can be had that tastes just as good, and has just as much "jizm" in it—and probably a good deal more—for from twenty-five cents to one dollar a gallon, somebody will surely make and sell that imitation.

Adulterating and imitating liquors is a very large business; and I don't know of anybody who will deny that this particular humbug is very extensively cultivated. There are a great many people, however, who will talk about it as they do in Western towns about fever and ague: "We don't do anything of the kind here, but those other people over there do!"

There is very little pure liquor, either malt or spirituous, to be obtained in any way. The more you pay for it, as a rule, the more the publican gains, but what you drink is none the purer. Importing don't help you. Port is—or used to be, for very little is now made, comparatively—imitated in immense quantities at Oporto; and in the logwood trade, the European winemakers competed with the dyers. It is a London proverb, that if you want genuine port-wine, you have got to go to Oporto and make your own wine, and then ride on the barrel all the way home. It is perhaps possible to get pure wine in France by buying it at the vineyard; but if any dealer has had it, give up the idea!

As for what is done this side of the water, now for it. I do not rely upon the old work of Mr. "Death- in-the-pot Accum," printed some thirty years ago, in England. My statements come mostly from a New York book put forth within a few years by a New York man, whose name is now in the Directory, and whose business is said to consist to a great extent in furnishing one kind or another of the queer stuff he talks about, to brewers, or distillers, or wine and brandy merchants.

This gentleman, in a sweet alphabetical miscellany of drugs, herbs, minerals, and groceries commonly used in manufacturing our best Old Bourbon whisky, Swan gin, Madeira wine, pale ale, London brown stout, Heidsieck, Clicquot, Lafitte, and other nice drinks; names the chief of such ingredients as follows:

Aloes, alum, calamus (flag-root) capsicum, *cocculus indicus*, copperas, coriander-seed, gentian-root, ginger, grains-of-paradise, honey, liquorice, logwood, molasses, onions, opium, orange-peel, quassia, salt, stramonium-seed (deadly nightshade), sugar of lead, sulphite of soda, sulphuric acid, tobacco, turpentine, vitriol, yarrow. I have left strychnine out of the list, as some persons have doubts about this poison ever being used in adulterating liquors. A wholesale liquor-dealer in New York city, however, assures me that more than one-half the so-called whisky is poisoned with it.

Besides these twenty-seven kinds of rum, here come twenty-three more articles, used to put the right color to it when it is made; by making a soup of one or another, and stirring it in at the right time. I alphabet these, too: alkanet-root, annatto, barwood, blackberry, blue-vitriol, brazil-wood, burnt sugar, cochineal, elderberry, garancine (an extract of madder), indigo, Nicaragua-wood, orchil, poke-berry, potash, quercitron, red beet, red cabbage, red carrots, saffron, sanders-wood, turmeric, whortleberry.

In all, in both lists, just fifty. There are more, however. But that's enough. Now then, my friend, what did you drink this morning? You called it Bourbon, or Cognac, or Old Otard, very likely, but what was it? The "glorious uncertainty" of drinking liquor under these circumstances is enough to make a man's head swim without his getting drunk at all. There might, perhaps, be found a consolation like that of the Western traveller about the hash. "When I travel in a canal-boat or steamboat," quoth this brave and stout-stomached man, "I always eat the hash, because then I know what I've got!"

It was a good many years ago that the Parliament of England found it necessary to make a law to prevent sophisticating malt liquors. Here is the list of things they forbid to put into beer: "molasses, honey, liquorice, vitriol, quassia, *cocculus indicus*, grains-of-paradise, Guinea-pepper, opium." The penalty was one thousand dollars fine on the brewer, and two thousand five hundred dollars on the druggist who supplied him.

I know of no such law in this country. The theory of our government leaves people to take care of themselves as much as possible. But now let us see what some of these fifty ingredients will do. Beets and carrots, honey and liquorice, orange-peel and molasses, will not do much harm; though I should think tipplers would prefer them as the customer at the eating-house preferred his flies, "on a separate plate." But the case is different with *cocculus indicus*, and stramonium, and sulphuric acid, and sugar of lead, and the like. I take the following accounts, so far as they are medical, from a standard work by Dr. Dunglison:—Aloes is a cathartic. Cocculus indicus contains picrotoxin, which is an "acrid narcotic poison;" from five to ten grains will kill a strong dog. The boys often call it "cockle-cinders;" they pound it and mix it in dough, and throw it into the water to catch fish. The poor fish eat it, soon become delirious, whirling and dancing furiously about on the top of the water, and then die. Copperas tends to produce nausea, vomiting, griping, and purging. Grains-of-paradise, a large kind of cardamom, is "strongly heating and carminative" (i.e., anti-flatulent and antispasmodic.) Opium is known well enough. Stramonium-seed would seem to have been made on purpose for the liquor business. In moderate doses it is a powerful narcotic, producing vertigo, headache, dimness or perversion of vision (i.e., seeing double) and confusion of thought. (N.B. What else does liquor do?) In larger doses (still like liquor,) you obtain these symptoms aggravated; and then a delirium, sometimes whimsical (snakes in your boots) and sometimes furious, a stupor, convulsions, and death. A fine drink this stramonium? Sugar of lead is what is called a cumulative poison; having the quality of remaining in the system when taken in small quantities, and piling itself up, as it were, until there is enough to accomplish something, when it causes debility, paralysis, and other things. Sulphuric acid is strongly corrosive—a powerful caustic, attacking the teeth, even when very dilute; eating up flesh and bones alike when strong enough; and, if taken in a large enough dose, an awfully tearing and agonizing fatal poison.

The way to use these delectable nutriments is in part as follows:—Stir a little sulphuric acid into your beer. This will give you a fine "old ale" in about a quarter of a minute. Take a mixture of alum, salt, and copperas, ground fine, and stir into your beer, and this will make it froth handsomely. Cocculus indicus, tobacco-leaves, and stramonium, cooked in the beer, etc., give it force. Potash is sometimes stirred into wine to correct acidity. Sulphite of soda is now very commonly stirred into cider, to keep it from fermenting further. Sugar of lead is stirred into wines to make them clear, and to keep them sweet. And so on, through the whole long list.

It is a curious instance of people's quiet acknowledgment of their own foolishness, that a popular form of the invitation to take a drink is, "Come and h'ist in some pizen!"

I know of no plan by which anybody can be sure of obtaining pure liquor of any description. Some persons always purchase their wines and liquors while they are under the customhouse lock and consequently before they have reached the hands of the importer. Yet there are scores of men in New York and Philadelphia who have made large fortunes by sending whisky to France, there refining, coloring, flavoring, and doctoring it, then re-shipping it to New York as French brandy, paying the duty, and selling it before it has left the customhouse! There is a locality in France where a certain brand of wine is made. It is adulterated with red-lead, and every year more or less of the inhabitants of that locality are attacked with "lead-colic," caused by drinking this poisoned wine right at the fountainhead where it is made. There is more bogus champagne drank in any one year, in the city of Paris alone, than there is genuine champagne made in any one year in the world. America ordinarily consumes more so-called champagne annually than is made in the world, and yet nearly all the genuine champagne in the world is taken by the courts of Europe. The genuine Hock wine made at Johannisberg on the Rhine is worth three dollars per bottle by the large quantity, and nearly all of it is shipped to Russia; yet, at any of the hotels in the village of Johannisberg, within half a mile from the winepresses of the pure article, you can be supplied for a dollar per bottle with what purports to be the genuine Hock wine. Since chemistry has enabled liquor dealers to manufacture any description of wine or liquor for twenty-five cents to a dollar a gallon, there are annually made and sold thousands of gallons of wine and brandy that never smelt a grape.

Suppose a wholesale liquor-merchant imports genuine brandy. He usually "rectifies" and adulterates it by adding eighty-five gallons of pure spirits (refined whisky,) to fifteen gallons of brandy, to give it a flavor; then colors and "doctors" it, and it is ready for sale. Suppose an Albany wholesale-dealer purchases, for pure brandy, ten pipes of this adulterated brandy from a New York importer. The Albany man immediately doubles his stock by adding an equal quantity of pure spirits. There are then seven and a half gallons of brandy in a hundred. A Buffalo liquor-dealer buys from the Albany man, and he in turn adds one-half pure spirits. The Chicago dealer buys from the Buffalo dealer, and as nearly all spirit-dealers keep large quantities of pure spirits on hand, and know how to use it, he again doubles the quantity of his brandy by adding pure spirits; and the Milwaukee liquor-dealer does the same, after purchasing from the Chicago man. So, in the ordinary course of liquor transactions, by the time a hundred gallon pipe of pure brandy reaches Wisconsin, at a cost of five or perhaps ten dollars per gallon, ninety-nine gallons and one pint of it is the identical whisky that was shipped from Wisconsin the same year at fifty cents per gallon. Truly a homeoopathic dose of genuine brandy! And even that whisky when it left Wisconsin was only half whisky; for there are men in the whisky-making States who make it a business to take whisky direct from the distillery, add to it an equal quantity of water, and then bring it up to a bead and the power of intoxication, by mixing in a variety of the villainous drugs and deadly poisons enumerated in this chapter. The annual loss of strength, health, and life caused by the adulteration of liquor is truly appalling. Those who have not examined the subject can form no just estimate of the atrocious and extensive effects of this murderous humbug.

Chapter 20

*The Peter Funks and their functions—The rural divine
and the watch—Rise and progress of mock
auctions—Their decline and fall.*

Not many years ago, a dignified and reverend man, whose
name is well known to me, was walking sedately down
Broadway. He was dressed in clerical garb of black garments
and white neckcloth. He was a man of great learning, profound thought, long experience, unaffected piety, and pure
and high reputation.

All at once, a kind of chattering shout smote him fair in
the left ear:

"Narfnarfnarf! Three shall I have? Narfnarfnarfnarfnarf!
Going at two and a half! Gone!!"

And the grave divine, pausing, beheld a doorway, over
which waved a little red flag. Within, a company of eager
bidders thronged around an auctioneer's stand; and the auctioneer himself, a well-dressed man with a highly respectable
look, was just handing over to the delighted purchaser a
gold watch.

"It would be cheap at one hundred dollars," said he, in a
despondent tone. "It's mere robbery to sell it for that price.
I'd buy it myself if 'twas legal."

And while the others, with exclamations of surprise and congratulation, crowded to see this famous purchase, and the buyer exhibited it with a joyful countenance close by the door, the divine, just out of curiosity, stepped in. He owned no watch; he was a country clergyman, and poor in this world's goods; so poor that, to use a familiar phrase, "if steamboats were selling at a dime a piece, he would hardly be able to buy a gangplank." But what if he could, by good luck, buy a good gold watch for two dollars and a half in this wonderful city!

Somehow, that watch was snapped open and closed again right under his ministerial nose about six times. The auctioneer held up another of exactly the same kind, and began to chatter again.

"Now gentlemen, what 'moffered f'this first-class M. I. Tobias gold English lever watch—full jeweled, compensation-balance, anchor-escapement, hunting case? One, did I hear? Say two cents, won't yer? Two and a half! narfnarfnarfnarf-narf and a half! Two and a half, and three quarters. Thank you, Sir," to a sailor-like man in the corner.

"Three," said a tall and well-dressed young gentleman with short hair, near the clergyman, adding, in an undertone, "I can sell it for fifty this afternoon."

"Three I am offered," says Mr. Auctioneer, and chattered on as before: "And a half, did you say, Sir? Thank you, Sir. And a halfnarfnarf!"

The reverend divine had said, "And a half." The Peter Funks had got him! But he didn't find it out quite yet. The bidding was run up to four dollars; the clergyman took the watch, opened and examined it; was convinced, handed it back, ventured another half, and the watch was knocked down to him. The auctioneer fumbled in some papers, and, in a moment, handed him his bargain neatly done up.

"This way to the clerk's office if you please, Sir," he added, with a civil bow. The clergyman passed a little further in; and while the sales proceeded behind him, the clerk made out a bill and proffered it.

"Fifty-four dollars and a half!" read the country divine, astounded. "Four and a half is what I bid!"

"Four and a half!" exclaimed the clerk, with sarcastic indignation; "Four dollars and a half! A pretty story! A minister to have the face to say he could buy an M. I. Tobias gold watch, full jeweled, for four dollars and a half! I'll thank you for the money, Sir. Fifty-four, fifty, if you please."

The auctioneer, as if interrupted by the loud tones of the indignant clerk, stopped the sale to see what was the matter. On hearing the statement of the two parties, he cast a glance of angry contempt upon the poor clergyman, who, by this time, was uneasy enough at their scowling faces. Then, as if relenting, he said half-sneeringly:

"I don't think you look very well in this business, Sir. But you are evidently a clergyman, and we wish everybody to have fair treatment in this office. We won't be imposed upon, Sir, by any man!" (Here his face darkened, and his fists could be seen to clench with much meaning.) "Pay that money, Sir! This establishment is not to be humbugged. But you needn't be afraid of losing anything. You may let me take the watch and sell it for you again on the spot. Very likely you can get more for it. You can't lose. The clergyman hesitated. The tall and well-dressed young man with short hair pushed up and said:

"Don't want it? Put her up again. G—! I'd like another chance myself!"

A heavily-built fellow with one eye, observed over the auctioneer's shoulder, with an evil look at the divine, "D—d if I don't believe that cuss is a gambler, come in here to fool us country-folks. They allus wears white neckcloths. I say, search him and boot him out of the shop!"

"Hold your tongue!" answered the auctioneer, with dignity. "I will see you safe, Sir," to the clergyman. "But you bid that money, and you must pay it. We can't do this business on any other principles."

"You will sell it for me again at once?" asked the poor minister.

"Certainly," said the mollified auctioneer. And the humbugged divine, with an indistinct sense of something wrong, but not able to tell what, took out forty dollars from his lean wallet and handed it to the clerk.

"It's all I have to get home with," he said, simply.

"Never fear, old gentleman," said the clerk, affably; "You'll be all right in two minutes."

The watch was put up again. The clergyman, scarce able to believe his ears, heard it rapidly run up to sixty dollars and knocked down at that price. The cash was handed to the clerk, and another bill made out; ten percent, deducted, commission on sales. "Usual terms, Sir," observed the clerk, handing over the notes just received for the watch. And the divine, very thankful to get off for half a dollar, hurried off as fast as he could.

I need not say that his fifty-four dollars was all counterfeit money. When he went next morning, after endeavoring in vain to part with his new funds, to find the place where he had been humbugged, it was close shut, and he could hardly identify even the doorway. He went to the police, and the shrewd captain told him that it was a difficult business; but sent an officer with him to look up the rascals. Officer found one; demanded redress; clergyman did the same. Rascal asked clergyman's name; got it; told him he could prosecute if he liked. Clergyman looked at officer; officer, with indifference, observed:

"Means to stick your name in the papers."

Clergyman said he would take further advice; did take it; thought he wouldn't be shown up as a "greeny" in the police reports; borrowed money enough to get home with, and if he has a gold watch now—which I really hope he has—got it either for its real value, or as a "testimonial."

There, that (with many variations) is the whole story of Peter Funk. These "mock auctioneers," sometimes, as in the case I have mentioned, take advantage of the respectability of their victims, sometimes of their haste to leave the city on business. When they could not possibly avoid it, they disgorged their prey. No instance is known to me of any legal penalty being inflicted on them by a magistrate; but they were always, until 1862, treated by police, by magistrate, and by mayor, just as thieves would be who should always be let off on returning their stealings; so that they could not lose by thieving, and might gain.

These rascally mock-auctioneers, thus protected by the authorities, used to fleece the public out of not less than sixty thousand dollars a year. One of them cleared twelve thousand dollars during the year 1861 alone. And this totally shameless and brazen-faced humbug flourished in New York for twenty-five years!

About the first day of June, 1862, the Peter Funks had eleven dens, or traps, in operation in New York; five in Broadway below Fulton Street, and the others in Park row, and Courtlandt, Greenwich, and Chatham Streets.

The name, Peter Funk, is said to have been that of the founder of their system; but I know nothing more of his career. At this date, in 1862, the system was in a high state of organization and success, and included the following constituents:

1. Eight chief Funks, or capitalists, and managers, whose names are well enough known. I have them on record.

2. About as many more salesmen, who took turns with the chiefs in selling and clerking.

3. Seventy or eighty, rank and file, or ropers-in. These acted the part of buyers, like the purchaser whose delight over his watch helped to deceive the minister and the other bidders on that occasion. These fellows dressed up as countrymen, sailors, and persons of miscellaneous respectability. They bid and talked when that was sufficient, or helped the managers thrash any troublesome person, if necessary. Once in a long time they met their match; as, for instance, when the mate of a ship brought up a squad of his crew, burst into one of their dens, and beat and battered up the whole gang within an inch of their lives. But, in most cases, the reckless infamy of these dregs of city vice gave them an immense advantage over a decent citizen; for they could not be defiled nor made ridiculous, and he could.

4. Two or three traders in cheap jewelry and fancy-goods supplied the Funks with their wares. One of these fellows used to sell them fifty or a hundred dollars' worth of this trash a day; and he lamented as much over their untimely

end as the Ephesian silversmiths did over the loss of their trade in shrines.

5. A lawyer received a regular salary of $1,200 a year to defend all the Funk cases.

6. The city politicians, in office and out of it, who were wont to receive the aid of the Funks (a very energetic cohort) at elections, and who in return unscrupulously used both power and influence to keep them from punishment.

All this cunning machinery was brought to naught and New York relieved of a shame and a pest by the courage, energy, perseverance, and good sense of one Yankee officer— Russell Wells, a policeman. Mr. Wells took about six months to finish up his work. He began it of his own accord, finding that the spirit of the police regulations required it; prosecuted the undertaking without fear or favor, finding not very much support from the judicial authorities, and sometimes actual and direct discouragement. His method was to mount guard over one auction shop at a time, and warn all whom he saw going in, and to follow up all complaints to the utmost until that shop was closed, when he laid siege to another. Various offers of money, direct and indirect, were made him. One fellow offered him $500 to walk on the other side of the street. Another offered him $1,000 to drop the undertaking. Another hinted at a regular salary of hush-money, saying "he had now got these fellows where he could make as much out of them as he wanted to, right along."

Sometimes they threatened him with "murder and sudden death." Several times they got out an injunction upon him, and several times sued him for slander. One of their complaints charged, with ludicrous hypocrisy, that the defendant, "with malicious intent, stood round the door uttering slanderous charges against the good name, fame, and credit of the defendant," just as foolish old lawyers used to argue that "the greater the truth the greater the libel." Sometimes they argued and indignantly denounced. One of them told him, "he was a thief and a murderer, driving men out of employment whose wives and children depended on their business for support."

Another contended that their business was just as fair as that of the stock-operators in Wall Street. I fear that wasn't making out much of a case.

But their threats were idle; their suits, and prosecutions, and injunctions, never came to a head; their bribes did not operate. The officer, imperturbably good-natured, but horribly diligent, watched, and warned, and hunted, and complained, and squeezed back their money at the rate of $500 or $1,000 every month, until they were perfectly sickened. One by one they shut up shop. One went to his farm, another to his merchandise, another to emigrant running, another (known by the elegant surname of Blur-eye Thompson) to raising recruits, several into the bounty jumping business.

Such was the life and death of an outrageous humbug and nuisance, whose like was not to be found in any other city on Earth; and would not have been endured in any except this careless, money-getting, misgoverned one of New York.

Chapter 21

*Lottery sharks—Boult and his brothers—Kenneth,
Kimball and Company—A more central location wanted
for business—Two seventeenth lies—Strange coincidence.*

I have before me a mass of letters, printed and lithographed circulars, and the like, which illustrate well two or three of the most foolish and vicious swindles [it is wrong to call them humbugs] now extant. They also prove that there are a good many more fools alive in our Great Republic than some of us would like to admit.

These letters and papers are signed, respectively, by the following names: Alexander Van Dusen; Thomas Boult & Co.; E. F. Mayo; Geo. P. Harper; Browne, Sherman & Co.; Hammett & Co.; Charles A. Herbert; Geo. C. Kenneth; T. Seymour & Co.; C. W. White, Purchasing Agency; C. J. Darlington; B. H. Robb & Co.; James Conway; S. B. Goodrich; Egerton Brothers; C. F. Miner; E. J. Kimball; E. A. Wilson; and J. T. Small.

All these productions, with one or two exceptions, are dated during the last three months of 1864, and January 1865. They are mailed from a good many different places, and addressed to respectable people in all directions.

In particular, should be noticed, however, two lots of them.

The first lot are signed either by Thomas Boult & Co., Hammett & Co., Egerton Brothers, or T. Seymour & Co. When these four documents are placed together, each with its enclosure, a story is told that seems clear enough to explain itself to the greenest fool in the world.

These fellows—Boult and the rest of them, I mean—are lottery sharks. Now, those who buy lottery tickets are very silly and credulous, or very lazy, or both. They want to get money without earning it. This foolish and vicious wish, however, betrays them into the hands of these lottery sharks. I wish that each of these poor foolish, greedy creatures could study on this set of letters awhile. Look at them. You see that the lithographed handwriting in all four is in the same hand. You observe that each of them encloses a printed handbill with "scheme," all looking as like as so many peas. They refer, you see, to the same "Havana scheme," the same "Shelby College Lottery," the same "managers," and the same place of drawing. Now, see what they say. Each knave tells his fool his only object is to put said fool in possession of a handsome prize, so that fool may run round and show the money, and rope in more fools. What an ingenious way to make the fool think he will return value for the prize! Each knave further says to his fool (I copy the words of the knave from his lithograph letter:) "We are so certain that we know how to select a lucky certificate, that if the one we select for you does not, at the very least, draw a $5,000 prize, we will"—what? Pay the money ourselves? Oh no. Knave does not offer to pay half of it. "Will send you another package in one of our extra lotteries for nothing!"

Observe how particularly every knave is to tell his fool to

"give us the name of the nearest bank," so that the draft for the prize-money can be forwarded instantly.

And in return for all this kindness, what do Messrs. Boult and-so-forth want? Why, almost nothing. "The ridiculously small sum," as Mr. Montague Tigg observed to Mr. Pecksniff, of $10. You observe that Hammett & Co., in one circular, demand $20, for the same $5,000 prize. But the amount, they would say, is too trifling to be so particular about!

I will suggest a form for answering these gentlemen. Let every one of my readers who receives one of their circulars just copy and date and sign, and send them the following:

"Gentlemen:—I thank you for your great kindness in wishing to make me the possessor of a $5,000 prize in your truly rich and splendid Royal Havana Lottery. I fully believe that you know, as you say, all about how to get these prizes, and that you can make it a big thing. But I cannot think of taking all that money from such kind of people as you. I must insist upon your having half of it, and I will not hear of any refusal, I therefore hereby authorize you to invest for me the trifle of $10, which you mention; and when the prize is drawn, to put half of it, and $10 over, right into your own benevolent pantaloons-pocket, and to remit the other half to me, addressed as follows: (Here give the name of the 'nearest bank.')

"I have not the least fear that you will cheat me out of my half; and, as you see, I thus place myself confidently in your hands. With many thanks for your great and undeserved kindness, I remain your obliged and obedient servant. Etc., Etc."

My readers will observe that this mode of replying affords full swing to the expansive charities of Boult and his brethren, and is a sure method of saving the expenditure of $10, although Boult is to get that amount back when the prize is drawn.

I charge nothing for these suggestions; but will not be so discourteous as to refuse a moderate percentage on all amounts received in pursuance of them from Brother Boult & Co.

Here is the second special lot of letters I spoke of. I lay them out on my desk as before: There are six letters signed respectively by Kimball, Goodrich, Darlington, Kenneth, Harper, and Herbert. Now notice, first the form, and next the substance.

As to form—they are all written, not, lithographed; they are on paper of the same make and size, and out of the same lot, as you observe by the manufacturer's stamp—a representation of the Capitol in the upper corner. They are in the same hand, an easy legible business-hand, though three of them are written with a backward slope. Those who sent them have not sent me the envelopes with them, except in one case, so that I cannot tell where they were mailed. Neither is any one of them dated inside at any town or post-office. But, by a wonderful coincidence, every one of them is dated at "No. 17 Merchants' Exchange." A busy mart that No. 17 must be! And it is a still more curious coincidence that every one of these six industrious chaps has been unable to find a sufficiently central location for transacting his business. Every letter you see, contains a printed slip advising of a removal, as follows:

"Removal.—Desiring a more central location for transacting my business, I have removed my office to No. 17 Merchants Exchange." Where? One says to West Troy, New York; another to Patterson, New Jersey; another to Bronxville, New York; another, to Salem, New-York, and so on! It is a new thing to find how central all those places are. Undeveloped metropolises seem to exist in every corner. Well, the slip ends with a notice that in future letters must be directed to the new place.

Next, as to substance. The six letters all tell the same story. They are each the second letter; the first one having been sent to the same person, and having contained a lottery-ticket, as a gift of love or free charity. This second letter is the one which is expected to "fetch." It says in substance: "Your ticket has drawn a prize of $200,"—the letters all name the same amount—but you didn't pay for it; and therefore are not entitled to it. Now send me $10 and I will cheat the lottery-man by altering the postmark of your letter so that the money shall seem to have been sent before the lottery was drawn. This forgery will enable me to get the $200, which I will send you."

How cunning that is! It is exactly calculated to hit the notions of a vulgar, ignorant, lazy, greedy, and unprincipled bumpkin. Such a fellow would see just far enough into the millstone to be tickled at the idea of cheating those lottery fellows. And the knave ends his letter with one more touch most delicately adapted to make Master Bumpkin feel certain that his cash is coming. He says, "Be sure to show your prize to all your friends, so as to make them buy tickets at my office."

Moreover, these letters enclose each a "report of the seventeenth monthly drawing of the Cosmopolitan Art Union Association." You may observe that one of these "seventeenth drawings" took place November 7 1864, and another December 5, 1864; so that seventeenthly came twice. What is a far more remarkable coincidence is this; that in each of these "reports" is a list of a hundred and thirty or forty numbers that drew prizes, and it is exactly the same list each time, and the same prize to each number! There is a third coincidence; that one of these two drawings is said to have been at London, New York, and the other at London, New Jersey. And lastly, there is a fourth coincidence, viz., that neither of these places exists.

Now, what a transparent swindle this is! how plain, how impudent, how rascally! And all done entirely by the use of the Post Office privileges of the United States. Try to catch this fellow. You can find where he mailed his circular; but he probably stopped there overnight to do so, and nobody knew it. In each circular, he wrote to his dupes to address him at that new "more central location" that he struggles after so hard; and how is the pursuer to find it? Would anybody naturally go and watch the Post Office at Bronxville, New York, for instance, as a particularly central location for business?

Besides, no one person is cheated out of enough to make him follow up the affair, and probably nobody who sends the cash wants to say much about it afterward. He wants to wait and show the prize!

These dirty sharking traps will always be set, and will always catch silly people, as long as there are any to catch. The only means of stopping such trickery is to diffuse the conviction that the best way to get a living is, to go to work like a man and earn it honestly.

Chapter 22

Another lottery humbug—Two hundred and fifty recipes—Vile books—"Advantage-cards"—A package for you; Please send the money—Peddling in western New York.

The readiness with which people will send off their money to a swindler is perfectly astounding. It does really seem as if an independent fortune could be made simply by putting forth circulars and advertisements, requesting the receiver to send five dollars to the advertiser, and saying that "it will be all right."

I have already given an account of the way in which lottery dealers operate. From among the same pile of documents which I used then, I have selected a few others, as instances in part, of a class of humbugs sometimes of a kind even far more noxious, and which show that their devisers and patrons are not only sharpers or fools, but often also very cold-blooded villains or very nasty ones. Some of them are managed by printed circulars and written letters, such as those before me; some of them by newspaper advertisements. Some are only to cheat you out of money, and others offer in return for money some base gratification. But whatever means are used, and whatever purpose is sought, they are all alike in one thing—they depend entirely on the monstrous number of simpletons who will send money to people they know nothing about.

Of the nasty ones, I can give no details. Vile books, pictures, etc., are from time to time advertised, sold, and forwarded, by circular, and through the mails, and for large prices.

There have been some cases where a funny sort of swindle has been effected by these peddlers of pruriency, by selling some dirty-minded dupe a cheap good book, at the extravagant price of a dear bad one. More than one foolish youth has received, instead of the vile thing that he sent five dollars for, a nice little New Testament. It is obvious that no very loud complaints are likely to be made about such cheating as that. It is, perhaps, one of the safest swindles ever contrived.

The first document which I take from my pile is the announcement of a fellow who operates lottery-wise. His scheme appeals at once to benevolence and to greediness. He says: "The profits of the distribution are to be given to the Sanitary Commission;" and secondly, "Every ticket brings a prize of at least its full value, and some of them $5,000."

If, therefore you won't buy tickets for filthy lucre's sake, buy for the sake of our soldiers.

"But," somebody says, "how can you afford this arrangement, which is a direct loss of the whole cost of working your lottery, and moreover of the whole value of all prizes costing more than a ticket?"

"Oh," replies our benevolent friend, "a number of manufacturers in New England have asked me to do this, and the prizes are given by them as friends of the soldier."

One observation will sufficiently show what an impudent mess of lies this story is, namely;—If the manufacturers of

New England wanted to give money to the Sanitary Commission, they would give money; if goods, they would give goods. They certainly would not put their gifts through the additional roundabout, useless nonsense of a lottery, which is to turn over only the same amount of funds to the Commission.

The next document is a circular sent from a Western town by a fellow who claims also to be a master of arts, doctor of medicines, and doctor of laws, but whose handwriting and language are those of a stable-boy. This chap sends round a list of two hundred and fifty recipes at various prices, from twenty-five cents to a dollar each. Send him the money for any you wish, and he promises to return you the directions for making the stuff. You are then to go about and peddle it, and swiftly become independently rich. You can begin with a dollar, he says; in two days make fifty dollars, and then sweep on in a grand career of affluence, making from $75 to $200 a day, "if you are industrious." What is petroleum to this? It is a mercy that we don't all turn to and peddle to each other; we should all get too rich to speak!

The fellow, out of pure kindness and desire for your good, recommends you to buy all his recipes, as then you will be sure to sell something to everybody. Most of these recipes are for sufficiently harmless purposes—shaving-soap, cement, inks—five gallons of good ink for fifteen cents"—tooth-powders, etc. Some of them are arrant nonsense; such as "tea—better than the Chinese," which is as if he promised something wetter than water; "to make thieves' vinegar;" "prismatic diamond crystals for windows;" "to make yellow butter"—is the butter blue where the man lives? Others are of a sort calculated to attract foolish rustic rascals who would like to gain an easy living by cheating, if they were only smart enough. Thus, there is "Rothschild's great secret; or how to make common gold." My readers shall have a better recipe than this swindler's—work hard, think hard, be honest, and spend little—this will "make common gold," and this is all the secret Rothschild ever had. A number of these recipes are barefaced quackeries; such as cures for consumption, cancer, rheumatism, and sundry other diseases; to make whiskers and mustaches grow—ah, boys, you can't hurry up those things. Greasing your cheeks is just as good as trying to whistle the hair out, but not a bit better. Don't hurry; you will be old quite soon enough! But this fellow is ready for old fools as well young ones, for he has recipes for curing baldness and removing wrinkles. And last, but not least, quietly inserted among all these fooleries and harmless humbugs, are two or three recipes which promise the safe gratification of the basest vices. Those are what he really hoped to get money for.

I have carefully refrained from giving any names or information which would enable anybody to address any of these folks. I do not propose to cooperate with them, if I know it.

The next is a circular only to be very briefly alluded to: it promises to furnish, on receipt of the price, and "by mail or express, with perfect safety, so as to defy detection," any of twenty-two wholly infamous books, and various other cards and commodities, well suited to the public of Sodom and Gomorrah, etc. The most honest and decent things advertised in this unclean list are "advantage-cards" which enable the player to swindle his adversary by reading off his hand by the backs of the cards.

The next paper I can copy verbatim, except some names, etc., is a letter as follows:

"Dear Sir—There is a Package in My care for a Mrs. preston New Griswold wich thare is 48 cts. fratage. Pleas forward the same. I shall send it Per Express Your recpt."

It is some little comfort to know that this gentleman, who is so much opposed to the present prevailing methods of spelling, lost the three cents which he invested in seeking "fratage." But a good many sensible people have carelessly sent away the small amounts demanded by letters like the above, and have wondered why their prepaid parcels never came.

Next, is an account by a half amused and half indignant eyewitness, of what happened in a well known town in Western New York, on Friday, January 6, 1865. A personage described as "dressed in Yankee style," drove into the principal street of the place with a horse and buggy, and began to sell what is called in some parts of New England "Attleboro," that is, imitation jewelry, but promising to return the customers their money, if required, and doing so. After a number of transactions of this kind, he bawls out, like the sorcerer in Aladdin, who went around crying new lamps for old, "Who will give me four dollars for this five-dollar greenback?"

He found a customer; sold a one-dollar greenback for ninety cents; then sold some half-dollar bills for twenty-five cents each; then flung out among the crowd what a fisherman would call ground bait, in the shape of a handful of "currency."

Everybody scrambled for the money. This liberal trader

now drove slowly a little way along, and the crowd pressed after him.

He now began, without any further promises, to sell a lot of bogus lockets at five dollars each, and in a few minutes had disposed of about forty. Having, therefore, about two hundred dollars in his pocket, and trade slackening, he coolly observes, with a terseness and clearness of oratory that would not discredit General Sherman:

"Gentlemen—I have sold you those goods at my price. I am a licensed peddler. If I give you your money back you will think me a lunatic. I wish you all success in your ordinary vocations! Good morning!"

And sure enough, he drove off. That same cunning chap has actually made a small fortune in this way. He really is licensed as a peddler, and though arrested more than once, has consequently not been found legally punishable.

I will specify only one more of my collection, of yet another kind. This is a printed circular appealing to a class of fools, if possible, even shallower, sillier, and more credulous than any I have named yet. It is headed "The Gypsies' Seven Secret Charms." These charms consist of a kind of hellbroth or decoction. You are to wet the hands and the forehead with them, and this is to render you able to tell what any person is thinking of; upon taking anyone by the hand, you will be able to entirely control the mind and will of such person (it is unnecessary to specify the purpose intended to be believed possible). These charms are also to enable you to buy lucky lottery-tickets, discover things lost or hid, dream correctly of the future, increase the intellectual faculties, secure the affections of the other sex, etc. These precious conceits are set forth in a ridiculous hodgepodge of statements. The "charms," it says, were used by the "Antedeluvians;" were the secret of the Egyptian enchanters and of Moses, too; of the Pythoness and the heathen conjurors and humbugs generally; and (which will be news to the geographers of today) "are used by the Psyli (the swindler misspells again) of South America to charm Beasts, Birds, and Serpents." The way to control the mind, he says, was discovered by a French traveler named Tunear. This Frenchman is perhaps a relative of the equally celebrated Russian traveller, Toofaroff.

But here is the point, after all. You send the money, we will say, for one of these charms—for they are for sale separately. You receive in return a second circular, saying that they work a great deal better all together, and so the man will send you all of them when you send the rest of the money. Send it, if you choose!

Now, how is it possible for people to be living among us here, who are fooled by such wretched balderdash as this? There are such, however, and a great many of them. I do not imagine that there are many of these addlepates among my readers; but there is no harm in giving once more a very plain and easy direction which may possibly save somebody some money and some mortification. Be content with what you can honestly earn. Know whom you deal with. Do not try to get money without giving fair value for it. And pay out no money on strangers' promises, whether by word of mouth, written letters, advertisements, or printed circulars.

Chapter 23

A California coal mine—A Hartford coal mine—Mysterious subterranean canal on the isthmus.

Some twelve years ago or so, in the early days of Californian immigration, a curious little business humbug came off about six miles from Monterey. A United States officer, about the year 1850, was on his way into the interior on a surveying expedition, with a party of men, a portable forge, a load of coal, and sundry other articles. At the place in question, six miles inland, the Lieutenant's coal wagon "stalled" in a "tule" swamp. With true military decision the greater part of the coal was thrown out to extricate the team, and not picked up again. The expedition went on and so did time, and the latter, in his progress, had some years afterward dried up the tule swamp. Some enterprising prospectors, with eyes wide open to the nature of things, now espied one fine morning the lumps of coal, sticking their black noses up out of the mud. It was a clear case—there was a coal mine there! The happy discoverers rushed into town. A company was at once organized under the mining laws of the state of California. The corporators at first kept the whole matter totally secret except from a few particular friends who were as a very great favor allowed to buy stock for cash. A "compromise" was made with the owner of the land, largely to his advantage. When things had thus been set properly at work, specimens of coal were publicly exhibited at Monterey. There was a gigantic excitement; shares went up almost out of sight. Twelve hundred dollars in coin for one share (par $100) was laughed at. About this time a quiet honest Dutchman of the vicinity passing along by the "mine" one evening with his cart, innocently and unconsciously picked up the whole at one single load and carried it home. Prompt was the discovery of the "sell" by the stockholders, and voluble and intense, it is said, their profane expressions of dissatisfaction. But the original discoverers of the mine vigorously protested that they were "sold" themselves, and that it was only a case of common misfortune. It is however reported that a number of persons in Monterey, *after* the explosion of the speculation, remembered all about the coal-wagon part of the business, which they said, the excitement of the "company" had put entirely out of their heads.

An equally unfounded but not quite so barefaced humbug came off a good many years ago in the good old city of Hartford, in Connecticut, according to the account given me by an old gentleman now deceased, who was one of the parties interested. This was a coal mine in the State House yard. It sounds like talking about getting sunbeams out of cucumbers—but something of the sort certainly took place.

Coal is found among rocks of certain kinds, and not elsewhere. Among strata of granite or basalt for instance, nobody expects to find coal. But along with a certain kind of sandstone it may reasonably be expected. Now the Hartford wiseacres found that tremendously far down under their city, there was *a* sort of sandstone, and they were sure that it was *the* sort. So they gathered together some money—there is a vast deal of *that* in Hartford, coal or no coal—organized a company, employed a Mining Superintendent, set up a boring apparatus, and down went their hole into the ground—an orifice some four or six inches across. Through the surface stratum of earth it went, and bang it came against the sandstone. They pounded away, with good courage, and got some fifties or hundreds of feet further. Indefinable sensations were aroused in their minds at one time by the coming up among the products of boring, of some chips of wood. Now wood, shortly coal, they thought. They might, I imagine, have brought up some pieces of boiled potato or even of fresh shad, provided it had fallen down first. They dug on until they got tired, and then they stopped. If they had gone down ten thousand feet they would have found no coal. Coal is found in the new red sandstone; but theirs was the old red sandstone, which is a very fine old stone itself, but in which no coal was ever found, except what might have been put there on purpose, or possibly some faint indications. The hole they made, however, as my informant gravely observed, was left sticking in the ground, and if he is right is to this day a sort of appendix or tail to the well northwest corner of the State House Square. So, I suppose, anyone who chooses can go and poke down there after it and satisfy himself about the accuracy of this account. Such an inquirer ought to find satisfaction, for "truth lies in the bottom of a well" says the proverb. Yet some ill natured skeptics have construed this to mean that all will tell lies sometimes, for—as they accent it, even "Truth *lies*, at the bottom of a well!"

Still a different sort of business humbug, again, was a wonderful story which went the rounds about fifteen years ago, and which was cooked up to help some one or other of the various enterprises for new routes by Central America to California. This story started, I believe, in the *New Orleans Courier*. It was, that a French Doctor of Vera Paz in Guatemala, while making a canal from his estate to the sea, discovered, away up at the very furthest extremity of the Gulf of Honduras, a vast ancient canal, two hundred and forty feet wide, seventy feet deep, and walled in on both sides with gigantic masses of rough cut stone. The Doctor at once gave up his own trifling modern excavation, and plunged into an explanation of this vast ancient one, as zealously as if he were probing after some uncertain bullet in a poor fellow's leg. The monstrous canal carried him in a straight line up the country, to the southwestward. Some twenty miles or so inland it plunged under a *volcano*!

But see what a French doctor is made of!

Cutting down the great, old trees that obstructed the entrance, and procuring a canoe with a crew of Indians, in he went. The canal became a prodigious tunnel, of the same width and depth of water, and vaulted three hundred and thirty five feet high in the living rock. Nothing is said about the bowels of the volcano, so that we must conclude either that such affairs are not planted so deep as is supposed, or that the fire-pot of the concern was shoved one side or bridged over by the canallers, or that the Frenchman had some remarkably good style of Fire Annihilator, or else that there is some mistake!

Eighteen hours of incessant travel brought our intrepid M.D. safe through to the Pacific Ocean; during which time, if the maps of that country are of any authority, he passed under quite a number of mountains and rivers. The trip was not dark at all, as shafts were sunk every little way, which lighted up the interior quite well, and then the volcano gave—or ought to have given—some light inside. Indeed, if the doctor had only thought of it, I presume he would have noticed double rows of street gas lamps on each side of the canal! The exclusive right to use this excellent transit route has not, to my knowledge, been secured to anybody yet. It will be observed that ships as large as the Great Eastern could easily pass each other in this canal, which renders it a sure thing for any other vessel unless that shrewd and grasping fellow the Emperor Louis Napoleon, has got hold of this canal and is keeping it dark for some still darker purposes of his own—as for instance to run his puppet Maximilian into for refuge, when he is run out of Mexico—it is therefore still in the market. And my publication of the facts effectually disposes of the Emperor's plan of secrecy, of course.

Part IV

MONEY MANIAS

Chapter 24

*The petroleum humbug—The New York and Rangoon
Petroleum Company.*

Every sham, as has often been said, proves some reality.
Petroleum exists, no doubt, and is an important addition to
our national wealth. But the petroleum humbug or mania or
superstition, or whatever you choose to call it, is a humbug,
just as truly, and a big one, whether we use the word in its
milder or its bitterer sense.

There are more than six hundred petroleum companies.
The capital they call for, is certainly not less than five hundred
million dollars. The money invested in the notorious South
Sea Bubble was less than two-fifths as much—only about
$190,000,000.

Now, this petroleum business—very much of it—is just as
thorough a gambling business as any faro bank ever set up in
Broadway, or any other stock speculation ever conjured up
in Wall Street—as much so, for instance, as the well known
Parker Vein coal company.

I shall here tell exactly how those well known and enterprising financiers, Messrs. Peter Rolleum and Diddle Digwell proceeded in organizing the New-York and Rangoon
Petroleum Company, of which all my readers have seen

the advertisements everywhere, and of which the former is the Vice President and managing officer, and the latter Secretary. In June 1864, neither of these worthy gentleman was worth a cent. Rolleum shinned up and down in some commission agency or other, and Digwell had a small salary as clerk in some insurance or money concern. They barely earned a living. Now, Rolleum says he is worth $200,000; and Mr. Secretary Digwell, besides about $10,000 worth of stock in the New York and Rangoon, has his comfortable salary and his highly respectable "posish"—to use a little bit of business slang.

Mr. Rolleum was the originator of the scheme, and let Digwell into it; and together they went to work. They had a few hundred dollars in cash, no particular credit, an entirely unlimited fund of lies, a good deal of industry, plausibility, talk, and cheek, considerable acquaintance with business, and an instinctive appreciation of some of the more selfish motives commonly influential among men.

First of all, Rolleum made a trip into the oil country. Here, while picking up some of his ordinary agency business, he looked around among the wells and oil lands, talking, and examining and inquiring of everybody about everything, with a busy, solemn face, and the air of one who does *not wish* it to be supposed that he has important interests in his care. Then he talked with some men at (we will say) Titusville and thereabouts; told all about his valuable business connections in New York City: and after getting a little acquainted, he laid before each of half-a-dozen or so of them, this proposition:

"You can have a good many shares of a first class new oil company about to be formed just for permitting your name to be used in its interest, and for being a trustee." A thousand shares apiece, he said; to be valued at five dollars each, the par value however, being ten dollars. Five thousand dollars each man, and to be made ten thousand, as soon as the proposed puffing should enable them to sell out. After a little hesitation, a sufficient number consented. There was nothing to pay, something handsome to get, and all they were asked for it was, to let a man talk about them. What if he did lie? That was his business.

This fixed four out of the nine intended trustees.

Rolleum also obtained memoranda or printed circulars showing the amounts for which a number of oil land owners would sell their holes in the ground or the room for making others, and describing the premises. He now flew back to New York, and went to sundry persons of some means and some position but of no great nobility, and thus he said:

"Here are these wealthy and distinguished oil men right there on the ground who are going to be trustees of my new company.

"You serve too, won't you? One thousand shares for your trouble—five thousand dollars. No money to pay—I will see to all that. Here are the lands we can buy,"—and he showed his lists. The bribe, and the names of those already bribed, influenced them, and this secured three more trustees. Two more were needed, namely the President and Vice President. Rolleum himself was to be the latter; his next move was to secure the former.

This, the most critical part of the scheme, was cunningly delayed until this time. Rolleum went to the Honorable A. Bee, a gentleman of a good deal of ability, pretty widely known, not very rich, believed (perhaps for that reason) to be honest, no longer young, and of a reverend yet agreeable presence. Him the plausible Rolleum told all about the new Company; what a respectable board of trustees there was going to be—and he showed the names; all either experienced and substantial men of the oil country, or reputable business men of New York City. And they have agreed to serve, in part because they know what a very honest company this is, and still more because they hope that the Honorable A. Bee will become President.

"My dear Sir," urged Rolleum, sweetly, "this legitimate business enterprise *must* succeed, and *must* secure wealth, reputation, and influence to all connected with it. We know that you are above pecuniary considerations, and that you do not need our influence, or anybody's. We need yours. And you need not do any work. I will do that. We only need your name. And merely as a matter of form, because the officers are expected to be interested in their own company, I have set apart two thousand shares, being at half par or $5 a share, $10,000 of stock, to stand in your name. See how respectable all these Trustees are!" And he showed the list and preached upon the items of it.

"This man is worth so many millions, that man is such an influential editor. Could I have obtained such names if this were not a perfectly square thing?"

Ten thousand dollars will go some ways towards squaring almost anything, with many people, even if it is a mere matter of form; and so the old gentleman consented. This fixed the whole official "slate."

Now to set up the machine.

In a few days of sharp running and talking, Rolleum and Digwell accomplished this, as follows:

First, they hired and furnished handsomely, paying cash

whenever they couldn't help it, a couple of pleasant first floor rooms close to Wall Street. No dingy desk-room up in some dark corner or attic, for them. Respectability is the thing for Rolleum.

Second, they hired a lawyer to draft the proper papers, and had the New York and Rangoon Petroleum Company "Duly incorporated under the mining and statute laws of the State of New York," with charter, bylaws, seal, officers' names, and everything fine, new, grand, magnificent, impressive, formal, respectable and businesslike.

Third, they now had every requisite of a powerful, enterprising and highly successful corporation, except the small trifles of money, land and oil. But what are these, to such geniuses as Rolleum and Digwell? Singular if having invented and set the trap, they could not catch the birds!

They *bought* about three pints of oil, for one dollar; and that settled one part of the question. They bought it ready sorted and vialled and labelled; some crude and green, some yellowish, some limpid as water, half a dozen or so of different specimens. These, in their tall vials of most respectable appearance, they placed casually on the mantelpiece of the outer office. They were specimens of the oils which the company's wells are confidently expected to yield—when they get 'em!

Last of all—land and money. Subscriptions to capital stock are to furnish money, money will buy land. And *saying we've got land* will procure subscriptions.

"It's not much of a lie, after all," said Rolleum, confidentially, to brother Digwell. "When we've *said* we've got it for awhile, we *shall* get it. It's not a lie at all. It's only discounting the truth at sixty days!"

So he and Digwell went to work and made a splendid prospectus and advertisement, the latter an abridged edition of the former. This prospectus was a great triumph of business lying mixed with plums and spices of truth, and all set forth with taking "display lines."

It began with a stately row of names: New York and Rangoon Petroleum Company; Honorable Abraham Bee, President; Peter Rolleum, Esq., Vice President; Diddle Digwell, Esq., Secretary; and so on. With cool impudence it then gave a list headed "Lands and Property"—not saying "of the Company" for fear of a prosecution for swindling. But the list below began with the words "the oil lands *to be conveyed* to the Company are as follows:" "that's exactly it" quoth Rolleum—no lie there, at any rate. They *are* to 'to be conveyed' to us—if we choose—just as soon as we can pay for them." And then the list went on from "No. 1" to "No. 43," giving in a row all those memoranda which Rolleum had obtained in Venango County and the region round about, of the descriptions of the real estate which the landsharks up there would be glad to sell for what they asked for it.

The Prospectus said the capital of the company was one million dollars, in one hundred thousand shares at ten dollars each. But *in order to obtain a* **working capital**, twenty thousand shares are offered for a *limited period* at five dollars each, not subject to further assessment.

And it added, though with more phrases, something to the following effect: Hurry! Pay quick! Or you will lose your chance! In conclusion the whole was wound up with many wise and moral observations about legitimate business, interests of stockholders, heavy capitalists, economical management, and other such things; and it bestowed some rather fat compliments upon the honorable Abraham Bee and the Trustees.

Having concocted this choice morsel of bait, they set it in the great stream of newspapers, there to catch fish. In plain terms, with some cash and some credit—for their means would not even reach to pay in advance the whole of their first advertising bill—they managed to have their advertisement published during several weeks in a carefully chosen group of about thirty of the principal newspapers of the United States.

The whole web was now woven; and Rolleum and Digwell, like two hungry spiders, squatted in their den, every nerve thrilling to feel the first buzz of the first fly. It was natural that the scamps should feel a good deal excited: it was life or death with them. If a confiding public, in answer to their impassioned appeal, should generously remit, they were made men for life. If not, instead of being rich and respected gentlemen, they were ridiculous, detected swindlers.

Well—they succeeded. So truthful is our Great American Nation—so confiding, so sure of the truth of what is said in print, even if only in the advertising columns of a newspaper—so certain of the good faith of people who have their names printed in large capitals and with a handle at one end—that actually these fellows had a hundred thousand dollars in bank within ten weeks—before they owned one foot of land, or one inch of well, or one drop of oil, except those three pints in the vials on the office shelf!

And remember this is no imaginary case. I am giving point by point the exact transactions of a real Petroleum Company.

Everything I have told was done, only if possible with a more false and baseless impudence than I have described.

And scores and scores of other Petroleum Companies have been organized in ways exactly as unprincipled. Some of them may perhaps have proceeded as real business concerns. Some have stopped and disappeared as soon as the managers could get a handsome sum of money into their pockets for stock.

What the result will be, in the present case, I don't know. The New York and Rangoon Petroleum Company, when I last knew about it, "still lived." They had—or said they had—bought some land. I have not heard of their receiving any oil raised from their own wells. They have sent off a monstrous quantity of circulars, prospectuses and advertisements. They caused a portrait and biography of the Honorable A. Bee to be printed in a very respectable periodical, and paid five hundred dollars for it. They had themselves systematically puffed up to the seventh heaven in a long series of articles in another periodical, and paid the owner of it $2,000 or so *in stock*. They talk very big about a dividend. But although they have received a great deal of money, and paid out a great deal, I do not know of their paying their stockholders any yet. If they should, it would not prove much. For it is sometimes considered "a good dodge" to declare and pay a large dividend before any real profits have been earned; as this is calculated to enhance the price of shares, and to make them "go off like hot cakes."

I shall not make any "moral" about this story. It teaches its own. It is a very mild statement of what was done to establish an actual specimen—and far from being of the worst description—of a great part of the Petroleum Company enterprises of the day.

It is whispered that somehow or other the trustees and

officers of the New York and Rangoon do not own so much stock of their company as they did, having managed to have their stock sold to subscribers as if it were company stock. If this is so, those gentlemen have made their reward sure; and Mr. Peter Rolleum, having the cash in hand for that very liberal allotment of stock which he gave himself for his trouble in getting up the New York and Rangoon Petroleum Company, is very likely half or a quarter as rich as he says.

Chapter 25

The Tulipomania.

Alboni, the singer, had an exquisitely sweet voice, but was a very big fat woman. Somebody accordingly remarked that she was an elephant that had swallowed a nightingale. About as incongruous is the idea of a nation of damp, foggy, fat, full-figured, broad-sterned, gin-drinking, tobacco-smoking Dutchmen in Holland, going crazy over a flower. But they did so, for three or four years together. Their craze is known in history as the Tulipomania, because it was a mania about tulips.

Just a word about the Dutchmen first.

These stout old fellows were not only hardy navigators, keen discoverers, ingenious engineers, laborious workmen, able financiers, shrewd and rich merchants, enthusiastic patriots and tremendous fighters, but they were eminently distinguished (as they still are to a considerable extent) by a love of elegant literature, poetry, painting, music and other fine arts, including horticulture. It was a Fleming that invented painting in oils. Before him, white of egg was used, or gum-water, or some such imperfect material, for spreading the color. Erasmus, one of the most learned, ready-minded, acute, graceful and witty scholars that ever lived, was a

Dutchman. All Holland and Flanders, in days when they were richer, and stronger compared with the rest of the world than they are now, were full of singing societies and musical societies and poetry making societies. The universities of Leyden and Utrecht and Louvain are of highly an ancient European fame. And as for flowers, and bulbs in particular, Holland is a principal home and market of them now, more than two hundred years after the time I am going to tell of.

Tulips grow wild in Southern Russia, the Crimea and Asia Minor, as potatoes do in Peru. The first tulip in Christian Europe was raised in Augsburg, in the garden of a flower-loving lawyer, one Counsellor Herwart, in the year 1559, thirteen years after Luther died. This tulip bulb was sent to Herwart from Constantinople. For about eighty years after this the flower continually increased in repute and became more and more known and cultivated, until the fantastic eagerness of the demand for fine ones and the great prices that they brought, resulted in a real mania like that about the *morus multicaulis*, or the petroleum mania of today, but much more intense. It began in the year 1635, and went out with an explosion in the year 1837.

This tulip business is, I believe, the only speculative excitement in history whose subject-matter did not even claim to have any real value. Petroleum is worth some shillings a gallon for actual use for many purposes. Stocks always claim to represent some real trade or business. The *morus multicaulis* was to be as permanent a source of wealth as corn, and was expected to produce the well known mercantile substance of silk. But nobody ever pretended that tulips could be eaten, or manufactured, or consumed in any way of practical usefulness. They have not one single quality of the kind termed useful. They have nothing desirable except the beauty of a peculiarly short-lived blossom. You can do absolutely nothing with them except to look at them. A speculation in them is exactly as reasonable as one in butterflies would be.

In the course of about one year, 1634–5, the tulip frenzy, after having increased for fifteen or twenty years with considerable speed, came to a climax, and poisoned the whole Dutch nation. Prices had at the end of this short period risen from high to extravagant, and from extravagant to insane. High and low, counts, burgomasters, merchants, shopkeepers, servants, shoeblacks, all were buying and selling tulips like mad. In order to make the commodity of the day accessible to all, a new weight was invented, called a perit, so small that there were about eight thousand of them in one pound avoirdupois, and a single tulip root weighing from half an ounce to an ounce, would contain from 200 to 400 of these perits. Thus, anybody unable to buy a whole tulip, could buy a perit or two, and have what the lawyers call an "undivided interest" in a root. This way of owning shows how utterly unreal was the pretended value. For imagine a small owner attempting to take his own perits and put them in his pocket. He would make a little hole in the tulip-root, would probably kill it, and would certainly obtain a little bit of utterly worthless pulp for himself, and no value at all. There was a whole code of business regulations made to meet the peculiar needs of the tulip business, besides, and in every town were to be found "tulip-notaries," to conduct the legal part of the business, take acknowledgments of deeds, note protests, etc.

To say that the tulips were worth their weight in gold would be a very small story. It would not be a very great exaggeration to say that they were worth their size in diamonds. The most valuable species of all was named *Semper Augustus*, and a bulb of it which weighed 200 perits, or less than half an ounce avoirdupois, was thought cheap at 5,500 florins. A florin may be called about 40 cents; so that the little brown root was worth $2,200, or 220 gold eagles, which would weigh, by a rough estimate, eight pounds four ounces, or 132 ounces avoirdupois. Thus this half ounce *Semper Augustus* was worth—I mean he would bring—two hundred and sixty-four times his weight in gold!

There were many cases where people invested whole fortunes equal to $40,000 or $50,000 in collections of forty or fifty tulip roots. Once there happened to be only two *Semper Augustus*es in all Holland, one in Haarlem and one in Amsterdam. The Haarlem one was sold for twelve acres of building lots, and the Amsterdam one for a sum equal to $1,840.00, together with a new carriage, span of grey horses and double harness, complete.

Here is the list of merchandise and estimated prices given for one root of the Viceroy tulip. It is interesting as showing what real merchandise was worth in those days by a cash standard, aside from its exhibition of tremendous speculative bedlamism:

160 bushels wheat	$179
320 bushels rye	223.
Four fat oxen	192.
Eight fat hogs	96.0
Twelve fat sheep	48.0
Two hogsheads wine	28.0
Four tuns beer	12.8
Two tuns butter	76.8
1000 lbs. cheese	48.0
A bed all complete	40.0
One suit clothes	32.0
A silver drinking cup	24.0
Total exactly	$1,0

In 1636, regular tulip exchanges were established in the nine Dutch towns where the largest tulip business was done, and while the gambling was at its intensest, the matter was managed exactly as stock gambling is managed in Wall Street today. You went out into "the street" without owning a tulip or a perit of a tulip in the world, and met another fellow with just as many tulips as yourself. You talk and "banter" with him, and finally (we will suppose) you "sell short" ten *Semper Augustus*es, "seller three," for $2,000 each, in all $20,000. This means in ordinary English, that without having any tulips (i.e., short,) you promise to deliver the ten roots as above in three days from date. Now when the three days are up, if *Semper Augustus*es are worth in the market only $1,500, you could, if this were a real transaction, buy ten of them for $15,000, and deliver them to the other gambler for $20,000, thus winning from him the difference of $5,000. But if the roots have risen and are worth $2,500 each, then if the transactions were real you would have to pay $25,000 for the ten roots and could only get $20,000 from the other gambler, and he, turning round and selling them at the market price, would win from you this difference of $5,000. But in fact the transaction was not real, it was a stock gambling one; neither party owned tulips or meant to, or expected the other to; and the whole was a pure game of chance or skill, to see which should win and which should lose that $5,000 at the end of three days. When the time came, the affair was settled, still without any tulips, by the loser paying the difference to the winner, exactly as one loses what the other wins at a game of poker or faro. Of course if you can set afloat a smart lie after making your bargain, such as will send prices up or down as your profit requires, you make money by it, just as stock gamblers do every day in New York, London, Paris, and other Christian commercial cities.

While this monstrous Dutch gambling fury lasted, money was plenty, everybody felt rich and Holland was in a whiz of windy delight. After about three years of fool's paradise, people began to reflect that the shuttlecock could not be knocked about in the air forever, and that when it came down somebody would be hurt. So first one and then another began quietly to sell out and quit the game, without buying in again. This cautious infection quickly spread like a pestilence, as it always does in such cases, and became a perfect panic or fright. All at once, as it were, rich people all over Holland found themselves with nothing in the world except a pocket full or a garden-bed full of flower roots that nobody would buy and that were not good to eat, and would not have made more than one tureen of soup if they were.

Of course this state of things caused innumerable bankruptcies, quarrels, and refusals to complete bargains, everywhere.

The government and the courts were appealed to, but with Dutch good sense they refused to enforce gambling transactions, and though the cure was very severe because very sudden, they preferred to let "the bottom drop out" of the whole affair at once. So it did. Almost everybody was either ruined or impoverished. The very few who had kept any or all of their gains by selling out in season, remained so far rich. And the vast actual business interests of Holland received a damaging check, from which it took many years to recover.

There were some curious incidents in the course of the tulipomania. They have been told before, but they are worth telling again, as the poet says, "To point the moral or adorn the tale."

A sailor brought to a rich Dutch merchant news of the safe arrival of a very valuable cargo from the Levant. The old hunks rewarded the mariner for his good tidings with one red herring for breakfast. Now Ben Bolt (if that was his name—perhaps as he was a Dutchman it was something like Benje Boltje) was very fond of onions, and spying one on the counter as he went out of the store, he slipped it into his pocket, and strolling back to the wharf, sat down to an odoriferous breakfast of onions and herring. He munched away without finding anything unusual in the flavor, until just as he was through, down came Mr. Merchant, tearing along like a madman at the head of an excited procession of clerks, and flying upon the luckless son of Neptune, demanded what he had carried off besides his herring?

"An onion that I found on the counter."

"Where is it? Give it back instantly!"

"Just ate it up with my herring, mynheer."

Wretched merchant! In a fury of useless grief he apprised

the sailor that his sacrilegious back teeth had demolished a *Semper Augustus* valuable enough, explained the unhappy old fellow, to have feasted the Prince of Orange and the Stadtholder's whole court. "Thieves!" he cried out—Seize the rascal!" So they did seize him, and he was actually tried, condemned and imprisoned for some months, all of which however did not bring back the tulip root. It is a question after all in my mind, whether that sailor was really as green as he pretended, and whether he did not know very well what he was taking. It would have been just like a reckless seaman's trick to eat up the old miser's twelve hundred dollar root, to teach him not to give such stingy gifts next time.

An English traveller, very fond of botany, was one day in the conservatory of a rich Dutchman, when he saw a strange bulb lying on a shelf. With that extreme coolness and selfishness which too many travellers have exercised, what does he do but take out his penknife and carefully dissect it, peeling off the outer coats, and quartering the innermost part, making all the time a great many wise observations on the phenomena of the strange new root. In came the Dutchman all at once, and seeing what was going on, he asked the Englishman, with rage in his eyes, but with a low bow and that sort of restrained formal civility which sometimes covers the most furious anger, if he knew what he was about?

"Peeling a very curious onion," answered Mr. Traveller, as calmly as if one had a perfect right to destroy other people's property to gratify his own curiosity.

"One hundred thousand devils!" burst out the Dutchman, expressing the extent of his anger by the number of evil spirits he invoked—It is an Admiral van der Eyck!"

"Indeed?" remarked the scientific traveller, "thank you. Are there a good many of these admirals in your country?" and he drew forth his note book to write down the little fact.

"Death and the devil!" swore the enraged Dutchman again—come before the Syndic and you shall find out all about it!" So he collared the astounded onion-peeler, and despite all he could say, dragged him straightway before the magistrate, where his scientific zeal suffered a dreadful quencher in the shape of an affidavit that the "onion" was worth four thousand florins—about $1,600—and in the immediate judgment of the Court, which "considered" that the prisoner be forthwith clapt into jail until he should give security for the amount. He had to do so accordingly, and doubtless all his life retained a distaste for Dutchmen and Dutch onions.

These stories about such monstrous valuations of flower roots recall to my mind another anecdote which I shall tell, not because it has anything to do with tulips, but because it is about a Dutchman, and shows in striking contrast an equally low valuation of human life. It is this. Once, in time of peace, an English and a Dutch Admiral met at sea, each in his flag ship, and for some reason or other exchanged complimentary salutes. By accident, one of the Englishman's guns was shotted and misdirected, and killed one of the Dutch crew. On hearing the fact the Englishman at once manned a boat and went to apologize, to inquire about the poor fellow's family and to send them some money, provide for the funeral, etc., etc., as a kind hearted man would naturally do. But the Dutch commander, on meeting him at the quarterdeck, and learning his errand, at once put all his kindly intentions completely one side, saying in imperfect English:

"It'sh no matter, it'sh no matter—*dere's blaanty more Tutch-men in Holland!*"

Chapter 26

John Bull's great money humbug—The south sea bubble in 1720.

The "South Sea Bubble" is one of the most startling lessons which history gives us of the ease with which the most monstrous, and absurd, and wicked humbugs can be crammed down the throat of poor human nature. It ought also to be a useful warning of the folly of mere "speculation," as compared with real "business undertakings." The history of the South Sea Bubble has been told, before, but it is too prominent a case to be entirely passed over. It occupied a period of about eight months, from February 1, 1720, to the end of the following September. It was an unreasonable expansion of the value of the stock of the "South Sea Company." This Company was formed in 1711; its stock was at first about $30,000,000, subscribed by the public and handed over by the corporators to Government to meet certain troublesome public debts. In return, Government guaranteed the stockholders a dividend of six percent, and gave the Company sundry permanent important duties and a monopoly of all trade to the South Pacific, or "South Sea." This matter went on with fair success as a money enterprise, until the birth of the "Bubble," which was as follows:—In the end of January,

1720, probably in consequence of catching infection from "Law's Mississippi Scheme" in France, the South Sea Company and the Bank of England made competing propositions to the English Government, to repeat the original South Sea Company financiering plan on a larger scale. The proposition of the Company, which was accepted by Government, was: to assume as before the whole public debt, now amounting to over one hundred and fifty millions of dollars; and to be guaranteed at first a five percent dividend, and afterward a four percent one, to thestockholders by Government. For this privilege, the Company agreed to pay outright a bonus of more than seventeen million dollars. This plan is said to have been originated and principally carried through by Sir John Blunt, one of the Company's directors. Parliament adopted it after two months' discussion—the Bubble having, however, been swelling monstrously all the time.

It must be remembered that the wonderful profits expected from the Company were to come from their monopoly of the South Sea trade. Tremendous stories were told by Blunt and his friends, who can hardly have believed more than one half of their own talk, about a free trade with all the Spanish Pacific colonies, the importation of silver and gold from Peru and Mexico in return for dry goods, etc., etc.; all which fine things were going to produce two or three times the amount of the Company's stock every year. When the bill authorizing the arrangement passed, South Sea stock had already reached a price of four hundred percent. The bill was stoutly opposed in Parliament by Mr.— afterwards Sir—Robert Walpole, and a few others but in vain. Under the operation of the beautiful stories of the speculative Blunt and his friends, South Sea stock, after a short lull in April, began to rise again, and the bubble swelled and swelled to a size so monstrous, and with colors so gay, that it filled the whole horizon of poor foolish John Bull:—perfectly turned his bull-headed brain, and made him for the time absolutely crazy. The directors opened books on April 12th for £5,000,000 new stock, charging, however, £300 for each share of £100, or three hundred percent to begin with. Double the amount was subscribed in a few days; that is, John Bull subscribed thirty million dollars for ten millions of stock, where only five millions were to be had. In a few days more, these subscribers were selling at double what they paid. April 21st, a ten percent dividend was voted for midsummer. In a day or two, another five million subscription was opened at four hundred percent to begin with. The whole, and half as much more, was taken in a few hours. In the end of May, South Sea stock was worth five hundred to one. On the 28th, it was five hundred and fifty. In four days more, for some reason or other, it jumped up to eight hundred and ninety. The speculating Blunt kept all this time blowing and blowing at his bubble. All summer, he and his friends blew and blew; and all summer the bubble swelled and floated, and shone; and high and low, men and women, lords and ladies, clergymen, princesses and duchesses, merchants, gamblers, tradesmen, dressmakers, footmen, bought and sold. In the beginning of August, South Sea stock stood at one thousand percent! It was really worth about twenty-five percent. The crowding in Exchange Alley, the Wall Street of the day, was tremendous. So noisy, and unmanageable and excited was this mob of greedy fools, that the very same stock was sometimes selling ten percent higher at one end of the Alley than at the other.

The growth of this monstrous, noxious bubble hatched out

a multitude of young cockatrices. Not only was the stock of the India Company, the Bank of England, and other sound concerns, much increased in price by sympathy with this fury of speculation, but a great number of utterly ridiculous schemes and barefaced swindles were advertised and successfully imposed on the public. Any piece of paper purporting to be stock could be sold for money. Not the least thought of investigating the solvency of advertisers seems to have occurred to anybody. Nor was any rank free from the poison. Almost a hundred projects were before the public at once, some of them incredibly brazen humbugs. There were schemes for a wheel for perpetual motion—capital, $5,000,000; for trading in hair (for wigs), in those days "a big thing;" for furnishing funerals to any part of Britain; for "improving the art of making soap;" for importing walnut-trees from Virginia—capital, $10,000,000; for insuring against losses by servants—capital, $15,000,000; for making quicksilver malleable; "Puckle's Machine Company," for discharging cannonballs and bullets, both round and square, and so on. One colossal genius in humbugging actually advertised in these words: "A company for carrying on an undertaking of great advantage, but nobody to know what it is." The capital he called for was $2,500,000, in shares of $500 each; deposit on subscribing, $10 per share. Each subscriber was promised $500 per share per annum, and full particulars were to be given in a month, when the rest of the subscription was to be paid. This great financier, having put forth his prospectus, opened his office in Cornhill next morning at nine o'clock. Crowds pressed upon him. At three p.m., John Bull had paid this immense humbug $10,000, being deposits on a thousand shares subscribed for. That night, the financier—a shrewd man!—modestly retired to an unknown place upon the Continent, and was never heard of again. Another humbug almost as preposterous, was that of the "Globe Permits." These were square pieces of playing-cards with a seal on them, having the picture of the Globe Tavern, and with the words, "Sailcloth Permits." What they "permitted" was a subscription at some future period to a sailcloth-factory, projected by a certain capitalist. These "permits" sold at one time for $300 each.

But the more sensible members of Government soon exerted their influence against these lesser and more palpable humbugs. Some accounts say that the South Sea Company itself grew jealous, for it was reckoned that these "sideshows" called for a total amount of $1,500,000,000, and itself took legal means against them. At any rate, an "order in council" was published, peremptorily dismissing and dissolving them all.

During August, it leaked out that Sir John Blunt and some other "insiders" had sold out their South Sea stock. There was also some charges of unfairness in managing subscriptions. After so long and so intense an excitement, the time for reaction and collapse was come. The price of stock began to fall in spite of all that the directors could do. September 2, it was down to 700.

A general meeting of the company was held to try to whitewash matters, but in vain. The stock fell, fell, fell. The great humbug had received its deathblow. Thousands of families saw beggary staring them in the face, grasping them with its iron hand. The consternation was inexpressible. Out of it a great popular rage began to flame up, just as fires often break out among the prostrate houses of a city ruined by an earthquake. Efforts were meanwhile vainly made to stay the ruin by help from the Bank of England. Bankers and goldsmiths (then often doing a banking business) absconded daily. Business corporations failed. Credit was almost paralyzed. In the end of September, the stock fell to 175, 150, 135.

Meanwhile violent riots were feared. South Sea directors could not be seen in the streets without being insulted. The King, then in Hanover, was imperatively sent for home, and had to come. So extensive was the misfortune and the wrath of the people, so numerous the public meetings and petitions from all over the kingdom, that Parliament found it necessary to grant the public demand, and to initiate a formal inquiry into the whole enterprise. This was done; and the foolish, swindled, disappointed, angry nation, through this proceeding, vented all the wrath it could upon the persons and estates of the managers and officers of the South Sea Company. They were forbidden to leave the kingdom, their property was sequestrated, they were placed in custody and examined. Those of them in Parliament were insulted there to their faces, several of them expelled, the most violent charges made against them all. A secret investigating committee was set to rip up the whole affair. Knight, the treasurer, who possessed all the dangerous secrets of the concern, ran away to Calais and the Continent, and so escaped.

The books were found to have been either destroyed, secreted, or mutilated and garbled. Stock bribes of $250,000, $150,000, $50,000 had been paid to the Earl of Sunderland, the Duchess of Kendal (the King's favorite,) Mr. Craggs (one of the Secretaries of State,) and others. Mr. Aislabie, the Chancellor of the Exchequer, had accumulated $4,250,000 and more out of the business. Many other noblemen, gentlemen, and reputable merchants were disgracefully involved.

The trials that were had resulted in the imprisonment, expulsion or degradation of Aislabie, Craggs, Sir George Caswell (a banker and member of the House,) and others. Blunt, a Mr. Stanhope, and a number more of the chief criminals were stripped of their wealth, amounting to from $135,000 to $1,200,000 each, and the proceeds used for the partial relief of the ruined, except amounts left to the culprits to begin the world anew. Blunt, the chief of all the swindlers, was stripped of about $925,000, and allowed only $5,000. By this means and by the use of such actual property as the Company did possess, about one-third of the money lost by its means was ultimately paid to the losers. It was a long time, however, before the tone of public credit was thoroughly restored.

The history of the South Sea bubble should always stand as a beacon to warn us that reckless speculation is the bane of commerce, and that the only sure method of gaining a fortune, and certainly of enjoying it, is to diligently prosecute some legitimate calling, which, like the quality of mercy, is "twice blessed." Every man's occupation should be beneficial to his fellow-man as well as profitable to himself. All else is vanity and folly.

Chapter 27

*Business humbugs—John Law—The Mississippi
scheme—Johnny Crapaud as greedy as Johnny Bull.*

In the "good old times," people were just as eager after money as they are now; and a great deal more vulgar, unscrupulous, and foolish in their endeavors to get it. During about two hundred years after the discovery of America, that continent was a constant source of great and little money humbugs. The Spaniards and Portuguese and French and English all insisted upon thinking that America was chiefly made of gold; perhaps believing, as the man said about Colorado, that the hardship of the place was, that you have to dig through three or four feet of solid silver before the gold could be reached. This curious delusion is shown by the fact that the early charters of lands in America so uniformly reserved to the King his proportion of all gold and silver that should be found. And if gold were not to be had, these lazy Europeans were equally crazy about the rich merchandise which they made sure of finding in the vast and solitary American mountains and forests.

In a previous letter, I have shown how one of those delusions, about the unbounded wealth to be obtained from the countries on the South Sea, caused the English South Sea bubble.

A similar belief, at the same time, in the neighboring country of France, formed the airy basis of a similar business humbug, even more gigantic, noxious, and destructive. This was John Law's Mississippi scheme, of which I shall give an account in this chapter. It was, I think, the greatest business humbug of history.

Law was a Scotchman, shrewd and able, a really good financier for those days, but vicious, a gambler, unprincipled, and liable to wild schemes. He had possessed a good deal of property, had traveled and gambled all over Europe, was witty, entertaining, and capital company, and had become a favorite with the Duke of Orleans and other French nobles. When the Duke became Regent of France at the death of Louis XIV, in 1715, that country was horribly in debt, and its people in much misery, owing to the costly wars and flaying taxations of the late King. When, therefore, Law came to Paris with a promising scheme of finance in his hand, the Regent was particularly glad to see him, both as financier and as friend.

The Regent quickly fell in with Law's plans; and in the spring of 1716, the first step—not, however, so intended at the time—toward the Mississippi Scheme was taken. This was, the establishment by royal authority of the banking firm of Law & Co., consisting of Law and his brother. This bank, by a judicious organization and issue of paper money, quickly began to help the distressed finances of the kingdom, and to invigorate trade and commerce. This success, which seems to have been an entirely sound and legitimate business success, made one sadly mistaken but very deep impression upon the ignorant and shallow mind of the Regent of France, which was the foundation of all the subsequent trouble. The Regent became firmly convinced, that if a certain quantity of bank bills could do so much good, a hundred thousand times as many bills would surely do a hundred thousand times as much. That is, he thought printing and issuing the bills was creating money. He paid no regard to the need of providing specie for them on demand, but thought he had an unlimited money factory in the city of Paris.

So far, so good. Next, Law planned, and, with the ever ready consent of the Regent, effected, an enlargement of the business of his bank, based on that delusion I spoke of about America. This enlargement was the formation of the Mississippi Company, and this was the contrivance which swelled into so tremendous a humbug. The company was closely connected with the banks, and received (to begin with) the monopoly of all trade to the Mississippi River, and all the country west of it. It was expected to obtain vast quantities of gold and silver from that region, and thus to make immense dividends on its stock. At home, it was to have the sole charge of collecting all the taxes and coining all the money. Stock was issued to the amount of one hundred thousand shares, at $200 (five hundred livres) each. And Law's help to the Government funds was continued by permitting this stock to be paid for in those funds, at their par value, though worth in market only about a third of it. Subscriptions came in rapidly—for the French community was far more ignorant about commercial affairs, finances, and the real resources of distant regions, than we can easily conceive of nowadays; and not only the Regent, but every man, woman, and child in France, except a very few tough and hardheaded old skeptics, believed every word Law said, and would have believed him if he had told stories a hundred times as incredible.

Well, pretty soon the Regent gave the associates—the bank and the company—two other monopolies: that of tobacco, always monstrously profitable, and that of refining gold and silver. Pretty soon, again, he created the bank a state institution, by the magnificent name of The Royal Bank of France. Having done this, the Regent could control the bank in spite of Law (or order either); for, in those days, the kings of France were almost perfectly despotic, and the Regent was acting king. I have mentioned the Regent's terrible delusion about paper-money. No sooner had he the bank in his power, than he added to the reasonable and useful total of $12,000,000 of notes already out, a monstrous issue of $200,000,000 worth in one vast batch, with the firm conviction that he was thus adding so much to the par currency of France.

The Parliament of France, a body mostly of lawyers, originating in the Middle Ages, a steady, conservative, wise, and brave assembly, was always hostile to Law and his schemes. When this great expansion of paper-currency began, the Parliament made a resolute fight against it, petitioning, ordaining, threatening to hang Law, and frightening him well, too; for the thorough enmity of an assembly of old lawyers may well frighten anybody. At last, the Regent, by the use of the despotic power of which the Kings of France had so much, reduced these old fellows to silence by sticking a few of them in jail.

The cross-grained Parliament thus disposed of, everything was quickly made to "look lovely." In the beginning of 1719, more grants were made to Law's associated concerns. The

Mississippi Company was granted the monopoly of all trade to the East Indies, China, the South Seas, and all the territories of the French India Company, and of the Senegal Company. It took a new and imposing name: "The Company of the Indies." They had already, by the way, also obtained the monopoly of the Canada beaver-trade. Of this colossal corporation, monopolizing the whole foreign commerce of France with two-thirds or more of the world, its whole home finances, and other important interests besides, fifty thousand new shares were issued, as before, at $100 each. These might be bought as before, with Government securities at par. Law was so bold as to promise annual dividends of $20 per share, which, as the Government funds stood, was one hundred and twenty percent per annum! Everybody believed him. More than three hundred thousand applications were made for the new shares. Law was besieged in his house by more than twice as many people as General Grant had to help him take Richmond. The Great Humbug was at last in full buzz. The street where the wonderful Scotchman lived was busy, filled, crowded, jammed, choked. Dangerous accidents happened in it every day, from the excessive pressure. From the princes of the blood down to cobblers and lackeys, all men and all women crowded and crowded to subscribe their money, and to pay their money, and to know how many shares they had gotten. Law moved to a roomier street, and the crazy mob crowded harder than ever; so that the Chancellor, who held his court of law hard by, could not hear his lawyers.

A tremendous uproar surely, that could drown the voices of those gentlemen! And so he moved again, to the great Hotel de Soissons, a vast palace, with a garden of some acres.

Fantastic circumstances variegated the wild rush of speculation. The haughtiest of the nobility rented mean rooms near Law's abode, to be able to get at him. Rents in his neighborhood rose to twelve and sixteen times their usual amount. A cobbler, whose lines had fallen in those pleasant places, made $40 a day by letting his stall and furnishing writing materials to speculators. Thieves and disreputable characters of all sorts flocked to this concourse. There were riots and quarrels all the time. They often had to send a troop of cavalry to clear the street at night. Gamblers posted themselves with their implements among the speculators, who gambled harder than the gamblers, and took an occasional turn at roulette by way of slackening the excitement; as people go to sleep, or go into the country. A hunchback fellow made a good deal of money by letting people write on his back. When Law had moved into the Hotel de Soissons, the former owner, the Prince de Carignan, reserved the gardens, procured an edict confining all stock-dealings to that place; put up five hundred tents there, leased them at five hundred livres a month each, and thus made money at the rate of $50,000 a month. There were just two of the aristocracy who were sensible and resolute enough not to speculate in the stock—the Duke de St. Simon and the old Marshal Villars.

Law became infinitely the most important person in the kingdom. Great and small, male and female, high and low, haunted his offices and antechambers, hunted him down, plagued his very life out, to get a moment's speech with him, and get him to enter their names as buyers of stock. The highest nobles would wait half a day for the chance. His servants received great sums to announce some visitor's name. Ladies of the highest rank gave him anything he would ask of them for leave to buy stock. One of them made her coachmen upset her out of her carriage as Law came by, to get a word with him. He helped her up; she got the word, and bought some stock. Another lady ran into the house where he was at dinner, and raised a cry of fire. The rest ran out, but she ran further in to reach Law, who saw what she was at, and like a pecuniary Joseph, ran away as fast as he could.

As the frenzy rose toward its height, and the Regent took advantage of it to issue stock enough to pay the whole national debt, namely, three hundred thousand new shares, at $1,000 each, or a thousand percent in the par value. They were instantly taken. Three times as many would have been instantly taken. So violent were the changes of the market, that shares rose or fell twenty percent within a few hours. A servant was sent to sell two hundred and fifty shares of stock; found on reaching the gardens of the Hotel de Soissons, that since he left his master's house the price had risen from $1,600 (par value $100 remember) to $2,000. The servant sold, gave his master the proceeds at $1,600 a share, put the remaining $100,000 in his own pocket, and left France that evening. Law's coachman became so rich that he left service, and set up his own coach; and when his master asked him to find a successor, he brought two candidates, and told Law to choose, and he would take the other himself. There were many absurd cases of vulgarians made rich. There were also many robberies and murders. That committed by the Count de Horn, one of the higher nobility and two accomplices, is a famous case. The Count, a dissipated rascal, poniarded a broker in a tavern for the money the broker carried with him. But he was taken, and, in spite of the utmost and most determined exertions of the nobility, the Regent had him broken on the wheel in public, like any other murderer.

The stock of the Company of the Indies, though it dashed up and down ten and twenty percent from day to day, was from the first immensely inflated. In August 1719, it sold at 610 percent; in a few weeks more it arose to 1,200 percent. All winter it still went up until, in April 1720, it stood at 2,050 percent. That is, one one-hundred dollar share would sell for two thousand and fifty dollars.

At this extreme point of inflation, the bubble stood a little, shining splendidly as bubbles do when they are nearest bursting, and then it received two or three quiet pricks. The Prince de Conti, enraged because Law would not send him some shares on his own terms, sent three wagon-loads of bills to Law's bank, demanding specie. Law paid it, and complained to the Regent, who made him put two-thirds of it back again. A shrewd stock-gambler drew specie by small sums until he had about $200,000 in coin, and lest he should be forced to return it, he packed it in a cart, covered it with manure, put on a peasant's disguise, and carted his fortune over the frontiers into Belgium. Some others quietly realized their means in like manner by driblets and funded them abroad.

By such means coin gradually grew very scarce, and signs of a panic appeared. The Regent tried to adjust matters by a decree that coin should be five percent less than paper; as much as to say, It is hereby enacted that there is a great deal more coin than there is! This did not serve, and the Regent decreed again, that coin should be worth ten percent less than paper. Then he decreed that the bank must not pay more than $22 at once in specie; and, finally, by a bold stretch of his authority, he issued an edict that no person should have over $100 in coin, on pain of fine and confiscation. These odious laws made a great deal of trouble, spying, and distress, and rapidly aggravated the difficulty they were meant to cure. The price of shares in the great company began to fall steadily and rapidly. Law and the Regent began to be universally hated, cursed, and threatened. Various foolish and vain attempts were made to stay the coming ruin, by renewing the stories about Louisiana sending out a lot of conscripted laborers, ordering that all payments must be made in paper, and printing a new batch of notes, to the amount of another $300,000,000. Law's two corporations were also doctored in several ways. The distress and fright grew worse. An edict was issued that Law's notes and shares should depreciate gradually by law for a year, and then be worth but half their face. This made such a tumult and outcry that the Regent had to retract it in seven days. On this seventh day, Law's bank stopped paying specie. Law was turned out of his public employments, but still well treated by the Regent in private. He was, however, mobbed and stoned in his coach in the street, had to have a company of Swiss Guards in his house, and at last had to flee to the Regent's own palace.

I have not space to describe in detail the ruin, misery, tumults, loss and confusion which attended the speedy descent of Law's paper and shares to entire worthlessness. Thousands of families were made paupers, and trade and commerce destroyed by the painful process. Law himself escaped out of France poor; and, after another obscure and disreputable career of gambling, died in poverty at Venice, in 1729.

Thus this enormous business-humbug first raised a whole nation into a fool's paradise of imaginary wealth, and then exploded, leaving its projector and many thousands of victims ruined, the country disturbed and distressed, long-enduring consequences, in vicious and lawless and unsteady habits, contracted while the delusion lasted, and no single benefit except one more most dearly-bought lesson of the wicked folly of mere speculation without a real business basis and a real business method. Let not this lesson be lost on the rampant and half-crazed speculators of the present day. Those who buy gold or flour, leather, butter, dry goods, groceries, hardware, or anything else on speculation, when prices are inflated far beyond the ordinary standard, are taking upon themselves great risks, for the bubble must eventually be pricked; and whoever is the "holder" when that time comes, must necessarily be the loser.

Part V

MEDICINE AND QUACKS

Chapter 28

Doctors And imagination—Firing a joke out of a cannon—The Paris eye water—Majendie on medical knowledge—Old sands of life.

Medical humbugs constitute a very critical subject indeed, because I shall be almost certain to offend some of three parties concerned, namely; physicians, quacks, and patients. But it will never do to neglect so important a division of my whole theme as this.

To begin with, it is necessary to suggest, in the most delicate manner in the world, that there is a small infusion of humbug among the very best of the regular practitioners. These gentlemen, for whose learning, kindheartedness, self-devotion, and skill I entertain a profound respect, make use of what I may call the gaseous element of their practice, not for the lucre of gain, but in order to enlist the imaginations of their patients in aid of nature and great remedies.

The stories are infinite in number, which illustrate the force of imagination, ranging through all the grades of mental action, from the lofty visions of good men who dream of seeing heaven opened to them, and all its ineffable glories and delights, down to the low comedy conceit of the fellow who put a smoked herring into the tail of his coat and imagined himself a mermaid.

Probably, however, imagination displays its real power more wonderfully in the operations of the mind on the body that holds it, than anywhere else. It is true that there are some people even so utterly without imagination that they cannot take a joke; such as that grave man of Scotland who was at last plainly told by a funny friend quite out of patience, "Why, you wouldn't take a joke if it were fired at you out of a cannon!"

"Sir," replied the Scot, with sound reasoning and grave thought, "Sir, you are absurd. You cannot fire a joke out of a cannon!"

But to return: It is certainly the case that frequently "the doctor" takes great care not to let the patient know what is the matter, and even not to let him know what he is swallowing. This is because a good many people, if at a critical point of disease, may be made to turn toward health if made to believe that they are doing so, but would be frightened, in the literal sense of the words, to death, if told what a dangerous state they are in.

One sort of regular practice humbug is rendered necessary by the demands of the patients. This is giving good big doses of something with a horrid smell and taste. There are plenty of people who don't believe the doctor does anything to earn his money, if he does not pour down some dirty brown or black stuff very nasty in flavor. Some, still more exacting, wish for that sort of testimony which depends on internal convulsions, and will not be satisfied unless they suffer torments and expel stuff enough to quiet the inside of Mount Vesuvius or Popocatepetl.

"He's a good doctor," was the verdict of one of this class of leather-boweled fellows—he'll work your innards for you!"

It is a milder form of this same method to give what the learned faculty term a placebo. This is a thing in the outward form of medicine, but quite harmless in itself. Such is a bread-pill, for instance; or a draught of colored water, with a little disagreeable taste in it. These will often keep the patient's imagination headed in the right direction, while good old Dame Nature is quietly mending up the damages in "the soul's dark cottage."

One might almost fancy that, in proportion as the physician is more skillful, by so much he gives less medicine, and relies more on imagination, nature, and, above all, regimen and nursing. Here is a story in point. There was an old gentleman in Paris, who sold a famous eye-water, and made much gain thereby. He died, however, one fine day, and unfortunately forgot to leave the recipe on record. "His disconsolate widow continued the business at the old stand," however—to quote another characteristic French anecdote—and being a woman of ready and decisive mind, she very quietly filled the vials with water from the river Seine, and lived respectably on the proceeds, finding, to her great relief, that the eye-water was just as good as ever. At last however, she found herself about to die, and under the stings of an accusing conscience she confessed her trick to her physician, an eminent member of the profession. "Be entirely easy, Madam," said the wise man; "don't be troubled at all. You are the most innocent physician in the world; you have done nobody any harm."

It is an old and illiberal joke to compare medicine to war, on the ground that the votaries of both seek to destroy life. It is, however, not far from the truth to say that they are alike in this; that they are both preeminently liable to mistakes, and that in both he is most successful who makes the fewest.

How can it be otherwise, until we know more than we do at present, of the great mysteries of life and death? It seems risky enough to permit the wisest and most experienced physician to touch those springs of life which God only understands. And it is enough to make the most stupid stare, to see how people will let the most disgusting quack jangle their very heartstrings with his poisonous messes, about as soon as if he were the best doctor in the world. A true physician, indeed, does not hasten to drug. The great French surgeon, Majendie, is even said to have commenced his official course of lectures on one occasion by coolly saying to his students: "Gentlemen, the curing of disease is a subject that physicians know nothing about." This was doubtless an extreme way of putting the case. Yet it was in a certain sense exactly true. There is one of the geysers in Iceland, into which visitors throw pebbles or turfs, with the invariable result of causing the disgusted geyser in a few minutes to vomit the dose out again, along with a great quantity of hot water, steam, and stuff. Now the doctor does know that some of his doses are pretty sure to work, as the traveler knows that his dose will work on the geyser. It is only the exact how and why that is not understood.

But however mysterious is nature, however ignorant the doctor, however imperfect the present state of physical science, the patronage and the success of quacks and quackeries are infinitely more wonderful than those of honest and laborious men of science and their careful experiments.

I have come about to the end of my tether for this time;

and quackery is something too monstrous in dimensions as well as character to be dealt with in a paragraph. But I may with propriety put one quack at the tail of this letter; it is but just that he should let decent people go before him. I mean "Old Sands of Life." Everybody has seen his advertisement, beginning "A retired Physician whose sands of life have nearly run out," etc. And everybody—almost— knows how kind the fellow is in sending gratis his recipe. All that is necessary is (as you find out when you get the recipe) to buy at a high price from him one ingredient which (he says) you can get nowhere else. This swindling scamp is in fact a smart brisk fellow of about thirty-five years of age, notwithstanding the length of time during which—to use a funny phrase which somebody got up for him—he has been "afflicted with a loose tailboard to his mortal sand-cart." Some benevolent friend was so much distressed about the feebleness of "Old Sands of Life" as to send him one day a large parcel by express, marked "C.O.D.," and costing quite a figure. "Old Sands" paid, and opening the parcel, found half a bushel of excellent sand.

Chapter 29

The consumptive remedy—E. Andrews, M.D.—Born without birthrights—Hasheesh candy—Roback the Great—A conjurer opposed to lying.

There is a fellow in Williamsburg who calls himself a clergyman, and sells a "consumptive remedy," by which I suppose he means a remedy for consumption. It is a mere slop corked in a vial; but there are a good many people who are silly enough to buy it of him. A certain gentleman, during last November, earnestly sought an interview with this reverend brother in the interests of humanity, but he was as inaccessible as a chipmunk in a stone fence. The gentleman wrote a polite note to the knave asking about prices, and received a printed circular in return, stating in an affecting manner the good man's grief at having to raise his price in consequence of the cost of gold "with which I am obliged to buy my medicines" saith he, "in Paris." This was both sad and unsatisfactory; and the gentleman went over to Williamsburg to seek an interview and find out all about the prices. He reached the abode of the man of piety, but, strange to relate, he wasn't at home.

Gentleman waited.

Reverend brother kept on not being at home. When gentleman had waited to his entire satisfaction he came back.

It is understood it is practically out of the question to see the reverend brother. Perhaps he is so modest and shy that he will not encounter the clamorous gratitude which would obstruct his progress through the streets, from the millions saved by his consumptive remedy. It is a pity that the reverend man cannot enjoy the still more complete seclusion by which the state of New York testifies its appreciation of unobtrusive and retiring virtues like his, in the salubrious and quiet town of Sing Sing.

A quack in an inland city, who calls himself E. Andrews, M.D., prints a "semi-occasional" document in the form of a periodical, of which a copy is lying before me. It is an awful hodgepodge of perfect nonsense and vulgar rascality. He calls it "The Good Samaritan and Domestic Physician," and this number is called "volume twenty." Only think what a great man we have among us—unless the Doctor himself is mistaken. He says: "I will here state that I have been favored by nature and Providence in gaining access to stores of information that has *fell* to the lot of but very few persons heretofore, during the past history of mankind." Evidently these "stores" were so vast that the great doctor's brain was stuffed too full to have room left for English Grammar. Shortly, the Doctor thus bursts forth again with some views having their own merits, but not such as concern the healing art very directly: "The automaton powers of machinery"—there's a new style of machinery, you observe—must be made to **work for**, *instead* of *as now*, against mankind; the Land of *all nations* must be made **free** to Actual Settlers in **limited** quantities. No one must be born without *his birthright* being born with him." The italics, etc., are the Doctor's. What an awful thought is this of being born without any birthright, or, as the Doctor leaves us to suppose possible, having one's birthright born first, and dodging about the world like a stray canary-bird, while the unhappy and belated owner tries in vain to put salt on its tail and catch it!

Well, this wiseacre, after his portentous introduction, fills the rest of his sixteen loosely printed double-columned octavo pages with a farrago of the most indescribable character, made up of brags, lies, promises, forged recommendations and letters, boasts of systematic charity, funny scraps of stuff in the form of little disquisitions, advertisements of remedies, hair-oils, cosmetics, liquors, groceries, thistle-killers, anti-bug mixtures, recipes for soap, ink, honey, and the Old Harry only knows what. The fellow gives a list of seventy-one specific diseases for which his Hasheesh Candy is a sure cure, and he adds that it is also a sure cure for all diseases of the liver, brain, throat, stomach, ear, and other internal disorders; also for "all long standing diseases"—whatever that means!— and for insanity! In this monstrous list are jumbled together the most incongruous troubles. "Bleeding at the nose, and abortions;" "worms, fits, poisons and cramps." And the impudent liar quotes General Grant, General Mitchell, the Rebel General Lee, General McClellan, and Doctor Mott of this city, all shouting in chorus the praises of the Hasheesh Candy! Next comes the "Secret of Beauty," a "preparation of Turkish Roses;" then alot of forged references, and an assertion that the Doctor gives to the poor five thousand pounds of bread every winter; then some fearful denunciations of the regular doctors.

But—as the auctioneers say—I can't dwell." I will only add

that the real villainy of this fellow only appears here and there, where he advertises the means of ruining innocence, or of indulging with impunity in the foulest vices. He will sell for $3.30, the "Mystic Weird Ring." In a chapter of infamous blatherumskite about this ring he says: "The wearer can drive from, or draw to him, anyone, and for any purpose whatever." I need not explain what this scoundrel means. He also will sell the professed means of robbery and swindling; saying that he is prepared to show how to remove papers, wills, titles, notes, etc., from one place to another "by invisible means." It is a wonder that the Bank of Commerce can keep any securities in its vaults—of course!

But enough of this degraded panderer to crime and folly. He is beneath notice, so far as he himself concerned; I devote the space to him, because it is well worth while to understand how base an imposture can draw a steady revenue from a nation boasting so much culture and intelligence as ours. It is also worth considering whether the authorities must not be remiss, who permit such odious deceptions to be constantly perpetrated upon the public.

I ought here to give a paragraph to the great C. W. Roback, one of whose Astrological Almanacs is before me. This erudite production is embellished in front with a picture of the doctor and his six brothers—for he is the seventh son of a seventh son. The six elder brethren—nice enough boys—stand submissively around their gigantic and bearded junior, reaching only to his waist, and gazing up at him with reverence, as the sheaves of Joseph's brethren worshipped his sheaf in his dream. At the end is a picture of Magnus Roback, the grandfather of C. W., a bullheaded, ugly old Dutchman, with a globe and compasses. This picture, by the way, is in fact a cheap likeness of the old discoverers or geographers. Within the book we find Gustavus Roback, the father of C. W., for whom is used a cut of Jupiter—or some other heathen god—half-naked, astraddle of an eagle, with a hook in one hand and a quadrant in the other; which is very much like the picture by one of the "Old Masters" of Abraham about to offer up Isaac, and taking a long aim at the poor boy with a flintlock horse-pistol. Doctor Roback is good enough to tell us where his brothers are: "One, a high officer in the Empire of China, another a Catholic Bishop in the city of Rome," and so on. There is also a cut of his sister, whom he cured of consumption. She is represented "talking to her bird, after the fashion of her country, when a maiden is unexpectedly rescued from the jaws of death!"

Roback cures all sorts of diseases, discovers stolen property, insures children a marriage, and so on, all by means of "conjurations." He also casts nativities and foretells future events; and he shows in full how Bernadotte, Louis Philippe, and Napoleon Bonaparte either did well or would have done well by following his advice. The chief peculiarity of this impostor is, that he really avoids direct pandering to vice and crime, and even makes it a specialty to cure drunkenness and—of all things in the world—lying! On this point Roback gives in full the certificate of Mrs. Abigail Morgan, whose daughter Amanda "was sorely given to fibbing, in so much that she would rather lie than speak the truth." And the delighted mother certifies that our friend and wizard "so changed the nature of the girl that, to the best of our knowledge and belief, she has never spoken anything but the truth since."

There is a conjurer "as is a conjurer."

What an uproar the incantation of the great Roback would

make, if set fairly to work among the politicians, for instance! But after all, on second thoughts, what a horrible mass of abominations would they lay bare in telling the truth about each other all round! No, no—it won't do to have the truth coming out, in politics at any rate! Away with Roback! I will not give him another word—not a single chance—not even to explain his great power over what he calls "Fits! Fits! Fits! Fits! Fits!"

Chapter 30

Monsignore Cristoforo Rischio; or, Il Creso, the nostrum-vender of Florence—A model for our quack doctors.

Every visitor to Florence during the last twenty years must have noticed on the grand piazza before the Ducal Palace, the strange genius known as Monsignore Créso, or, in plain English, Mr. Croesus. He is so called because of his reputed great wealth; but his real name is Christoforo Rischio, which I may again translate, as Christopher Risk. Mrs. Browning refers to him in one of her poems—the "Casa Guidi Windows," I think—and he has also been the staple of a tale by one of the Trollope brothers.

Twice every week, he comes into the city in a strange vehicle, drawn by two fine Lombardy ponies, and unharnesses them in the very center of the square. His assistant, a capital vocalist, begins to sing immediately, and a crowd soon collects around the wagon. Then Monsignore takes from the box beneath his seat a splendidly jointed human skeleton, which he suspends from a tall rod and hook, and also a number of human skulls. The latter are carefully arranged on an adjustable shelf, and Créso takes his place behind them, while in his rear a perfect chemist's shop of flasks, bottles, and pillboxes is disclosed. Very soon his singer ceases, and in the purest Tuscan dialect—the very utterance of which is music—the Florentine quack-doctor proceeds to address the assemblage. Not being conversant with the Italian, I am only able to give the substance of his harangue, and pronounce indifferently upon the merit of his elocution. I am assured, however, that not only the common people, who are his chief patrons, but numbers of the most intelligent citizens, are always entertained by what he has to say; and certainly his gestures and style of expressions seem to betray great excellence of oratory. Having turned the skeleton round and round on its pivot, and minutely explained the various anatomical parts, in order to show his proficiency in the basis of medical science, he next lifts the skulls, one by one, and descants upon their relative perfection, throwing in a shrewd anecdote now and then, as to the life of the original owner of each cranium.

One skull, for example, he asserts to have belonged to a lunatic, who wandered for half a lifetime in the Val d'Ema, subsisting precariously upon entirely vegetable food—roots, herbs, and the like; another is the superior part of a convict, hung in Arezzo for numerous offenses; a third is that of a very old man who lived a celibate from his youth up, and by his abstinence and goodness exercised an almost priestly influence upon the *borghesa*. When, by this miscellaneous lecture, he has both amused and edified his hearers, he ingeniously turns the discourse upon his own life, and finally introduces the subject of the marvellous cures he has effected. The story of his medical preparations alone, their components and method of distillation, is a fine piece of popularized art, and he gives a practical exemplification of his skill and their virtues by calling from the crowd successively, a number of invalid people, whom he examines and prescribes for on the spot. Whether these subjects are provided by himself or not, I am unable to decide; but it is very possible that by long experience, Christoforo—who has no regular diploma—has mastered the simpler elements of Materia Medica, and does in reality effect cures. I class him among what are popularly known as humbugs, however, for he is a pretender to more wisdom than he possesses. It was to me a strange and suggestive scene—the bald, beak-nosed, coal-eyed charlatan, standing in the marketplace, so celebrated in history, peering through his gold spectacles at the upturned faces below him, while the bony skeleton at his side swayed in the wind, and the grinning skulls below, made grotesque faces, as if laughing at the gullibility of the people. Behind him loomed up the massive Palazzo Vecchio, with its high tower, sharply cut, and set with deep machicolations; to the left, the splendid Loggia of Orgagna, filled with rare marbles, and the long picture-gallery of the Uffizi, heaped with the rarest art-treasures of the world; to his right, the Giant Fountain of Ammanato, throwing jets of pure water—one drop of which outvalues all the nostrums in the world; and in front, the Post Office, built centuries before, by Pisan captives. If any of these things moved the imperturbable Créso, he showed no feeling of the sort; but for three long hours, two days in the week, held his hideous clinic in the open daylight.

Seeing the man so often, and interested always in his manner—as much so, indeed, as the peasants or contadini, who bought his vials and pillboxes without stint—I became interested to know the main features of his life; and, by the aid of a friend, got some clues which I think reliable enough to publish. I do so the more willingly, because his career is illustrative, after an odd fashion, of contemporary Italian life.

He was the son of a small farmer, not far from Sienna, and grew up in daily contact with vinedressers and olive-gatherers, living upon the hard Tuscan fare of macaroni and maroon-nuts, with a cutlet of lean mutton once a day, and a pint of sour Tuscan wine. Being tolerably well educated for a peasant-boy, he imbibed a desire for the profession of an actor, and studied Alfieri closely.

Some little notoriety that he gained by recitations led him, in an evil hour, to venture an appearance *en grand role*, in Florence, at a third-rate theatre. His father had meanwhile deceased and left him the property; but to make the debut referred to, he sold almost his entire inheritance. As may be supposed, his failure was signal. However easy he had found it to amuse the rough, untutored peasantry of his neighborhood, the test of a large and polished city was beyond his merit.

So, poor and abashed, he sank to the lower walks of dramatic art, singing in choruses at the opera, playing minor parts in showpieces, and all the while feeling the sting of disappointed ambition and half-deserved penury.

One day found him, at the beginning of winter, without work, and without a soldo in his pocket. Passing a druggist's shop, he saw a placard asking for men to sell a certain new preparation. The druggist advanced him a small sum for travelling expenses, and he took to peripatetic lectures at once, going into the country and haranguing at all the villages.

Here he found his dramatic education available. Though not good enough for an actor, he was sufficiently clever for a nomadic eulogizer of a patent-medicine. His vocal abilities were also of service to him in gathering the people together. The great secret of success in anything is to get a hearing. Half the object is gained when the audience is assembled.

Well! poor, vagabond, peddling Christopher Risk, selling so much for another party, conceived the idea of becoming his own capitalist. He resolved to prepare a medicine of his own; and, profiting by the assistance of a young medical student, obtained bona fide prescriptions for the commonest maladies. These he had made up in gross, originated labels for them, and concealing the real essences thereof by certain harmless adulterations, began to advertise himself as the discoverer of a panacea.

To gain no ill-will among the priests, whose influence is paramount with the peasantry, he dexterously threw in a reverent word for them in his nomadic harangues, and now and then made a sounding present to the Church.

He profited also by the superstitions abroad, and to the skill of Hippocrates added the roguery of Simon Magus. By report, he was both a magician and physician, and a knack that he had of slight-of-hand was not the least influential of his virtues.

His bodily prowess was as great as his suppleness. One day, at Fiesole, a foreign doctor presumed to challenge Monsignore to a debate, and the offer was accepted. While the two stood together in Cristoforo's wagon, and the intruder was haranguing the people, the quack, without a movement of his face or a twitch of his body, jerked his foot against his rival's leg and threw him to the ground. He had the effrontery to proclaim the feat as magnetic entirely, accomplished without bodily means, and by virtue of his black-art acquirements.

An awe fell upon the listeners, and they refused to hear the checkmated disputant further.

As soon as Cristoforo began to thrive, he indulged his dramatic taste by purchasing a superb wagon, team, and equipments, and hired a servant. Such a turnout had never been seen in Tuscany since the Medician days. It gained for him the name of Créso straightway, and, enabling him to travel more rapidly, enlarged his business sphere, and so vastly increased his profits.

He arranged regular days and hours for each place in Tuscany, and soon became as widely known as the Grand Duke himself. When it was known that he had bought an old castle at Pontassieve on the banks of the Arno, his reputation still further increased. He was now so prosperous that he set the faculty at defiance. He proclaimed that they were jealous of his profounder learning, and threatened to expose the banefulness of their systems.

At the same time, his talk to the common people began to savor of patronage, and this also enhanced his reputation. It is much better, as a rule, to call attention up to you rather than charity down to you. The shrewd impostor became also more absolute now. It was known that the Grand Duke had once asked him to dine, and that Monsignore had the hardihood to refuse. Indeed, he sympathized too greatly with the aroused Italian spirit of unity and progress to compromise himself with the house of Austria. When at last the revolution came, Cristoforo was one of its best champions in Tuscany. His cantante sang only the march of Garibaldi and the victories of Savoy. His own speeches teemed with the gospel of Italy regenerated; and for a whole month he wasted no time in the sale of his bottighias and pillolas, but threw all his vehement, persuasive, and dramatic eloquence into the popular cause.

The end we know. Tuscany is a dukedom no longer, but a component part of a great peninsular kingdom with "Florence the Beautiful" for its capital.

And still before the ducal palace, where the deputies of Italy are to assemble, poor, vain Cristoforo Rischio makes his harangue every Tuesday and Saturday. He is now—or was four years ago—upward of sixty years of age, but spirited and athletic as ever, and so rich that it would be superfluous for him to continue his peripatetic career.

His life is to me noteworthy, as showing what may be gained by concentrating even humble energies upon a paltry thing. Had Créso persevered as well upon the stage, I do not doubt that he would have made a splendid actor. If he did so well with a mere nostrum, why should he not have gained riches and a less grotesque fame by the sale of a better article? He understood human nature, its credulities and incredulities, its superstitions, tastes, changefulness, and love of display and excitement. He has done no harm, and given as much amusement as he has been paid for. Indeed, I consider him more an ornamental and useful character than otherwise. He has brightened many a traveler's recollections, relieved the tedium of many a weary hour in a foreign city, and, with all his deception, has never severed himself from the popular faith, nor sold out the popular cause. I dare say his death, when it occurs, will cause more sensation and evoke more tears, than that of any better physician in Tuscany.

Part VI

HOAXES

Chapter 31

The Twenty-Seventh Street ghost—Spirits on ohe rampage.

In classing the ghost excitement that agitated our good people to such an extent some two years ago among the "humbugs" of the age, I must, at the outset, remind my readers that there was no little accumulation of what is termed "respectable" testimony, as to the reality of his ghostship in Twenty-seventh Street.

One fine Sunday morning, in the early part of 1863, my friends of the *Sunday Mercury* astonished their many thousands of patrons with an account that had been brought to them of a fearful spectre that had made its appearance in one of the best houses in Twenty-seventh Street. The narrative was detailed with circumstantial accuracy, and yet with an apparent discreet reserve, that gave the finishing touch of delightful mystery to the story.

The circumstances, as set forth in the opening letter (for many others followed) were briefly these:—A highly respectable family residing on Twenty-seventh Street, one of our handsome uptown thoroughfares, became aware, toward the close of the year 1862, that something extraordinary was taking place in their house, then one of the best in the neighborhood. Sundry mutterings and whisperings began to be heard among the servants employed about the domicile, and, after a little while it became almost impossible to induce them to remain there for love or money. The visitors of the family soon began to notice that their calls, which formerly were so welcome, particularly among the young people of the establishment, seemed to give embarrassment, and that the smiles that greeted them, as early as seven in the evening gradually gave place to uneasy gestures, and, finally to positive hints at the lateness of the hour, or the fatigue of their host by nine o'clock.

The head of the family was a plain, matter-of-fact old gentleman, by no means likely to give way to any superstitious terrors—one of your hardheaded business men who pooh-poohed demons, hobgoblins, and all other kinds of spirits, except the purest Santa Cruz and genuine old Otard; and he fell into a great rage, when upon his repeated gruff demands for an explanation, he was delicately informed that his parlor was "haunted." He vowed that somebody wanted to drive him from the house; that there was a conspiracy afoot among the women to get him still higher up town, and into a bigger brownstone front, and refused to believe one word of the ghost-story. At length, one day, while sitting in his "growlery," as the ladies called it, in the lower story, his attention was aroused by a clatter on the stairs, and looking out into the entry he saw a party of carpenters and painters who had been employed upon the parlor-floor, beating a precipitate retreat toward the front door.

"Stop!—stop! you infernal fools! What's all this hullabaloo about?" shouted the old gentleman.

No reply—no halt upon the part of the mechanics, but

away they went down the steps and along the street, as though Satan himself, or Moseby the guerrilla, was at their heels. They were pursued and ordered back, but absolutely refused to come, swearing that they had seen the Evil One, in propria persona; and threats, persuasions, and bribes alike proved vain to induce them to return. This made the matter look serious, and a family-council was held forthwith. It wouldn't do to let matters go on in this way, and something must be thought of as a remedy. It was in this half-solemn and half-tragic conclave that the paterfamilias was at last put in possession of the mysterious occurrences that had been disturbing the peace of his domestic hearth.

A ghost had been repeatedly seen in his best drawing-room!—a genuine, undeniable, unmitigated ghost!

The spectre was described by the female members of the family as making his appearance at all hours, chiefly, however in the evening, of course. Now the good old orthodox idea of a ghost is, of a very long, cadaverous, ghastly personage, of either sex, appearing in white draperies, with uplifted finger, and attended or preceded by sepulchral sounds— whist! hush! and sometimes the rattling of casements and the jingling of chains. A bluish glare and a strong smell of brimstone seldom failed to enhance the horror of the scene. This ghost, however, came it seems, in more ordinary guise, but none the less terrible for his natural style of approach and costume. He was usually seen in the front parlor, which was on the second story and faced the street. There he would be found seated in a chair near the fire place, his attire the garb of a carman or "carter" and hence the name "Carter's Ghost" afterward frequently applied to him. There he would sit entirely unmoved by the approach of living denizens of the house, who, at first, would suppose that he was some drunken or insane intruder, and only discover their mistake as they drew near, and saw the firelight shining through him, and notice the glare of his frightful eyes, which threatened all comers in a most unearthly way. Such was the purport of the first sketch that appeared in the *Sunday Mercury*, stated so distinctly and impressively that the effect could not fail to be tremendous among our sensational public. To help the matter, another brief notice, to the same effect, appeared in the Sunday issue of a leading journal on the same morning. The news dealers and street-carriers caught up the novelty instanter, and before noon not a copy of the *Sunday Mercury* could be bought in any direction. The country issue of the *Sunday Mercury* had still a larger sale.

On Sunday morning, every sheet in town made some allusion to the Ghost, and many even went so far as to give the very (supposed) number of the house favored with his visitations. The result of this enterprising guess was ludicrous enough, bordering a little, too, upon the serious. Indignant householders rushed down to the *Sunday Mercury* office with the most amusing wrath, threatening and denouncing the astonished publishers with all sorts of legal action for their presumed trespass, when in reality, their paper had designated no place or person at all. But the grandest demonstration of popular excitement was revealed in Twenty-seventh Street itself. Before noon a considerable portion of the thoroughfare below Sixth Avenue was blocked up with a dense mass of people of all ages, sizes, sexes, and nationalities, who had come "to see the Ghost." A liquor store or two, near by, drove a splendid "spiritual" business; and by evening "the fun" grew so "fast and furious" that a whole squad of police had to be employed to keep the sidewalks and even the carriageway clear. The "Ghost" was shouted for to make a speech, like any other new celebrity, and old ladies and gentlemen peering out of upper-story windows were saluted with playful tokens of regard, such as turnips, eggs of ancient date, and other things too numerous to mention, from the crowd. Nor was the throng composed entirely of Gothamites. The surrounding country sent in its contingent. They came on foot, on horseback, in wagons, and arrayed in all the costumes known about these parts, since the days of Rip Van Winkle. Cruikshanks would have made a fortune from his easy sketches of only a few figures in the scene. And thus the concourse continued for days together, arriving at early morn and staying there in the street until "dewy eve."

As a matter of course, there were various explanations of the story propounded by various people—all wondrously wise in their own conceit. Some would have it that "the Ghost" was got up by some of the neighbors, who wished, in this manner, to drive away disreputable occupants; others insisted that it was the revenge of an ousted tenant, etc., etc. Everybody offered his own theory, and, as is usual, in such cases, nobody was exactly right.

Meanwhile, the *Sunday Mercury* continued its publications of the further progress of the "mystery," from week to week, for a space of nearly two months, until the whole country seemed to have gone ghost-mad. Apparitions and goblins dire were seen in Washington, Rochester, Albany, Montreal, and other cities.

The spiritualists took it up and began to discuss "the Carter Ghost" with the utmost zeal. One startling individual—a physician and a philosopher—emerged from his professional shell into full-fledged glory, as the greatest canard of all, and published revelations of his own intermediate intercourse with the terrific "Carter." In every nook and corner of the land, tremendous posters, in white and yellow, broke out upon the walls and windows of news-depots, with capitals a foot long, and exclamation-points like drumsticks, announcing fresh installments of the "Ghost" story, and it was a regular fight between go-ahead vendors who should get the next batch of horrors in advance of his rivals.

Nor was the effect abroad the least feature of this stupendous "sell." The English, French, and German press translated some of the articles in epitome, and wrote grave commentaries thereon. The stage soon caught the blaze; and Professor Pepper, at the Royal Polytechnic Institute, in London, invented a most ingenious device for producing ghosts which should walk about upon the stage in such a perfectly-astounding manner as to throw poor Hamlet's father and the evil genius of Brutus quite into the "shade." "Pepper's Ghost" soon crossed the Atlantic, and all our theatres were speedily alive with nocturnal apparitions. The only real ghosts, however—four in number—came out at the Museum, in an appropriate drama, which had an immense run—all for twenty-five cents," or only six and a quarter cents per ghost!

But I must not forget to say that, really, the details given in the *Sunday Mercury* were well calculated to lead captive a large class of minds prone to luxuriate in the marvelous when well mixed with plausible reasoning. The most circumstantial accounts were given of sundry "gifted young ladies," "grave and learned professors," "reliable gentlemen"—where are those not found?—lonely watchers," and others, who had sought interviews with the "ghost," to their own great enlight-

enment, indeed, but, likewise, complete discomfiture. Pistols
were fired at him, pianos played and songs sung for him, and,
finally, his daguerreotype taken on prepared metallic plates
set upright in the haunted room. One shrewd artist brought
out an "exact photographic likeness" of the distinguished
stranger on cartes de visite, and made immense sales. The
apparitions, too, multiplied. An old man, a woman, and a
child made their appearance in the house of wonders, and, at
last, a gory head with distended eyeballs, swimming in a sea
of blood, upon a platter—like that of Holofernes—capped
the climax.

Certain wiseacres here began to see political allusions in
the Ghost, and many actually took the whole affair to be
a cunningly devised political satire upon this or that party,
according as their sympathies swayed them.

It would have been a remarkable portion of "this strange,
eventful history," of course, if "Barnum" could have escaped
the accusation of being its progenitor.

I was continually beset, and frequently, when more than
usually busy, thoroughly annoyed by the innuendoes of my
visitors, that I was the father of "the Ghost."

"Come, now, Mr. Barnum— this is going a little too far!"
some good old dame or grandfather would say to me. "You
oughtn't to scare people in this way. These ghosts are ugly
customers!"

"My dear Sir," or "Madam," I would say, as the case might
be, "I do assure you I know nothing whatever about the
Ghost—and as for 'spirits,' you know I never touch them,
and have been preaching against them nearly all my life."

"Well! well! you will have the last turn," they'd retort, as they edged away; "but you needn't tell us. We guess we've found the ghost."

Now, all I can add about this strange hallucination is, that those who came to me to see the original "Carter," really saw the "Elephant."

The wonderful apparition disappeared, at length, as suddenly as he had come. The "Bull's-Eye Brigade," as the squad of police put on duty to watch the neighborhood, for various reasons, was termed, hung to their work, and flashed the light of their lanterns into the faces of lonely couples, for some time afterward; but quiet, at length, settled down over all: and it has been it seems, reserved for my pen to record briefly the history of "The Twenty-seventh Street Ghost."

Chapter 32

The moon-hoax.

The most stupendous scientific imposition upon the public that the generation with which we are numbered has known, was the so-called "Moon-Hoax," published in the columns of the *New York Sun,* in the months of August and September, 1835. The sensation created by this immense imposture, not only throughout the United States, but in every part of the civilized world, and the consummate ability with which it was written, will render it interesting so long as our language shall endure; and, indeed, astronomical science has actually been indebted to it for many most valuable hints—a circumstance that gives the production a still higher claim to immortality.

At the period when the wonderful "yarn" to which I allude first appeared, the science of astronomy was engaging particular attention, and all works on the subject were eagerly bought up and studied by immense masses of people. The real discoveries of the younger Herschel, whose fame seemed destined to eclipse that of the elder sage of the same name, and the eloquent startling works of Dr. Dick, which the Harpers were republishing, in popular form, from the English edition, did much to increase and keep up this peculiar mania of the time, until the whole community at last were literally occupied with but little else than "stargazing." Dick's works on "The Sidereal Heavens," "Celestial Scenery," "The improvement of Society," etc., were read with the utmost avidity by rich and poor, old and young, in season and out of season. They were quoted in the parlor, at the table, on the promenade, at church, and even in the bedroom, until it absolutely seemed as though the whole community had "Dick" upon the brain. To the highly educated and imaginative portion of our good Gothamite population, the Doctor's glowing periods, full of the grandest speculations as to the starry worlds around us, their wondrous magnificence and ever-varying aspects of beauty and happiness were inexpressibly fascinating. The author's well-reasoned conjectures as to the majesty and beauty of their landscapes, the fertility and diversity of their soil, and the exalted intelligence and comeliness of their inhabitants, found hosts of believers; and nothing else formed the staple of conversation, until the beaux and belles, and dealers in small talk generally, began to grumble, and openly express their wishes that the Dickens had Doctor Dick and all his works.

It was at the very height of the furor above mentioned, that one morning the readers of the *Sun*— at that time only twenty-five hundred in number—were thrilled with the announcement in its columns of certain "Great Astronomical Discoveries Lately Made by Sir John Herschel, LL.D., F.R.S. etc., at the Cape of Good Hope," purporting to be a republication from a Supplement to the *Edinburgh Journal of Science*. The heading of the article was striking enough, yet was far from conveying any adequate idea of its contents. When the latter became known, the excitement went beyond all bounds, and grew until the *Sun* office was positively besieged with crowds of people of the very first class, vehemently applying for copies of the issue containing the wonderful details.

As the pamphlet form in which the narrative was subsequently published is now out of print, and a copy can hardly be had in the country, I will recall a few passages from a rare edition, for the gratification of my friends who have never seen the original. Indeed, the whole story is altogether too good to be lost; and it is a great pity that we can not have a handsome reprint of it given to the world from time to time. It is constantly in demand; and, during the year 1859, a single copy of sixty pages, sold at the auction of Mr. Haswell's library, brought the sum of $3.75. In that same year, a correspondent, in Wisconsin, writing to the *Sunday Times* of this city, inquired where the book could be procured, and was answered that he could find it at the old bookstore, No. 85 Center Street, if anywhere. Thus, after a search of many weeks, the Western bibliopole succeeded in obtaining a well-thumbed specimen of the precious work. Acting upon this chance suggestion, Mr. William Gowans, of this city, during the same year, brought out a very neat edition, in paper covers, illustrated with a view of the moon, as seen through Lord Rosse's grand telescope, in 1856. But this, too, has all been sold; and the most indefatigable book-collector might find it difficult to purchase a single copy at the present time. I, therefore, render the inquiring reader no slight service in culling for him some of the flowers from this curious astronomical garden.

The opening of the narrative was in the highest *Review* style; and the majestic, yet subdued, dignity of its periods, at once claimed respectful attention; while its perfect candor, and its wealth of accurate scientific detail exacted the homage of belief from all but cross-grained and inexorable skeptics.

It commences thus:

> "In this unusual addition to our Journal, we have the happiness to make known to the British public, and thence to the whole civilized world, recent discoveries in Astronomy, which will build an imperishable monument to the age in which we live, and confer upon the present generation of the human race a proud distinction through all future time. It has been poetically said, that the stars of heaven are the hereditary regalia of man, as the intellectual sovereign of the animal creation. He may now fold the Zodiac around him with a loftier consciousness of his mental superiority," etc., etc.

The writer then eloquently descanted upon the sublime achievement by which man pierced the bounds that hemmed him in, and with sensations of awe approached the revelations of his own genius in the far-off heavens, and with intense dramatic effect described the younger Herschel surpassing all that his father had ever attained; and by some stupendous apparatus about to unveil the remotest mysteries of the sidereal space, pausing for many hours ere the excess of his emotions would allow him to lift the veil from his own overwhelming success.

I must quote a line or two of this passage, for it capped the climax of public curiosity:

"Well might he pause! He was about to become the sole depository of wondrous secrets which had been hid from the eyes of all men that had lived since the birth of time. He was about to crown himself with a diadem of knowledge which would give him a conscious preeminence above every individual of his species who then lived or who had lived in the generations that are passed away. He paused ere he broke the seal of the casket that contained it."

Was not this introduction enough to stimulate the wonder bump of all the stargazers, until

"Each particular hair did stand on end,
Like quills upon the fretful porcupine?"

At all events, such was the effect, and it was impossible at first to supply the frantic demand, even of the city, not to mention the country readers.

I may very briefly sum up the outline of the discoveries alleged to have been made, in a few paragraphs, so as not to protract the suspense of my readers too long.

It was claimed that the *Edinburgh Journal* was indebted for its information to Doctor Andrew Grant—a savant of celebrity, who had, for very many years, been the scientific companion, first of the elder and subsequently of the younger Herschel, and had gone with the latter in September, 1834, to the Cape of Good Hope, whither he had been sent by the British Government, acting in conjunction with the Governments of France and Austria, to observe the transit of Mercury over the disc of the sun—an astronomical point of great importance to the lunar observations of longitude, and consequently to the navigation of the world. This transit was not calculated to occur before the 7th of November, 1835 (the year in which the hoax was printed;) but Sir John Herschel set out nearly a year in advance, for the purpose of thoroughly testing a new and stupendous telescope devised by himself under this peculiar inspiration, and infinitely surpassing anything of the kind ever before attempted by mortal man. It has been discovered by previous astronomers and among others, by Herschel's illustrious father, that the sidereal object becomes dim in proportion as it is magnified, and that, beyond a certain limit, the magnifying power is consequently rendered almost useless. Thus, an impassable barrier seemed to lie in the way of future close observation, unless some means could be devised to illuminate the object to the eye. By intense research and the application of all recent improvements in optics, Sir John had succeeded in securing a beautiful and perfectly lighted image of the moon with a magnifying power that increased its apparent size in the heavens six thousand times. Dividing the distance of the moon from the Earth, viz.: 240,000 miles, by six thousand, we have forty miles as the distance at which she would then seem to be seen; and as the elder Herschel, with a magnifying power, only one thousand, had calculated that he could distinguish an object on the moon's surface not more than 122 yards in diameter, it was clear that his son, with six times the power, could see an object there only twenty-two yards in diameter. But, for any further advance in power and light, the way seemed insuperably closed until a profound conversation with the great savant and optician, Sir David Brewster, led Herschel to suggest to the latter the idea of the readoption of the old fashioned telescopes, without tubes, which threw their images upon reflectors in a dark apartment, and then the illumination of these images by the intense hydro-oxygen light used in the ordinary illuminated microscope. At this suggestion, Brewster is represented by the veracious chronicler as leaping with enthusiasm from his chair, exclaiming in rapture to Herschel:

"Thou art the man!"

The suggestion, thus happily approved, was immediately acted upon, and a subscription, headed by that liberal patron of science, the Duke of Sussex, with £10,000, was backed by the reigning King of England with his royal word for any sum that might be needed to make up £70,000, the amount required. No time was lost; and, after one or two failures, in January 1833, the house of Hartley & Grant, at Dumbarton, succeeded in casting the huge object-glass of the new apparatus, measuring twenty-four feet (or six times that of the elder Herschel's glass) in diameter; weighing 14,826 pounds, or nearly seven tons, after being polished, and possessing a magnifying power of 42,000 times!—a perfectly pure, spotless, achromatic lens, without a material bubble or flaw!

Of course, after so elaborate a description of so astounding a result as this, the *Edinburg Scientific Journal* (i.e., the writer in the "*New York Sun*") could not avoid being equally precise in reference to subsequent details, and he proceeded to explain that Sir JohnHerschel and his amazing apparatus having been selected by the Board of Longitude to observe the transit of Mercury, the Cape of Good Hope was chosen because, upon the former expedition to Peru, acting in conjunction with one to Lapland, which was sent out for the same purpose in the eighteenth century, it had been noticed that the attraction of the mountainous regions deflected the plumb-line of the large instruments seven or eight seconds from the perpendicular, and, consequently, greatly impaired the enterprise. At the Cape, on the contrary, there was a magnificent tableland of vast expanse, where this difficulty could not occur. Accordingly, on the 4th of September, 1834, with a design to become perfectly familiar with the working of his new gigantic apparatus, and with the Southern Constellations, before the period of his observations of Mercury, Sir John Herschel sailed from London, accompanied by Doctor Grant (the supposed informant,) Lieutenant Drummond, of the Royal Engineers, F.R.A.S., and a large party of the best English workmen. On their arrival at the Cape, the apparatus was conveyed, in four days' time, to the great elevated plain, thirty-five miles to the N.E. of Cape Town, on trains drawn by two relief-teams of oxen, eighteen to a team, the ascent aided by gangs of Dutch boors. For the details of the huge fabric in which the lens and its reflectors were set up, I must refer the curious reader to the pamphlet itself—not that the presence of the "Dutch boors" alarms me at all, since we have plenty of boors at home, and one gets used to them in the course of time, but because the elaborate scientific description of the structure would make most readers see "stars" in broad daylight before they get through.

I shall only go on to say that, by the 10th of January, everything was complete, even to the two pillars "one hundred and fifty feet high!" that sustained the lens. Operations then commenced forthwith, and so, too, did the "special wonder" of the readers. It is a matter of congratulation to mankind that the writer of the hoax, with an apology (Heaven save

the mark!) spared us Herschel's notes of "the Moon's tropi-
cal, sidereal, and synodic revolutions," and the "phenomena
of the syzygies," and proceeded at once to the pith of the
subject. Here came in his grand stroke, informing the world
of complete success in obtaining a distinct view of objects
in the moon "fully equal to that which the unaided eye
commands of terrestrial objects at the distance of a hundred yards, affirmatively settling the question whether the
satellite be inhabited, and by what order of beings," "firmly
establishing a new theory of cometary phenomena," etc., etc.
This announcement alone was enough to take one's breath
away, but when the green marble shores of the *Mare Nubium*;
the mountains shaped like pyramids, and of the purest and
most dazzling crystalized, wine-colored amethyst, dotting
green valleys skirted by "round-breasted hills;" summits of
the purest vermilion fringed with arching cascades and but-
tresses of white marble glistening in the sun—when these
began to be revealed, the delight of our Lunatics knew no
bounds—and the whole town went moon-mad! But even
these immense pictures were surpassed by the "lunatic" animals discovered. First came the "herds of brown quadrupeds"
very like a—no! not a whale, but a bison, and "with a tail
resembling that of the *bos grunniens*"— the reader probably
understands what kind of a "bos" that is, if he's apprenticed
to a theatre in midsummer with musicians on a strike; then
a creature, which the hoax-man naively declared "would be
classed on Earth as a monster"—I rather think it would!—of
a bluish lead color, about the size of a goat, with a head and
a beard like him, and a single horn, slightly inclined forward
from, the perpendicular"—it is clear that if this goat was
cut down to a single horn, other people were not! I could

not but fully appreciate the exquisite distinction accorded by the writer to the female of this lunar animal—for she, while deprived of horn and beard, he explicitly tells us, "had a much larger tail!" When the astronomers put their fingers on the beard of this "beautiful" little creature (on the reflector, mind you!) it would skip away in high dudgeon, which, considering that 240,000 miles intervened, was something to show its delicacy of feeling.

Next in the procession of discovery, among other animals of less note, was presented "a quadruped with an amazingly long neck, head like a sheep, bearing two long spiral horns, white as polished ivory, and standing in perpendiculars parallel to each other. Its body was like that of a deer, but its forelegs were most disproportionately long, and its tail, which was very bushy and of a snowy whiteness, curled high over its rump and hung two or three feet by its side. Its colors were bright bay and white, brindled in patches, but of no regular form." This is probably the animal known to us on Earth, and particularly along the Mississippi River, as the "guyascutus," to which I may particularly refer in a future article.

But all these beings faded into insignificance compared with the first sight of the genuine Lunatics, or men in the moon, "four feet high, covered, except in the face, with short, glossy, copper-colored hair," and "with wings composed of a thin membrane, without hair, lying snugly upon their backs from the top of their shoulders to the calves of their legs," "with faces of a yellowish flesh-color—a slight improvement on the large orangutan." Complimentary for the Lunatics! But, says the chronicler, Lieutenant Drummond declared that "but for their long wings, they would look as well on a parade-ground as some of the cockney militia!" A little rough, my friend the reader will exclaim, for the aforesaid militia.

Of course, it is impossible, in a sketch like the present, to do more than give a glimpse of this rare combination of astronomical realities and the vagaries of mere fancy, and I must omit the Golden-fringed Mountains, the Vale of the Triads, with their splendid triangular temples, etc., but I positively cannot pass by the glowing mention of the inhabitants of this wonderful valley—a superior race of Lunatics, as beautiful and as happy as angels, "spread like eagles" on the grass, eating yellow gourds and red cucumbers, and played with by snow-white stags, with jet-black horns! The description here is positively delightful, and I even now remember my poignant sigh of regret when, at the conclusion, I read that these innocent and happy beings, although evidently "creatures of order and subordination," and "very polite," were seen indulging in amusements which would not be deemed "within the bounds of strict propriety" on this degenerate ball. The story wound up rather abruptly by referring the reader to an extended work on the subject by Herschel, which has not yet appeared.

One can laugh very heartily, now, at all this; but nearly everybody, the gravest and the wisest, too, was completely taken in at the time: and the *Sun*, then established at the corner of Spruce Street, where the *Tribune* office now stands, reaped an increase of more than fifty thousand to its circulation—in fact, there gained the foundation of its subsequent prolonged success. Its proprietors sold no less than $25,000 worth of the "Moon Hoax" over the counter, even exhausting an edition of sixty thousand in pamphlet form. And who was the author? A literary gentleman, who has devoted very many years of his life to mathematical and astronomical studies, and was at the time connected as an editor with the *Sun*—one whose name has since been widely known in literature and politics—Richard Adams Locke, Esq., then in his youth, and now in the decline of years. Mr. Locke, who still survives, is a native of the British Isles, and, at the time of his first connection with the New York press, was the only shorthand reporter in this city, where he laid the basis of a competency he now enjoys. Mr. Locke declares that his original object in writing the Moon story was to satirize some of the extravagances of Doctor Dick, and to make some astronomical suggestions which he felt diffident about offering seriously.

Whatever may have been his object, his hit was unrivaled; and for months the press of Christendom, but far more in Europe than here, teemed with it, until Sir John Herschel was actually compelled to come out with a denial over his own signature. In the meantime, it was printed and published in many languages, with superb illustrations. Mr. Endicott, the celebrated lithographer, some years ago had in his possession a splendid series of engravings, of extra folio size, got up in Italy, in the highest style of art, and illustrating the "Moon Hoax."

Here, in New York, the public were, for a long time, divided on the subject, the vast majority believing, and a few grumpy customers rejecting the story. One day, Mr. Locke was introduced by a mutual friend at the door of the *Sun* office to a very grave old orthodox Quaker, who, in the calmest manner, went on to tell him all about the embarkation of Herschel's apparatus at London, where he had seen it with his own eyes. Of course, Locke's optics expanded somewhat while he listened to this remarkable statement, but he wisely kept his own counsel.

The discussions of the press were very rich; the *Sun*, of course, defending the affair as genuine, and others doubting it. The *Mercantile Advertiser*, the *Albany Daily Advertiser*, the *New York Commercial Advertiser*, the *New York Times*, the *New Yorker*, the *New York Spirit of '76*, the *Sunday News*, the *United States Gazette*, the *Philadelphia Inquirer*, and hosts of other papers came out with the most solemn acceptance and admiration of these "wonderful discoveries," and were eclipsed in their approval only by the scientific journals abroad. The *Evening Post*, however, was decidedly skeptical, and took up the matter in this irreverent way:

"It is quite proper that the Sun should be the means of shedding so much light on the Moon. That there should be winged people in the moon does not strike us as more wonderful than the existence of such a race of beings on the Earth; and that there does still exist such a race, rests on the evidence of that most veracious of voyagers and circumstantial of chroniclers, Peter Wilkins, whose celebrated work not only gives an account of the general appearance and habits of a most interesting tribe of flying Indians; but, also, of all those more delicate and engaging traits which the author was enabled to discover by reason of the conjugal relations he entered into with one of the females of the winged tribe."

The moon-hoax had its day, and some of its glory still survives. Mr. Locke, its author, is now quietly residing in the beautiful little home of a friend on the Clove Road, Staten

Island, and no doubt, as he gazes up at the evening luminary, often fancies that he sees a broad grin on the countenance of its only well-authenticated tenant, "the hoary solitary whom the criminal code of the nursery has banished thither for collecting fuel on the Sabbath-day."

Chapter 33

The miscegenation hoax—A great literary sell—Political humbugging—Tricks of the wire-pullers—Machinery employed to render the pamphlet notorious—Who were sold and how it was done.

Some persons say that "all is fair in politics." Without agreeing with this doctrine, I nevertheless feel that the history of Ancient and Modern Humbugs would not be complete without a record of the last and one of the most successful of known literary hoaxes. This is the pamphlet entitled "Miscegenation," which advocates the blending of the white and black races upon this continent, as a result not only inevitable from the freeing of the negro, but desirable as a means of creating a more perfect race of men than any now existing. This pamphlet is a clever political quiz; and was written by three young gentlemen of the *World* newspaper, namely. D. G. Croly, George Wakeman, and E. C. Howell.

The design of "Miscegenation" was exceedingly ambitious, and the machinery employed was probably among the most ingenious and audacious ever put into operation to procure the endorsement of absurd theories, and give the subject the widest notoriety. The object was to so make use of the prevailing ideas of the extremists of the Anti-Slavery party, as to induce them to accept doctrines which would be obnoxious to the great mass of the community, and which would, of course, be used in the political canvass which was to ensue. It was equally important that the "Democrats" should be made to believe that the pamphlet in question emanated from a "Republican" source. The idea was suggested by a discourse delivered by Mr. Theodore Tilton, at the Cooper Institute, before the American Anti-Slavery Society, in May 1863, on the negro, in which that distinguished orator argued, that in some future time the blood of the negro would form one of the mingled bloods of the great regenerated American nation. The scheme once conceived, it began immediately to be put into execution. The first stumbling-block was the name "amalgamation," by which this fraternizing of the races had been always known. It was evident that a book advocating amalgamation would fall stillborn, and hence some new and novel word had to be discovered, with the same meaning, but not so objectionable. Such a word was coined by the combination of the Latin *miscere*, to mix, and *genus*, race: from these, miscegenation—a mingling of the races. The word is as euphonious as "amalgamation," and much more correct in meaning. It has passed into the language, and no future dictionary will be complete without it. Next, it was necessary to give the book an erudite appearance, and arguments from ethnology must form no unimportant part of this matter. Neither of the authors being versed in this science, they were compelled to depend entirely on encyclopedias and books of reference. This obstacle to a New York editor or reporter was not so great as it might seem. The public are often favored in our journals with dissertations upon various abstruse matters by men who are entirely ignorant of what they are writing about. It was said of Cuvier that he could restore the skeleton of an extinct animal if he were only given one of its teeth, and so a competent editor or reporter of a city journal can get up an article of any length on any given subject, if he is only furnished one word or name to start with. There was but one writer on ethnology distinctly known to the authors, which was Prichard; but that being secured, all the rest came easily enough. The authors went to the Astor Library and secured a volume of Prichard's works, the perusal of which of course gave them the names of many other authorities, which were also consulted; and thus a very respectable array of scientific arguments in favor of Miscegenation were soon compiled. The sentimental and argumentative portions were quickly suggested from the knowledge of the authors of current politics, of the vagaries of some of the more visionary reformers, and from their own native wit.

The book was at first written in a most cursory manner the chapters got up without any order or reference to each other, and afterward arranged. As the impression sought to be conveyed was a serious one, it would clearly not do to commence with the extravagant and absurd theories to which it was intended that the reader should gradually be led. The scientific portion of the work was therefore given first, and was made as grave and terse and unobjectionable as possible; and merely urged, by arguments drawn from science and history, that the blending of the different races of men resulted in a better progeny. As the work progressed, they continued to "pile on the agony," until, at the close, the very fact that the statue of the Goddess of Liberty on the

Capitol, is of a bronze tint, is looked upon as an omen of the color of the future American!

"When the traveler approaches the City of Magnificent Distances," it says, "the seat of what is destined to be the greatest and most beneficent power on Earth, the first object that will strike his eye will be the figure of Liberty surmounting the Capitol; not white, symbolizing but one race, nor black, typifying another, but a statue representing the composite race, whose sway will extend from the Atlantic to the Pacific Ocean, from the Equator to the North Pole—the Miscegens of the Future."

The Book once written, plans were laid to obtain the endorsement of the people who were to be humbugged. It was not only necessary to humbug the members of the Reform and Progressive party, but to present—as I have before said—such serious arguments that Democrats should be led to believe it as a bona fide revelation of the "infernal" designs of their antagonists. In both respects there was complete success. Although, of course, the mass of the Republican leaders entirely ignored the book, yet a considerable number of Anti-Slavery men, with more transcendental ideas, were decidedly "sold." The machinery employed was exceedingly ingenious. Before the book was published, proof-copies were furnished to every prominent abolitionist in the country, and also to prominent spiritual mediums, to ladies known to wear Bloomers, and to all that portion of our population who are supposed to be a little "soft" on the subject of reform. A circular was also enclosed, requesting them, before the publication of the book, to give the author the benefit of their opinions as to the value of the arguments presented, and the desirability of the immediate publication of the work; to be enclosed to the American News Company, 121 Nassau Street, New York—the agents for the publishers. The bait took. Letters came pouring in from all sides, and among the names of prominent persons who gave their endorsements were Albert Brisbane, Parker Pillsbury, Lucretia Mott, Sarah M. Grimke, Angelina G. Weld, Dr. J. McCune Smith, Wm. Wells Brown. Mr. Pillsbury was quite excited over the book, saying; "Your work has cheered and gladdened a winter-morning, which I began in cloud and sorrow. You are on the right track. Pursue it, and the good God speed you." Mr. Theodore Tilton, upon receiving the pamphlet, wrote a note promising to read it, and to write the author a long and candid letter as soon as he had time; and saying, that the subject was one to which he had given much thought. The promised letter, I believe, however, was never received; probably because, on a careful perusal of the book, Mr. Tilton "smelt a rat." He might also have been influenced by an ironical paragraph relating to himself, and arguing that, as he was a "pure specimen of the blonde," and "when a young man was noted for his angelic type of feature," his sympathy for the colored race was accounted for by the natural love of opposites. Says the author with much gravity:

"The sympathy Mr. Greeley, Mr. Phillips and Mr. Tilton feel for the negro is the love which the blonde bears for the black; it is the love of race, a sympathy stronger to them than the love they bear to woman. It is founded upon natural law. We love our opposites. It is the nature of things that we should do so, and where Nature has free course, men like those we have indicated, whether Anti-Slavery or Pro-Slavery, Conservative or Radical, Democrat or Republican, will marry and be given in marriage to the most perfect specimens of the colored race."

So far, things worked favorably; and, having thus bagged a goodly number of prominent reformers, the next effort was to get the ear of the public. Here, new machinery was brought into play. A statement was published in the *Philadelphia Inquirer* (a paper which, ever since the war commenced, has been notorious for its "sensation" news,) that a charming and accomplished young mulatto girl was about to publish a book on the subject of the blending of the races, in which she took the affirmative view. Of course, so piquant a paragraph was immediately copied by almost every paper in the country. Various other stories, equally ingenious and equally groundless, were set afloat, and public expectation was riveted on the forthcoming work.

Some time in February last, the book was published. Copies, of course, were sent to all the leading journals. The "Anglo-African," the organ of the colored population of New York, warmly, and at great length, endorsed the doctrine. The *Anti-Slavery Standard*, edited by Mr. Oliver Johnson, gave over a column of serious argument and endorsement to the work. Mr. Tilton, of the *Independent*, was not to be caught napping. In that journal, under date of February 25, 1864, he devoted a two-column leader to the subject of Miscegenation and the little pamphlet in question. Mr. Tilton was the first to announce a belief that the book was a hoax. I quote from his article:

"Remaining a while on our table unread, our attention was specially called to it by noticing how savagely certain newspapers were abusing it."

"The authorship of the pamphlet is a well-kept secret; at least it is unknown to us. Nor, after a somewhat careful reading, are we convinced that the writer is in earnest. Our first impression was, and remains, that the work was meant as a piece of pleasantry—a burlesque upon what are popularly called the extreme and fanatical notions of certain radical men named therein. Certainly, the essay is not such a one as any of these gentlemen would have written on the subject, though some of their speeches are conspicuously quoted and commended in it."

"If written in earnest, the work is not thorough enough to be satisfactory; if in jest, we prefer Sydney Smith—or McClellan's Report. Still, to be frank, we agree with a large portion of these pages, but disagree heartily with another portion."

"The idea of scientifically undertaking to intermingle existing populations according to a predetermined plan for reconstructing the human race—for flattening out its present varieties into one final unvarious dead-level of humanity—is so absurd, that we are more than ever convinced such a statement was not written in earnest!"

Mr. Tilton, however, hints that the colored race is finally in some degree to form a component part of the future American; and that, in time, "the negro of the South, growing paler with every generation, will at last completely hide his face under the snow."

One of the editorial writers for the *Tribune* was so impressed with the book that he wrote an article on the subject, arguing about it with apparent seriousness, and in a manner with some readers supposed to be rather favorable than otherwise to the doctrine. Mr. Greeley and the publishers, it is understood, were displeased at the publication of the article. The next morning nearly all the city journals had editorial articles upon the subject.

The next point was, to get the miscegenation controversy into Congress. The book, with its endorsements, was brought to the notice of Mr. Cox, of Ohio (commonly called "Sunset Cox;") and he made an earnest speech on the subject. Mr. Washburne replied wittily, reading and commenting on extracts from a work by Cox, in which the latter deplored the existence of the prejudice against the Africans. A few days after, Mr. Kelly, of Pennsylvania, replied very elaborately to Mr. Cox, bringing all his learning and historical research to bear on the topic. It was the subject of a deal of talk in Washington afterward. Mr. Cox was charged by some of the more shrewd members of Congress with writing it. It was said that Mr. Sumner, on reading it, immediately pronounced it a hoax.

Through the influence of the authors, a person visited James Gordon Bennett, of the *Herald*, and spoke to him about *Miscegenation*. Mr. Bennett thought the idea too monstrous and absurd to waste an article upon.

"But," said the gentleman, "the Democratic papers are all noticing it."

"The Democratic editors are asses," said Bennett.

"Senator Cox has just made a speech in Congress on it."

"Cox is an ass," responded Bennett.

"Greeley had an article about it the other day."

"Well, Greeley's a donkey."

"The *Independent* yesterday had a leader of a column and a half about it."

"Well, Beecher is no better," said Bennett. "They're all asses. But what did he say about it?"

"Oh, he rather endorsed it."

"Well, I'll read the article," said Bennett. "And perhaps I'll have an article written ridiculing Beecher."

"It will make a very good handle against the radicals," said the other.

"Oh, I don't know," said Bennett. "Let them marry together, if they want to, with all my heart."

For some days, the *Herald* said nothing about it, but the occasion of the departure of a colored regiment from New York City having called forth a flattering address to them from the ladies of the "Loyal League," the *Herald*, saw a chance to make a point against Mr. Charles King and others; and the next day it contained a terrific article, introducing miscegenation in the most violent and offensive manner, and saying that the ladies of the "Loyal League" had offered to marry the colored soldiers on their return! After that, the *Herald* kept up a regular fusillade against the supposed miscegenic proclivities of the Republicans. And thus, after all, Bennett swallowed the "critter" horns, hoofs, tail, and all.

The authors even had the impudence to attempt to entrap Mr. Lincoln into an endorsement of the work, and asked permission to dedicate a new work, on a kindred subject,

"Melaleukation," to him. Honest Old Abe however, who can see a joke, was not to be taken in so easily.

About the time the book was first published, Miss Anne E. Dickinson happened to lecture in New York. The authors here exhibited a great degree of acuteness and tact, as well as sublime impudence, in seizing the opportunity to have some small hand bills, with the endorsement of the book, printed and distributed by boys among the audience. Before Miss Dickinson appeared, therefore, the audience were gravely reading the miscegenation handbill; and the reporters, noticing it, coupled the facts in their reports. From this, it went forth, and was widely circulated, that Miss Dickinson was the author!

Dr. Mackay, the correspondent of the *London Times*, in New York, was very decidedly sold, and hurled all manner of big words against the doctrine in his letters to "The Thunderer;" and thus "the leading paper of Europe" was, for the hundredth time during the American Rebellion, decidedly taken in and done for.

The *Saturday Review*— perhaps the cleverest and certainly the sauciest of the English hebdomadals—also berated the book and its authors in the most pompous language at its command. Indeed, the *Westminster Review* seriously refers to the arguments of the book in connection with Dr. Broca's pamphlet on Human Hybridity, a most profound work. "Miscegenation" was republished in England by Trübner & Co.; and very extensive translations from it are still passing the rounds of the French and German papers.

Thus passes into history one of the most impudent as well as ingenious literary hoaxes of the present day. There is probably not a newspaper in the country but has printed much about it; and enough of extracts might be collected from various journals upon the subject to fill my whale-tank.

It is needless to say that the book passed through several editions. Of course, the mass of the intelligent American people rejected the doctrines of the work, and looked upon it either as a political dodge, or as the ravings of some crazy man; but the authors have the satisfaction of knowing that it achieved a notoriety which has hardly been equalled by any mere pamphlet ever published in this country.

Part VII

GHOSTS AND WITCHCRAFTS

Chapter 34

Haunted houses—A night spent alone with a ghost—Kirby, the actor—Colt's pistols versus hobgoblins—The mystery explained.

A great many persons believe more or less in haunted houses. In almost every community there is some building that has had a mysterious history. This is true in all countries, and among all races and nations. Indeed it is to this very fact that the ingenious author of the "Twenty-seventh-street Ghost" may attribute his success in creating such an excitement. In fact, I will say, "under the rose," he predicted his hopes of success entirely upon this weakness in human nature. Even in "this day and age of the world" there are hundreds of deserted buildings which are looked upon with awe, or terror, or superstitious interest. They have frightened their former inhabitants away, and left the buildings in the almost undisputed possession of real moles, bats, and owls, and imaginary goblins and sprites.

In the course of my travels in both hemispheres I have been amazed at the great number of such cases that have come under my personal observation.

But for the present, I will give a brief account of a haunted house in Yorkshire, England, in which some twenty years ago, Kirby, the actor, who formerly played at the Chatham Theatre, passed a pretty strange night. I met Mr. Kirby in London in 1844, and I will give, in nearly his own language, a history of his lone night in this haunted house, as he gave it to me within a week after its occurrence. I will add, that I saw no reason to doubt Mr. Kirby's veracity, and he assured me upon his honor that the statement was literally true to the letter. Having myself been through several similar places in the daytime, I felt a peculiar interest in the subject, and hence I have a vivid recollection of nearly the exact words in which he related his singular nocturnal adventure. One thing is certain: Kirby was not the man to be afraid of trying such an experiment.

"I had heard wonderful stories about this house," said Mr. Kirby to me, "and I was very glad to get a chance to enter it, although, I confess, the next morning I was about as glad to get out of it."

"It was an old country-seat—a solid stone mansion which had long borne the reputation of a haunted house. It was watched only by one man. He was the old gardener—an ancient servant of the family that once lived there, and a person in whom the family reposed implicit confidence.

"Having had some inkling of this wonderful place, and having a few days to spare before going to London to fulfil an engagement at the Surry Theatre, I thought I would probe this haunted-house story to the bottom. I therefore called on the old gardener who had charge of the place, and introduced myself as an American traveller desirous of spending a night with his ghosts. The old man seemed to be about seventy-five or eighty years of age. I met him at the gate of the estate, where he kept guard. He told me, when

I applied, that it was a dangerous spot to enter, but I could pass it if I pleased. I should, however, have to return by the same door, if I ever came back again.

"Wishing to make sure of the job, I gave him a sovereign, and asked him to give me all the privileges of the establishment; and if his bill amounted to more, I would settle it when I returned. He looked at me with an expression of doubt and apprehension, as much as to say that he neither understood what I was going to do nor what was likely to happen. He merely remarked:

"'You can go in.'

"'Will you go with me, and show me the road?'

"'I will.'

"'Go ahead.'

"We entered. The gate closed. I suddenly turned on my man, the old gardener and custodian of the place, and said to him:

"'Now, my patriarchal friend, I am going to sift this humbug to the bottom, even if I stay here forty nights in succession; and I am prepared to lay all "spirits" that present themselves; but if you will save me all trouble in the matter and frankly explain to me the whole affair, I will never mention it to your injury, and I will present you with ten golden sovereigns.'

"The old fellow looked astonished; but he smirked, and whimpered, and trembled, and said:

"'I am afraid to do that; but I will warn you against going too far.'

"When we had crossed a courtyard, he rang a bell, and several strange noises were distinctly heard. I was introduced to the establishment through a well-constructed archway, which led to a large stairway, from which we proceeded to a great door, which opened into a very large room. It was a library. The old custodian had carried a torch (and I was prepared with a box of matches.) He was acting evidently 'on the square,' and I sat myself down in the library, where he told me that I should soon see positive evidence that this was a haunted house.

"Not being a very firm believer in the doctrine of houses really haunted, I proposed to keep a pretty good hold of my matchbox, and lest there should be any doubt about it, I had also provided myself with two sperm candles, which I kept in my pocket, so I should not be left too suddenly and too long in the dark.

"'Now Sir,' said he, 'I wish you to hold all your nerves steady and keep your courage up, because I intend to stand by you as well as I can, but I never come into this house alone.'

"'Well, what is the matter with the house?'

"'Oh! everything, Sir!'

"'What?'

"'Well, when I was much younger than I am now, the master of this estate got frightened here by some mysterious appearances, noises, sounds, etc., and he preferred to leave the place.'

"'Why?'

"'He had a tradition from his grandfather, and pretty well kept alive in the family, that it was a haunted house; and he let out the estate to the smaller farmers of the neighborhood, and quit the premises, and never returned again, except one night, and after that one night he left. We suppose he is dead. Now, Sir, if you wish to spend the night here as you have requested, what may happen to you I don't know; but I tell you it is a haunted house, and I would not sleep here tonight for all the wealth of the Bank of England!'

"This did not deter me in the least, and having the means of self-protection around me, and plenty of lucifer matches, etc., I thought I would explore this mystery and see whether a humbug which had terrified the proprietors of that magnificent house in the midst of a magnificent estate, for upward of sixty years, could not be explored and exploded. That it was a humbug, I had no doubt; that I would find it out, I was not so certain.

"I sat down in the library, fully determined to spend the night in the establishment. A door was opened into an adjoining room where there was a dust-covered lounge, and everything promised as much comfort as could be expected under the circumstances.

"However, before the old keeper of the house left, I asked him to show me over the building, and let me explore for myself the different rooms and apartments. To all this he readily consented; and as he had some prospect before him of making a good job out of it, he displayed a great deal of alacrity, and moved along very quick and smart for a man apparently eighty years of age.

"I went from room to room and story to story. Everything seemed to be well arranged, but somewhat dusty and time-worn. I kept a pretty sharp lookout, but I could see no sort of machinery for producing a grand effect.

"We finally descended to the library, when I closed the door, and bolting and locking it, took the key and put it in my pocket.

"'Now, Sir,' I said to the keeper, 'where is the humbug?'

"'There is no humbug here,' he answered.

"'Well, why don't you show me some evidence of the haunted house?'

"'You wait,' said he, 'till twelve o'clock tonight, and you will see "haunting" enough for you. I will not stay till then.'

"He left; I stayed. Everything was quiet for some time. Not a mouse was heard, not a rat was visible, and I thought I would go to sleep.

"I lay down for this purpose, but I soon heard certain extraordinary sounds that disturbed my repose. Chains were clanked, noises were made, and shrieks and groans were heard from various parts of the mansion. All of these I had expected. They did not frighten me much. A little while after, just as I was going to sleep again, a curious string of light burned around the room. It ran along on the walls in a zigzag line, about six feet high, entirely through the apartment. I did not smell anything bituminous or like sulphur. It flashed quicker than powder, and it did not smell like it. Thinks I: 'This looks pretty well, we will have some amusement now.' Then the jangling of bells, and clanking of chains, and flashes of light; then thumpings and knockings of all sorts came along, interspersed with shrieks and groans. I sat very quiet. I had two of Colt's best pistols in my pocket, and I thought I could shoot anything spiritual or material with these machines made in Connecticut. I took them out and laid them on the table. One of them suddenly disappeared! I did not like that, still my nerves were firm, for I knew it was all gammon. I took the other pistol in my hand and surveyed the room. Nobody was there; and, finally half suspicious that I had gone to sleep and had a dream, I woke up with a grasp on my hand which was holding the other pistol. This soon made me fully awake.

"I tried to recover my balance, and at this moment the candle went out. I lit it with one of my lucifers. No person was visible, but the noises began again, and they were infernal. I then took one of my sperm candles out, and went to unlock the door. I attempted to take the key out of my pocket. It was not there! Suddenly the door opened, I saw a man or a somebody about the size of a man, standing straight in front of me. I pointed one of Colt's revolvers at his head, for I thought I saw something human about him; and I told him that whether he was ghost or spirit, goblin or robber, he had better stand steady, or I would blow his brains out, if he had any. And to make sure that he should not escape I got hold of his arm, and told him that if he was a ghost he would have a tolerably hard time of it, and that if he was a humbug I would let him off if he would tell me the whole story about the trick.

"He saw that he was caught, and he earnestly begged me not to fire that American pistol at him. I did not; but I did not let go of him. I brought him into the library, and with pistol in hand I put him through a pretty close examination. He was clad in mailed armor, with breastplate and helmet, and a great sword, in the style of the Crusaders. He promised, on condition of saving his life, to give me an honest account of the facts.

"In substance they were, that he, an old family-servant, and ultimately a gardener in charge of the place, had been employed by an enemy of the gentleman who owned the property, to render it so uncomfortable that the estate should be sold for much less than its value; and that he had got an ingenious machinist and chemist to assist him in arranging such contrivances as would make the house so intolerable that they could not live there. A galvanic battery with wires were provided, and every device of chemistry and mechanism was resorted to in order to effect this purpose.

"One by one, the family left; and they had remained away for nearly two generations under the terror of such forms, and appearances, and sights and sounds, as frightened them almost to death. And furthermore, the old gardener added, that he expected his own granddaughter would become the lady of that house, when the property should have been neglected so long and the place became so fearful that no one in the neighborhood would undertake to purchase it, or to even pass one moment after dark in exploring its horrible mysteries.

"He begged on his knees that I would spare him with his gray hairs, since he had so short a time to live. He declared that he had been actuated by no other motive than pride and ambition for his child.

"I told the poor old fellow that his secret should be safe with me, and should not be made public so long as he lived. The old man grasped my hand eagerly and expressed his gratitude in the strongest terms. Thus, Mr. Barnum, I have given you the pure and honest facts in regard to my adventure in a so called haunted house. Don't make it public until you are convinced that the old gardener has shuffled off this mortal coil."

So much for Kirby's story of the haunted house. No doubt, the old gardener has before this become in reality a disembodied spirit, but that his granddaughter became legally possessed of the estate is not at all probable. Real estate does not change hands so easily in England. So powerful, however is the superstitious belief in haunted houses, that it is doubtful whether that property will for many years sustain half so great a cash value in the market as it would have done had it not been considered a "haunted house."

It is to be hoped that, as schools multiply and education increases, the follies and superstitions which underlie a belief in ghosts and hobgoblins will pass away.

Chapter 35

Haunted houses—Ghosts—Ghouls—Phantoms—
Vampires—Conjurors—Divining—
Goblins—Fortune-telling—Magic—Witches—Sorcery—
Obi—Dreams— Signs—Spiritual mediums—False
prophets—Demonology—Deviltry generally.

Whether superstition is the father of humbug, or humbug the mother of superstition (as well as its nurse,) I do not pretend to say; for the biggest fools and the greatest philosophers can be numbered among the believers in and victims of the worst humbugs that ever prevailed on the Earth.

As we grow up from childhood and begin to think we are free from all superstitions, absurdities, follies, a belief in dreams, signs, omens, and other similar stuff, we afterward learn that experience does not cure the complaint. Doubtless much depends upon our "bringing up." If children are permitted to feast their ears night after night (as I was) with stories of ghosts, hobgoblins, ghouls, witches, apparitions, bugaboos, it is more difficult in afterlife for them to rid their minds of impressions thus made.

But whatever may have been our early education, I am convinced that there is an inherent love of the marvelous in every breast, and that everybody is more or less superstitious;

and every superstition I denominate a humbug, for it lays the human mind open to any amount of belief, in any amount of deception that may be practised.

One object of these chapters consists in showing how open everybody is to deception, that nearly everybody "hankers" after it, that solid and solemn realities are frequently set aside for silly impositions and delusions, and that people, as a too general thing, like to be led into the region of mystery. As Hudibras has it:

"Doubtless the pleasure is as great
Of being cheated as to cheat;
As lookers-on feel most delight
That least perceive a juggler's sleight;
And still the less they understand,
The more they admire his sleight of hand."

The amount or strength of man's brains have little to do with the amount of their superstitions. The most learned and the greatest men have been the deepest believers in ingeniously-contrived machines for running human reason off the track. If any expositions I can make on this subject will serve to put people on their guard against impositions of all sorts, as well as foolish superstitions, I shall feel a pleasure in reflecting that I have not written in vain. The heading of this chapter enumerates the principal kinds of supernatural humbugs. These, it must be remembered, are quite different from religious impostures.

It is astonishing to reflect how ancient is the date of this class of superstitions (as well as of most others, in fact,) and how universally they have prevailed. Nearly thirty-six hundred years ago, it was thought a matter of course that Joseph, the Hebrew Prime Minister of Pharaoh, should have a silver cup that he commonly used to do his divining with: so that the practice must already have been an established one.

In Homer's time, about twenty-eight hundred years ago, ghosts were believed to appear. The Witch of Endor pretended to raise the ghost of Samuel, at about the same time.

Today, here in the City of New York, dream books are sold by the edition; a dozen fortune-tellers regularly advertise in the papers; a haunted house can gather excited crowds for weeks; abundance of people are uneasy if they spill salt, dislike to see the new moon over the wrong shoulder, and are delighted if they can find an old horseshoe to nail to their doorpost.

I have already told about one or two haunted houses, but must devote part of this chapter to that division of the subject. There are hundreds of such—that is, of those reputed to be such; and have been for hundreds of years. In almost every city, and in many towns and country places, they are to be found. I know of one, for instance, in New Jersey, one or two in New York, and have heard of several in Connecticut. There are great numbers in Europe; for as white men have lived there so much longer than in America, ghosts naturally accumulated. In this country there are houses and places haunted by ghosts of Hessians, and Yankee ghosts, not to mention the headless Dutch phantom of Tarrytown, that turned out to be Brom Bones; but who ever heard of the ghost of an Indian? And as for the ghost of a black man, evidently it would have to appear by daylight. You couldn't see it in the dark!

I have no room to even enumerate the cases of haunted

houses. One in Aix-la-Chapelle, a fine large house, stood empty five years on account of the knockings in it, until it was sold for almost nothing, and the new owner (lucky man!) discovered that the ghost was a draft through a broken window that banged a loose door. An English gentleman once died, and his heir, in a day or two, heard of mysterious knockings which the frightened servants attributed to the defunct. He, however, investigated a little, and found that a rat in an old store room, was trying to get out of an old-fashioned box trap, and being able to lift the door only partly, it dropped again, constituting the ghost. Better pleased to find the rat than his father, the young man exterminated rat and phantom together.

A very ancient and impressive specimen of a haunted house was the palace of Vauvert, belonging to King Louis IX, of France, who was so pious that he was called Saint Louis. This fine building was so situated as to become very desirable, in the year 1259, to some monks. So there was forthwith horrid shriekings at night-times, red and green lights shone through the windows, and, finally, a large green ghost, with a white beard and a serpent's tail, came every midnight to a front window, and shook his fist, and howled at those who passed by. Everybody was frightened—King Louis, good simple soul! as well as the rest. Then the bold monks appearing at the nick of time, intimated that if the King would give them the palace, they would do up the ghost in short order. He did it, and was very thankful to them besides. They moved in, and sure enough, the ghost appeared no more. Why should he?

The ghosts of Woodstock are well known. How they tormented the Puritan Commissioners who came thither in

1649, to break up the place, and dispose of it for the benefit of the Commonwealth! The poor Puritans had a horrid time. A disembodied dog growled under their bed, and bit the bedclothes; something invisible walked all about; the chairs and tables danced; something threw the dishes about (like the Davenport "spirits;") put logs for the pillows; flung brick-bats up and down, without regard to heads; smashed the windows; threw pebbles in at the frightened commissioners; stuck a lot of pewter platters into their beds; ran away with their breeches; threw dirty water over them in bed; banged them over the head—until, after several weeks, the poor fellows gave it up, and ran away back to London. Many years afterward, it came out that all this was done by their clerk, who was secretly a royalist, though they thought him a furious Puritan, and who knew all the numerous secret passages and contrivances in the old palace. Most people have read Sir Walter Scott's capital novel of "Woodstock," founded on this very story.

The well known "Demon of Tedworth," that drummed, and scratched, and pounded, and threw things about, in 1661, in Mr. Mompesson's house turned out to be a gypsy drummer and confederates.

The still more famous "Ghost in Cock Lane," in London in 1762, consisted of a Mrs. Parsons and her daughter, a little girl, trained by Mr. Parsons to knock and scratch very much after the fashion of the alphabet talking of the "spirits" of today. Parsons got up the whole affair, to revenge himself on a Mr. Kent. The ghost pretended to be that of a deceased sister-in-law of Kent, and to have been poisoned by him. But Parsons and his assistants were found out, and had to smart for their fun, being heavily fined, imprisoned, etc.

A very able ghost indeed, a Methodist ghost—the spectral property, consequently, of my good friends the Methodists—used to rattle, and clatter, and bang, and communicate, in the house of the Rev. Mr. Wesley, the father of John Wesley, at Epworth, in England. This ghost was very troublesome, and utterly useless. In fact, none of the ghosts that haunt houses are of the least possible use. They plague people, but do no good. They act like the spirits of departed monkeys.

I must add two or three short anecdotes about ghosts, got up in the devil-manner. They are not new, but illustrate very handsomely the state of mind in which a ghost should be met. One is, that somebody undertook to scare Cuvier, the great naturalist, with a ghost having an ox's head. Cuvier woke, and found the fearful thing glaring and grinning at his bedside.

"What do you want?"

"To devour you!" growled the ghost.

"Devour me?" quoth the great Frenchman—Hoofs, horns, graminivorous! You can't do it—clear out!"

And he did clear out.

A pious maiden lady, in one of our New-England villages, was known to possess three peculiarities. First, she was a very religious, honest, matter-of-fact woman. Second, she supposed everybody else was equally honest; hence she was very credulous, always believing everything she heard. And third, having "a conscience void of offense," she saw no reason to be afraid of anything; consequently, she feared nothing.

On a dark night, some boys, knowing that she would be returning home alone from prayer-meeting, through an unfrequented street, determined to test two of her peculiarities, viz., her credulity and her courage. One of the boys was sewed up in a huge shaggy bearskin, and as the old lady's feet were heard pattering down the street, he threw himself directly in her path and commenced making a terrible noise.

"Mercy!" exclaimed the old lady. "Who are you?"

"I am the devil!" was the reply.

"Well, you are a poor creature!" responded the antiquated virgin, as she stepped aside and passed by the strange animal, probably not for a moment doubting it was his Satanic Majesty, but certainly not dreaming of being afraid of him.

It is said that a Yankee tin peddler, who had frequently cheated most of the people in the vicinity of a New England village through which he was passing, was induced by some of the acute ones to join them in a drinking bout. He finally became stone drunk; and in that condition these wags carried him to a dark rocky cave near the village, then, dressing themselves in raw-head-and-bloody-bones' style, awaited his return to consciousness.

As he began rousing himself, they lighted some huge torches, and also set fire to some bundles of straw, and three or four rolls of brimstone, which they had placed in different parts of the cavern. The peddler rubbed his eyes, and seeing and smelling all these evidences of pandemonium, concluded he had died, and was now partaking of his final doom. But he took it very philosophically, for he complacently remarked to himself.

"In hell—just as I expected!"

A story is told of a cool old sea captain, with a virago of a wife, who met one of these artificial devils in a lonely place. As the ghost obstructed his path, the old fellow remarked:

"If you are not the devil, get out! If you are, come along with me and get supper. I married your sister!"

Chapter 36

Magical humbugs—Virgil—A pickled sorcerer—Cornelius Agrippa—His students and his black dog—Doctor Faustus—Humbugging horse-jockeys—Ziito and his large swallow—Salamanca—Devil take the hindmost.

Magic, sorcery, witchcraft, enchantment, necromancy, conjuring, incantation, soothsaying, divining, the black art, are all one and the same humbug. They show how prone men are to believe in *some* supernatural power, in *some* beings wiser and stronger than themselves, but at the same time how they stop short, and find satisfaction in some debasing humbug, instead of looking above and beyond it all to God, the only being that it is really worth while for man to look up to or beseech.

Magic and witchcraft are believed in by the vast majority of mankind, and by immense numbers even in Christian countries. They have always been believed in, so far as I know. In following up the thread of history, we always find conjuring or witch work of some kind, just as long as the narrative has space enough to include it. Already, in the early dawn of time, the business was a recognized and long established one. And its history is as unbroken from that day down to this, as the history of the race.

In the narrow space at my command at present, I shall only gather as many of the more interesting stories about these humbugs, as I can make room for. Reasoning about the subject, or full details of it, are at present out of the question. A whole library of books exists about it.

It is a curious fact that throughout the middle ages, the Roman poet Virgil was commonly believed to have been a great magician. Traditions were recorded by monastic chroniclers about him, that he made a brass fly and mounted it over one of the gates of Naples, having instilled into this metallic insect such potent magical qualities that as long as it kept guard over the gate, no mosquitoes, or flies, or cockroach, or other troublesome insects could exist in the city. What would have become of the celebrated Bug Powder man in those days? The story is told about Virgil as well as about Albertus Magnus, Roger Bacon, and other magicians, that he made a brazen head which could prophesy. He also made some statues of the gods of the various nations subject to Rome, so enchanted that if one of those nations was preparing to rebel, the statue of its god rung a bell and pointed a finger toward the nation. The same set of stories tells how poor Virgil came to an untimely end in consequence of trying to live forever. He had become an old man, it appears, and wishing to be young again, he used some appropriate incantations, and prepared a secret cavern. In this he caused a confidential disciple to cut him up like a hog and pack him away in a barrel of pickle, out of which he was to emerge in his new magic youth after a certain time. But by that special bad luck which seems to attend such cases, some malapropos traveller somehow made his way into the cavern, where he found the magic pork-barrel standing silently all alone in the middle of the place, and an ever-burning lamp illuminating the room, and slowly distilling a magic oil upon the salted sorcerer who was cooking below. The traveller rudely jarred the barrel, the light went out, as the torches flared upon it; and suddenly there appeared to the eyes of the astounded man, close at one side of the barrel, a little naked child, which ran thrice around the barrel, uttering deep curses upon him who had thus destroyed the charm, and vanished. The frightened traveller made off as fast as he could, and poor old Virgil, for what I know, is in pickle yet.

Cornelius Agrippa was one of the most celebrated magicians of the middle ages. He lived from the year 1486 (six years before the discovery of America) until 1534, and was a native of Cologne, Agrippa is said to have had a magic glass in which he showed to his customers such dead or absent persons as they might wish to see. Thus he would call up the beautiful Helen of Troy, or Cicero in the midst of an oration; or to a pining lover, the figure of his absent lady, as she was employed at the moment—a dangerous exhibition! For who knows, whether the consolation sought by the fair one, will always be such as her lover will approve? Agrippa, they say, had an attendant devil in the form of a huge black dog, whom on his deathbed the magician dismissed with curses. The dog ran away, plunged into the river Saone and was seen no more. We are of course to suppose that his Satanic Majesty got possession of the conjuror's soul however, as per agreement. There is a story about Agrippa, which shows conclusively how "a little learning" may be "a dangerous thing." When Agrippa was absent on a short journey, his student in magic slipped into the study and began to read spells out of a great book. After a little there was a knock at the door, but the young man paid no attention to it. In another moment there was another louder one, which startled him, but still he read on. In a moment the door opened, and in came a fine large devil who angrily asked, "What do you call me for?" The frightened youth answered very much like those naughty boys who say "I didn't do nothing!" But it will not do to fool with devils. The angry demon caught him by the throat and strangled him. Shortly, when Agrippa returned, lo and behold, a strong squad of evil spirits were kicking up their heels and playing tag all over the house, and crowding his study particularly full. Like a schoolmaster among mischievous boys, the great enchanter sent all the little fellows home, catechised the big one, and finding the situation unpleasant, made him reanimate the corpse of the student and walk it about town all the afternoon. The malignant demon however, was free at sunset, and let the corpse drop dead in the middle of the market place. The people recognized it, found the claw-marks and traces of strangling, suspected the fact, and Agrippa had to abscond very suddenly.

Another student of Agrippa's came very near an equally bad end. The magician was in the habit of enchanting a broomstick into a servant to do his housework, and when it was done, turning it back to a broomstick again and putting it behind the door. This young student had overheard the charm which made the servant, and one day in his master's absence, wanting a pail of water he said over the incantation and told the servant "Bring some water." The evil spirit promptly obeyed; flew to the river, brought a pailful and emptied it, instantly brought a second, instantly a third; and the student, startled, cried out, "that's enough!" But this was not the "return charm," and the ill tempered demon, rejoicing in doing mischief within the letter of his obligation, now flew backward and forward like lightning, so that he even began to flood the room about the rash student's feet. Desperate, he seized an axe and hewed this diabolical serving-man in two. *Two* serving-men jumped up, with two water-pails, grinning in devilish glee, and both went to work harder than ever. The poor student gave himself up for lost, when luckily the master came home, dismissed the over-officious water carrier with a word, and saved the student's life.

How thoroughly false all these absurd fictions are, and yet how ingeniously based on some fact, appears by the case of Agrippa's black dog. Wierus, a writer of good authority, and a personal friend of Agrippa's, reports that he knew very well all about the dog; that it was not a superhuman dog at all, but (if the term be admissible) a mere human dog—an animal which he, Wierus, had often led about by a string, and only a domestic pet of Agrippa.

Another eminent magician of those days was Doctor Faustus, about whom Goethe wrote "Faust," Bailey wrote "Festus," and whose story, mingled of human love and of the devilish tricks of Mephistopheles, is known so very widely. The truth about Faust seems to be, that he was simply a successful juggler of the sixteenth century. Yet the wonderful stories about him were very implicitly and extensively believed. It was the time of the Protestant Reformation, and even Melanchthon and Luther seem to have entirely believed that Faustus could make the forms of the dead appear, could carry people invisibly through the air, and play all the legendary tricks of the enchanters. So strong a hold does humbug often obtain even upon the noblest and clearest and wisest minds!

Faustus, according to the traditions, had a pretty keen eye for a joke. He once sold a splendid horse to a horse-jockey at a fair. The fellow shortly rode his fine horse to water. When he got into the water, lo and behold, the horse vanished, and the humbugged jockey found himself sitting up to his neck in the river on a straw saddle. There is something quite satisfactory in the idea of playing such a trick on one of that sharp generation, and Faust felt so comfortable over it that he entered his hotel and went quietly to sleep—or pretended to. Shortly in came the angry jockey; he shouted and bawled, but could not awaken the doctor, and in his anger he seized his foot and gave it a good pull. Foot and leg came off in his hand. Faustus screamed out as if in horrible agony, and the terrified jockey ran away as fast as he could, and never troubled his very loose-jointed customer for the money.

A magician named Ziito, resident at the court of Wenceslaus of Bohemia (AD 1368 to 1419,) appears to great advantage in the annals of these humbugs. He was a homely, crooked creature, with an immense mouth. He had a collision once in public on a question of skill with a brother conjuror, and becoming a little excited, opened his big mouth and swallowed the other magician, all to his shoes, which as he observed were dirty. Then he stepped into a closet, got his rival out of him somehow, and calmly led him back to the company. A story is told about Ziito and some hogs, just like that about Faust and the horse.

In all these stories about magicians, their power is derived from the devil. It was long believed that the ancient university of Salamanca in Spain, founded AD 1240, was the chief school of magic, and had regular professors and classes in it. The devil was supposed to be the special patron of this department, and he had a curious fee for his trouble, which he collected every commencement day. The last exercise of the graduating class on that day was, to run across a certain cavern under the University. The devil was always on hand at this time, and had the privilege of grabbing at the last man of the crowd. If he caught him, as he commonly did, the soul of the unhappy student became the property of his captor. Hence arose the phrase "Devil take the hindmost." Sometime it happened that some very brisk fellow was left last by some accident. If he were brisk enough to dodge the devil's grab, that personage only caught his shadow. In this case it was well understood that this particular enchanter never had any shadow afterwards, and he always became very eminent in his art.

Chapter 37

Witchcraft—New York witches—The Witch mania—How fast they burned them—The mode of trial—Witches today in Europe.

Witchcraft is one of the most baseless, absurd, disgusting and silly of all the humbugs. And it is not a dead humbug either; it is alive, busily exercised by knaves and believed by fools all over the world. Witches and wizards operate and prosper among the Hottentots and negroes and barbarous Indians, among the Siberians and Kirgishes and Lapps, of course. Everybody knows *that*—they are poor ignorant creatures! Yes: but are the French and Germans and English and Americans poor ignorant creatures too? They are, if the belief and practice of witchcraft among them is any test; for in all those countries there are witches. I take up one of the New York City dailies of this very morning, and find in it the advertisements of seven Witches. In 1858, there were in full blast in New York and Brooklyn sixteen witches and two wizards. One of these wizards was a black man; a very proper style of person to deal with the black art.

Witch means, a woman who practices sorcery under an agreement with the devil, who helps her. Before the Christian era, the Jewish witch was a mere diviner or at most a raiser of the dead, and the Gentile witch was a poisoner, a maker of philtres or love potions, and a vulgar sort of magician. The devil part of the business did not begin until a good while after Christ. During the last century or so, again, while witchcraft has been extensively believed in, the witch has degenerated into a very vulgar and poverty stricken sort of conjuring woman. Take our New York city witches, for instance. They live in cheap and dirty streets that smell bad; their houses are in the same style, infected with a strong odor of cabbage, onions, washing-day, old dinners, and other merely sublunary smells. Their rooms are very ill furnished, and often beset with washtubs, swill-pails, mops and soiled clothes; their personal appearance is commonly unclean, homely, vulgar, coarse, and ignorant, and often rummy. Their fee is a quarter or half of a dollar. Sometimes a dollar. Their divination is worked by cutting and dealing cards or studying the palm of your hand. And the things which they tell you are the most silly and shallow babble in the world; a mess of phrases worn out over and over again. Here is a specimen, as gabbled to the customer over a pack of cards laid out on the table; anybody can do the like: "You face a misfortune. I think it will come upon you within three weeks, but it may not. A dark complexioned man faces your life-card. He is plotting against you, and you must beware of him. Your marriage-card faces two young women, one fair and the other dark. One you will have, and the other you will not. I think you will have the fair one. She favors the dark complexioned man, which means trouble. You face money, but you must earn it. There is a good deal, but you may not get much of it" etc., etc. These words are exactly the sort of stuff that is sold by the witches of today. But the greatest witch humbug of all the witchcraft of history, is that of Christendom for about three hundred years, beginning about the time of the discovery of America. To that period belonged the Salem witchcraft of New England, the witch-finding of Matthew Hopkins in Old England, the Scotch witch trials, and the Swedish and German and French witch mania.

The peculiar traits of the witchcraft of this period are among the most mysterious of all humbugs. The most usual points in a case of witchcraft were, that the witch had sold herself to the devil for all eternity, in order to get the power during a few years of earthly life, to inflict a few pains on the persons of those she disliked, or to cause them to lose part of their property. This was almost always the whole story, except the mere details of the witch baptism and witch sabbath, parodies on the ceremonies of the Christian religion. And the mystery is, how anybody could believe that to accomplish such very small results, seldom equal even to the death of an enemy, one would agree to accept eternal damnation in the next world, almost certain poverty, misery, persecution and torment in this, besides having for an amusement performances more dirty, obscene and vulgar than I can even hint at.

But such a belief was universal, and hundreds of the witches themselves confessed as much as I have described, and more, with numerous details, and they were burnt alive for their trouble. The extent of wholesale murdering perpetrated under forms of law, on charges of witchcraft, is astonishing. A magistrate named Remigius, published a book in which he told how much he thought of himself for having condemned and burned nine hundred witches in sixteen years, in Lorraine. And the one thing that he blamed himself for was this: that out of regard for the wishes of a colleague, he had only caused certain children to be whipped naked three times round the market place where their parents had been burned, instead of burning them. At Bamberg, six hundred persons were burned in five years, at Wurzburg nine hundred in two years. Sprenger, a German inquisitor-general, and author of a celebrated book on detecting and punishing witchcraft, called *Malleus Maleficarum*, or "The Mallet of Malefactors," burned more than five hundred in one year. In Geneva, five hundred persons were burned during 1515 and 1516. In the district of Como in Italy, a thousand persons were burned as witches in the single year 1524, besides over a hundred a year for several years afterwards. *Seventeen thousand* persons were executed for witchcraft in Scotland during thirty-nine years, ending with 1603. *Forty thousand* were executed in England from 1600 to 1680. Bodinus, another of the witch killing judges, gravely announced that there were undoubtedly not less than three hundred thousand witches in France.

The way in which the witch murderers reasoned, and their modes of conducting trials and procuring confessions, were truly infernal. The chief rule was that witchcraft being an "exceptional crime," no regard need be had to the ordinary forms of justice. All manner of tortures were freely applied to force confessions. In Scotland "the boot" was used, being an iron case in which the legs are locked up to the knees, and an iron wedge then driven in until sometimes the bones were crushed and the marrow spouted out. Pin sticking, drowning, starving, the rack, were too common to need details. Sometimes the prisoner was hung up by the thumbs, and whipped by one person, while another held lighted candles to the feet and other parts of the body. At Arras, while the prisoners were being torn on the rack, the executioner stood by, sword in hand, promising to cut off at once the heads of those who did not confess. At Offenburg, when the prisoners had been tortured until beyond the power of speaking aloud, they silently assented to abominable confessions read to them out of a book. Many were cheated into confession by the promise of pardon and release, and then burned. A poor woman in Germany was tricked by the hangman, who dressed himself up as a devil and went into her cell. Overpowered by pain, fear and superstition, she begged him to help her out; her beseeching was taken for confession, she was burned, and a ballad which treated the trick as a jolly and comical device, was long popular in the country. Several of the judges in witch cases tell us how victims, utterly weary of their tormented lives, confessed whatever was required, merely as the shortest way to death, and an escape out of their misery. All who dared to argue against the current of popular and judicial delusion were instantly refuted very effectively by being attacked for witchcraft themselves; and once accused, there was little hope of escape. The Jesuit Delrio, in a book published in 1599, states the witch killers' side of the discussion very neatly indeed; for in one and the same chapter he defies any opponents to disprove the existence of witchcraft, and then shows that a denial of witchcraft is the worst of all heresies, and must be punished with death. Quite a number of excellent and sensible people were actually burnt on just this principle.

I do not undertake to give details of any witch trials; this sketch of the way in which they operated is all I can make room for, and sufficiently delineates this cruel and bloody humbug.

I have already referred to the fact that we have right here among us in this city a very fair supply of a vulgar, dowdy kind of witchcraft. Other countries are favored in like manner. I have not just now the most recent information, but in the year 1857 and 1858, for instance, mobbing and prosecutions growing out of a popular belief in witchcraft were quite plentiful enough in various parts of Europe. No less than eight cases of the kind in England alone were reported during those two years. Among them was the actual murder of a woman as a witch by a mob in Shropshire; and an attack by another mob in Essex, upon a perfectly inoffensive person, on suspicion of having "bewitched" a scolding ill-conditioned girl, from which attack the mob was diverted with much difficulty, and thinking itself very unjustly treated. Some others of those cases show a singular quantity of credulity among people of respectability.

While therefore some of us may perhaps be justly thankful for safety from such horrible follies as these, still we can not properly feel very proud of the progress of humanity, since after not less than six thousand years of existence and eighteen hundred of revelation, so many believers in witchcraft still exist among the most civilized nations.

Chapter 38

Charms and incantations—How Cato cured sprains—The secret name of God—Secret names of cities—Abracadabra—Cures for cramp—Mr. Wright's sigil—Whiskerifusticus—Witches' horses—Their curses—How to raise the devil.

It is worth while to print in plain English for my readers a good selection of the very words which have been believed, or are still believed, to possess magic power. Then any who choose, may operate by themselves or may put some bold friend up in a corner, and blaze away at him or her until they are wholly satisfied about the power of magic.

The Roman Cato, so famous for his grumness and virtue, believed that if he were ill, it would much help him, and that it would cure sprains in others, to say over these words: "Daries, dardaries, astaris, ista, pista, sista," or, as another account has it, "motas, daries, dardaries, astaries;" or, as still another account says, "Huat, huat, huat; ista, pista, sista; domiabo, damnaustra." And sure enough, nothing is truer, as any physician will tell you, that if the old censor only believed hard enough, it would almost certainly help him; not by the force of the words, but by the force of his own ancient Roman imagination. Here are some Greek words of no less virtue: *"Aski, Kataski, Tetrax."* When the Greek priests let out of their doors those who had been completely initiated in the Eleusinian mysteries, they said to them last of all the awful and powerful words, *"Konx, ompax."* If you want to know what the usual result was, just say them to somebody, and you will see, instantly. The ancient Hebrews believed that there was a secret name of God, usually thought to be inexpressible, and only to be represented by a mystic figure kept in the Temple, and that if anyone could learn it, and repeat it, he could rule the intelligent and unintelligent creation at his will. It is supposed by some, that Jehovah is the word which stands for this secret name; and some Hebraists think that the word "Yahveh" is much more nearly the right one. The Mohammedans, who have received many notions from the Jews, believe the same story about the secret name of God, and they think it was engraved on Solomon's signet, as all readers of the Arabian Nights will very well remember. The Jews believed that if you pronounced the word "Satan" any evil spirit that happened to be by could in consequence instantly pop into you if he wished, and possess you, as the devils in the New Testament possessed people.

Some ancient cities had a secret name, and it was believed that if their enemies could find this out, they could conjure with it so as to destroy such cities. Thus, the secret name of Rome was Valentia, and the word was very carefully kept, with the intention that none should know it except one or two of the chief pontiffs. Mr. Borrow, in one of his books, tells about a charm which a gypsy woman knew, and which she used to repeat to herself as a means of obtaining supernatural aid when she happened to want it. This was, *"Saboca enrecar maria ereria."* He induced her after much effort to repeat the words to him, but she always wished she had not, with an evident conviction that some harm would result. He explained to her that they consisted of a very simple phrase, but it made no difference.

An ancient physician named Serenus Sammonicus, used to be quite sure of curing fevers, by means of what he called Abracadabra, which was a sort of inscription to be written on something and worn on the patient's person. It was as follows:

ABRACADABRA
BRACADABR
RACADAB
ACADA
CAD
A.

Another gentleman of the same school used to cure sore eyes by hanging round the patient's neck an inscription made up of only two letters, A and Z; but how he mixed them we unfortunately do not know.

By the way, many of the German peasantry in the more ignorant districts still believe that to write Abracadabra on a slip of paper and keep it with you, will protect you from wounds, and that if your house is on fire, to throw this strip into it will put the fire out.

Many charms or incantations call on God, Christ or some saints, just as the heathen ones call on a spirit. Here is one for epilepsy that seems to appeal to both religions, as if with a queer proviso against any possible mistake about either. Taking the epileptic by the hand, you whisper in his ear "I adjure thee by the sun and the moon and the gospel of today, that thou arise and no more fall to the ground; in the name of the Father, Son and Holy Ghost."

A charm for the cramp found in vogue in some rustic regions is this:

> "The devil is tying a knot in my leg,
> Mark, Luke and John, unloose it, I beg,
> Crosses three we make to ease us—
> Two for the thieves, and one for Christ Jesus."

Here is another, often used in Ireland, which in the same spirit of superstition and ignorant irreverence uses the name of the Savior for a slight human occasion. It is to cure the toothache, and requires the repeating of the following string of words:

"St. Peter sitting on a marble stone, our Savior passing by, asked him what was the matter. 'Oh Lord, a toothache!' Stand up, Peter, and follow me; and whoever keeps these words in memory of me, shall never be troubled with a toothache, Amen."

The English astrologer Lilly, after the death of his wife, formerly a Mrs. Wright, found in a scarlet bag which she wore under her arm a pure gold "sigil" or round plate worth about ten dollars in gold, which the former husband of the defunct had used to exorcise a spirit that plagued him. In case any of my readers can afford bullion enough, and would like to drive away any such visitor, let them get such a plate and have engraved round the edge of one side, *"Vicit Leo de tribus Judae tetragrammaton."* Inside this engrave a "holy lamb." Round the edge of the other side engrave "Annaphel" and three crosses; and in the middle, *"Sanctus Petrus Alpha et Omega."*

The witches have always had incantations, which they have used to make a broomstick into a horse, to kill or to sicken animals and persons, etc. Most of these are sufficiently stupid, and not half so wonderful as one I know, which may be found in a certain mysterious volume called *The Girl's Own Book*, and which, as I can depose, has often power to tickle children. It is this:

"Bandy-legged Borachio Mustachio Whiskerifusticus, the bald and brave Bombardino of Bagdad, helped Abomilique Bluebeard Bashaw of Babelmandel beat down an abominable bumblebee at Balsora."

But to the other witches. Their charms were repeated sometimes in their own language and sometimes in gibberish. When the Scotch witches wanted to fly away to their "Witches' Sabbath," they straddled a broom-handle, a corn stalk, a straw, or a rush, and cried out "Horse and hattock, in the Devil's name!" and immediately away they flew, "forty times as high as the moon," if they wished. Some English witches in Somersetshire used instead to say, "Thout, tout, throughout and about;" and when they wished to return from their meeting they said *"Rentum, tormentum!"* If this form of the charm does not manufacture a horse, not even a sawhorse, then I recommend another version of it, thus:

"Horse and pattock, horse and go!
Horse and pellats, ho, ho, ho!"

German witches said (in High Dutch:)

"Up and away!
Hi! Up aloft, and nowhere stay!"

Scotch witches had modes of working destruction to the persons or property of those to whom they meant evil, which were strikingly like the negro obeah or mandinga. One of these was, to make a hash of the flesh of an unbaptised child, with that of dogs and sheep, and to put this goodly dish in the house of the victim, reciting the following rhyme:

"We put this until this hame
In our Lord the Devil's name;
The first hands that handle thee.
Burned and scalded may they be!
We will destroy houses and hald,
With the sheep and nolt (i.e. cattle) into the fauld;
And little shall come to the fore (i.e. remain,)
Of all the rest of the little store."

Another, used to destroy the sons of a certain gentleman named Gordon was, to make images for the boys, of clay and paste, and put them in a fire, saying:

"We put this water among this meal
For long pining and ill heal,
We put it into the fire
To burn them up stock and stour (i.e. stack and band.)
That they be burned with our will,
Like any stikkle (stubble) in a kiln."

In case any lady reader finds herself changed into a hare,

let her remember how the witch Isobel Gowdie changed herself from hare back to woman. It was by repeating:

> "Hare, hare, God send thee care!
> I am in a hare's likeness now;
> But I shall be woman even now—
> Hare, hare, God send thee care!"

About the year 1600 there was both hanged and burned at Amsterdam a poor demented Dutch girl, who alleged that she could make cattle sterile, and bewitch pigs and poultry by saying to them *"Turius und Shurius Inturius."* I recommend to say this first to an old hen, and if found useful it might then be tried on a pig.

Not far from the same time a woman was executed as a witch at Bamberg, having, as was often the case, been forced by torture to make a confession. She said that the devil had given her power to send diseases upon those she hated, by saying complimentary things about them, as "What a strong man!" "what a beautiful woman!" "what a sweet child!" It is my own impression that this species of cursing may safely be tried where it does not include a falsehood.

Here are two charms which the German witches used to repeat to raise the devil with in the form of a he goat:

> "Lalle, Bachea, Magotte, Baphia, Dajam,
> Vagoth Heneche Ammi Nagaz, Adomator
> Raphael Immanuel Christus, Tetragrammaton
> Agra Jod Loi. Konig! Konig!"

The two last words to be screamed out quickly. This second

one, it must be remembered, is to be read backward except the two last words. It was supposed to be the strongest of all, and was used if the first one failed:

"Anion, Lalle, Sabolos, Sado, Poter, Aziel,
Adonai Sado Vagoth Agra, Jod,
Baphra! Komm! Komm!"

In case the devil stayed too long, he could be made to take himself off by addressing to him the following statement, repeated backward:

"Zellianelle Heotti Bonus Vagotha
Plisos sother osech unicus Beelzebub
Dax! Komm! Komm!"

Which would evidently make almost anybody go away.

A German charm to improve one's finances was perhaps no worse than gambling in gold. It ran thus:

"As God be welcomed, gentle moon—
Make thou my money more and soon!"

To get rid of a fever in the German manner, go and tie up a bough of a tree, saying, "Twig, I bind thee; fever, now leave me!" To give your ague to a willow tree, tie three knots in a branch of it early in the morning, and say, "Good morning, old one! I give thee the cold; good morning, old one!" and turn and run away as fast as you can without looking back.

Enough of this nonsense. It is pure mummery. Yet it is worth while to know exactly what the means were which in ancient times were relied on for such purposes, and it is not useless to put this matter on record; for just such formulas are believed in now by many people. Even in this city there are "witches" who humbug the more foolish part of the community out of their money by means just as foolish as these.

Part VIII

ADVENTURERS

Chapter 39

The Princess Cariboo; or, The Queen Of The Isles.

Bristol was, in 1812, the second commercial city of Great Britain, having in particular an extensive East India trade. Among its inhabitants were merchants, reckoned remarkably shrewd, and many of them very wealthy; and quite a number of aristocratic families, who were looked up to with the abject toad-eating kind of civility that follows "the nobility." On the whole, Bristol was a very fashionable, rich, cultivated, and intelligent place—considering.

One fine evening in the winter of 1812–13, the White Lion hotel, a leading inn at Bristol, was thrown into a wonderful flutter by the announcement that a very beautiful and fabulously wealthy lady, the Princess Cariboo, had just arrived by ship from an oriental port. Her agent, a swarthy and wizened little Asiatic, who spoke imperfect English, gave this information, and ordered the most sumptuous suite of rooms in the house. Of course, there was great activity in all manner of preparations; and the mysterious character of this lovely but highborn stranger caused a wonderful flutter of excitement, which grew and grew until the fair stranger at length deigned to arrive. She came at about ten o'clock, in great state, and with two or three coaches packed with servants and luggage—the former of singularly dingy complexion and fantastic vestments, and the latter of the most curious forms and material imaginable. The eager anticipations of hosts and guests alike were not only fully justified but even exceeded by the rare beauty of the unknown, the oriental style and magnificence of her attire and that of her attendants, and the enormous bulk of her baggage—a circumstance that has no less weight at an English inn than anywhere else. The stranger, too, was most liberal with her fees to the servants, which were always in gold.

It was quickly discovered that her ladyship spoke not one word of English, and even her agent—a dark, wild, queer little fellow—got along with it but indifferently, preferring all his requests in very "broken China" indeed. The landlord thought it a splendid opportunity to create a long bill, and got up rooms and a dinner in flaring style, with wax candles, a mob of waiters, ringing of bells, and immense ceremony. But the lady, like a real princess, while well enough pleased and very gracious, took all this as a matter of course, and preferred her own cook, a flat-faced, pug-nosed, yellow-breeched and almond-eyed Oriental, with a pigtail dangling from his scalp, which was shaved clean, excepting at the back of the head. This gentleman ran about in the kitchen-yard with queer little brass utensils, wherein he concocted sundry diabolical preparations—as they seemed to the English servants to be—of herbs, rice, curry powder, etc., etc., for the repast of his mistress. For the next three or four days, the White Lion was in a state bordering upon frenzy, at the singular deportment of the "Princess" and her numerous attendants. The former arrayed herself in the most astonishing combinations of apparel that had ever been seen by the good gossips of Bristol, and the latter indulged in gymnastic antics and vocal chantings that almost deafened the neighborhood. There was a peculiar nasal ballad in which they were fond of indulging, that commenced about midnight and kept up until well nigh morning, that drove the neighbors almost beside themselves. It sounded like a concert by a committee of infuriated cats, and wound up with protracted whining notes, commencing in a whimper, and then with a sudden jerk, bursting into a loud, monotonous howl. Yet, withal, these attendants, who slept on mats, in the rooms adjacent to that of their mistress, and fed upon the preparations of her own cuisine, were, in the main, very civil and inoffensive, and seemed to look upon the Princess with the utmost awe. The "agent," or "secretary," or "prime-minister," or whatever he might be called, was very mysterious as to the objects, purposes, history, and antecedents of her Highness, and the quidnuncs were in despair until, one morning, the *Bristol Mirror*, then a leading paper, came out with a flaring announcement, expressing the pleasure it felt in acquainting the public with the fact, that a very eminent and interesting foreign personage had arrived from her home in the remotest East to proffer His Majesty, George III, the unobstructed commerce and friendship of her realm, which was as remarkable for its untold wealth as for its marvelous beauty. The lady was described as a befitting representative of the loveliness and opulence of this new Golconda and Ophir in one, since her matchless wealth and munificence were approached only by her ravishing personal charms. The other papers took up the topic, and were even more extravagant. *Felix Farley's Journal* gave a long narrative of her wanderings and extraordinary adventures in the uttermost East, as gleaned, of course, from her garrulous agent. The island of her chief residence was described as being of vast extent and fertility, immensely rich and populous, and possessing many rare and beautiful arts unknown to the nations of Europe. The princess had become desperately enamored of a certain young Englishman of high rank, who had been shipwrecked on her coast, but had afterward escaped, and as she learned, safely reached a port in China, and thence departed for Europe. The Princess had hereupon set out upon her journeyings over the world in search of him. In order to facilitate her enterprise, and softened by the deep affection she felt for the son of Albion, she had determined to break through the usages of her country, and form an alliance with that of her beloved.

Such were the statements everywhere put in circulation; and when the Longbows of the place got full hold of it, Gulliver, Peter Wilkins, and Sinbad the Sailor were completely eclipsed. Diamonds as big as hen's eggs, and pearls the size of hazelnuts, were said to be the commonest buttons and ornaments the Princess wore, and her silks and shawls were set beyond all price.

The announcement of this romantic and mysterious history, this boundless wealth, this interesting mission from majesty to majesty in person and the reality which everyone could see of so much grace and beauty, supplied all that was wanting to set the upper-tendom of the place in a blaze. It was hardly etiquette for a royal visitor to receive much company before having been presented at Court; but as this princely lady came from a point so far outside of the pale of Christendom, and all its formalities, it was deemed not out of place, to show her befitting attentions; and the ice once broken, there was no arresting the flood. The aristocracy of

Bristol vied with each other in seeing who should be first and most extravagant in their demonstrations. The street in front of the "White Lion" was day after day blocked up, with elegant equipages, and her reception-rooms thronged with "fair women and brave men." Milliners and mantuamakers pressed upon the lovely and mysterious Princess Cariboo the most exquisite hats, dresses, and laces, just to acquaint her with the fashionable style and solicit her distinguished patronage; dry-goodsmen sent her rare patterns of their costliest and richest stuffs, perfumers their most exquisite toilet-cases, filled with odors sweet; jewellers, their most superb sets of gems; and florists and visitors nearly suffocated her with the scarcest and most delicate exotics. Pictures, sketches, and engravings, oil-paintings, and portraits on ivory of her rapturous admirers, poured in from all sides, and her own fine form and features were reproduced by a score of artists. Daily she was fêted, and nightly serenaded, until the Princess Cariboo became the furore of the United Kingdom. Magnificent entertainments were given her in private mansions; and at length, to cap the climax, Mr. Worrall, the Recorder of Bristol, managed, by his influence, to bring about for her a grand municipal reception in the town-hall, and people from far and near thronged to it in thousands.

In the meantime the papers were gravely trying to make out whether the Cariboo country meant some remote portion of Japan, or the Island of Borneo, or some comparatively unfamiliar archipelago in the remotest East, and the *Mirror* was publishing type expressly cut for the purpose of representing the characters of the language in which the Princess spoke and wrote. They were certainly very uncouth, and pretended sages, who knew very well that there was no one to contradict them, declared that they were "ancient Coptic!"

Upon reading the sequel of the story, one is irresistibly reminded of the ancient Roman inscription discovered by one of Dickens' characters, which some irreverent rogue subsequently declared to be nothing more nor less than "Bil Stumps His Mark."

All this went on for about a fortnight, until the whole town and a good deal of the surrounding country had made complete fools of themselves, and only the "naughty little boys" in the streets held out against the prevailing mania, probably because they were not admitted to the sport. Their salutations took the form of an inharmonious thoroughfare-ballad, the chorus of which terminated with:

"Boo! hoo! hoo!
And who's the Princess Cariboo?"

yelled out at the top of their voices.

At length one day, the luggage of her Highness was embarked upon a small vessel to be taken round by water to London, while she announced, through her "agent," her intention to reach the capital by post-coaching.

Of course, the most superb traveling-carriages and teams were placed at her disposal; but, courteously declining all these offers, she set out in the nighttime with a hired establishment, attended by her retinue.

Days and weeks rolled on, and yet no announcement came of the arrival of her Highness at London or at any of the intervening cities after the first two or three towns eastward of Bristol. Inquiry began to be made, and, after long and patient but unavailing search, it became apparent to divers and sundry dignitaries in the old town that somebody had been very particularly "sold."

The landlord at the "White Lion" who had accepted the agent's order for £1,000 on a Calcutta firm in London; poor Mr. Worrall, who had been Master of Ceremonies at the town hall affair, and had spent large sums of money; and the tradespeople and others who sent their finest goods, all felt that they had "heard something drop." The Princess Cariboo had disappeared as mysteriously as she came.

For years, the people of Bristol were unmercifully ridiculed throughout the entire Kingdom on account of this affair, and burlesque songs and plays immortalized its incidents for successive seasons.

One of these insisted that the Princess was no other than an actress of more notoriety than note, humbly born in the immediate vicinity of the old city, where she practiced this gigantic hoax, and that she had been assisted in it by a set of dissolute young noblemen and actors, who furnished the money she had spent, got up the oriental dresses, published the fibs, and fomented the excitement. At all events, the net profit to her and her confederates in the affair must have been some £10,000.

Within a few months, and since the first publication of the above paragraphs, the English newspapers have recorded the death of the "Princess Cariboo," who it appears afterward married in her own rank in life and spent a considerable number of years of usefulness in the leech trade—an occupation not without a metaphorical likeness to her early and more ambitious exploit.

Chapter 40

Count Cagliostro, alias Joseph Balsamo, known also as "Cursed Joe."

One of the most striking, amusing, and instructive pages in the history of humbug is the life of Count Alessandro di Cagliostro, whose real name was Joseph or Giuseppe Balsamo. He was born at Palermo, in 1743, and very early began to manifest his brilliant talents for roguery.

He ran away from his first boarding-school, at the age of eleven or twelve, getting up a masquerade of goblins, by the aid of some scampish schoolfellows, which frightened the monkish watchmen of the gates away from their posts, nearly dead with terror. He had gained little at this school, except the pleasant surname of Beppo Maldetto (or cursed Joe.) At the age of thirteen he was a second time expelled from the convent of Cartegirone, belonging to the order of Benfratelli, the good fathers having in vain endeavored to train him up in the way he should go.

While in this convent, the boy was in charge of the apothecary, and probably picked up more or less of the smattering of chemistry and physics which he afterwards used. His final offense was a ridiculous and characteristic one. He was a greedy and thievish fellow, and was by way of penalty set to read aloud about the ancient martyrs, those dry though pious old gentlemen, while the monks ate dinner. Thus put to what he liked least, and deprived of what he liked best, he impudently extemporized, instead of the stories of holy agonies, all the indecorous scandal he could think of about the more notorious disreputable women of Palermo, putting their names instead of those of the martyrs.

After this, Master Joe proceeded to distinguish himself by forging opera-tickets, and even documents of various kinds, indiscriminate pilfering and swindling, interpreting visions, conjuring, and finally, it is declared, a touch of genuine assassination.

Pretty soon he made a foolish, greedy goldsmith, one Marano, believe that there was a treasure hidden in the sand on the seashore near Palermo, and induced the silly man to go one night to dig it up. Having reached the spot, the dupe was made to strip himself to his shirt and drawers, a magic circle was drawn round him with all sorts of raw-head and bloody-bones ceremonies, and Beppo, exhorting him not to leave the ring, lest the spirits should kill him, stepped out of sight to make the incantations to raise them. Almost instantly, six devils, horned, hoofed, tailed, and clawed, breathing fire and smoke, leaped from among the rocks and beat the wretched goldsmith senseless, and almost to death. They were of course Cursed Joe and some confederates; and taking Marano's money and valuables, they left him. He got home in wretched plight, but had sense enough left to suspect Master Joe, whom he shortly promised, after the Sicilian manner, to assassinate. So Joe ran away from Palermo, and went to Messina. Here he said he fell in with a venerable humbug, named Athlotas, an "Armenian Sage," who united his talents

with Beppo's own, in making a peculiar preparation of flax
and hemp and passing it off upon the people of Alexandria,
in Egypt, as a new kind of silk. This feat made not only a
sensation but plenty of money; and the two swindlers now
traversed Greece, Turkey, and Arabia, in various directions,
stirring up the Oriental "old fogies" in amazing style. Harems
and palaces, according to Cagliostro's own apocryphal story,
were thrown open to them everywhere, and while the Sharif
of Mecuca took Balsao under his high protection, one of
the Grand Muftis actually gave him splendid apartments
in his own abode. It is only necessary to reflect upon the
unbounded reverence felt by all good Mussulmen for these
exalted dignitaries, to comprehend the height of distinction
thus attained by the Palermo thimble-rigger. But, among
the many obscure records that exist in the Italian, French,
and German languages, touching this arch impostor, there
is a hint of a night adventure in the harem of a high and
mighty personage, at Mecca, whereby the latter was put out
of doors, with his robes torn and his beard singed, by his own
domestics, and left to wander in the streets, while Beppo,
in disguise, received the salaams and sequins of the establishment, including the attentions of the fair ones therein
caged, for an entire night. His escape to the seacoast after
this adventure was almost miraculous; but escape he did,
and shortly afterward turned up in Rome, with the title
(conferred by himself) of Count Cagliostro, the reputation
of enormous wealth, and genuine and enthusiastic letters of
recommendation from Pinto, Grand Master of the Knights of
Malta. Pinto was an alchemist, and had been fooled to the
top of his bent by the cunning Joseph.

These letters introduced our humbug into the first families

of Rome; who, like some other first families, were first also as fools. He also married a very beautiful, very shrewd, and very wicked Roman donzella, Lorenza Feliciani by name; and the worthy couple, combining their various talents, and regarding the world as their oyster, at once proceeded to open it in the most scientific style. I cannot follow this wonderful human chameleon in all his transformations under his various names of Fischio, Melissa, Fenice, Anna, Pellegrini, Harat, and Belmonte, nor state the studies and processes by which he picked up sufficient knowledge of physic, chemistry, the hidden properties of numbers, astronomy, astrology, mesmerism, clairvoyance, and the genuine old-fashioned "black art;" but suffice it to say, that he travelled through every part of Europe, and set it in a blaze with excitement.

There were always enough of silly coxcombs, young and old, of high degree, to be allured by the siren smiles of his "Countess;" and dupes of both sexes everywhere, to swallow his yarns and gape at his juggleries. In the course of his rambles, he paid a visit to his great brother humbug, the Count of St. Germain, in Westphalia, or Schleswig, and it was not long afterward that he began to publish to the world his grand discoveries in Alchemy, of the Philosopher's Stone, and the Elixir of Life, or Waters of Perpetual Youth. These and many similar wonders were declared to be the result of his investigations under the Arch of Old Egyptian Masonry, which degree he claimed to have revived. This notion of Egyptian Masonry, Cagliostro is said to have found in some manuscripts left by one George Cofton, which fell into our quack's hands. This degree was to give perfection to human beings, by means of moral and physical regeneration. Of these two the former was to be secured by means of a Pentagon, which removes original sin and renews pristine innocence. The physical kind of regeneration was to be brought about by using the "prime matter" or philosopher's stone, and the "Acacia," which two ingredients will give immortal youth. In this new structure, he assumed the title of the "Grand Cophta" and actually claimed the worship of his followers; declaring that the institution had been established by Enoch and Elias, and that he had been summoned by "spiritual" agencies to restore it to its pristine glory. In fact, this pretension, which influenced thousands upon thousands of believers, was one of the most daring impostures that ever saw the light; and it is astounding to think that, so late as 1780, it should, for a long time, have been entirely successful. The preparatory course of exercises for admission to the mystic brotherhood has been described as a series of "purgation, starvation, and desperation," lasting for forty days! and ending in "physical regeneration" and an immortality on Earth. The celebrated Lavater, a mild and genial, but feeble man, became one of Cagliostro's disciples, and was bamboozled to his heart's content—in fact, made to believe that the Count could put the devil into him, or take him out, as the case might be.

The wondrous "Water of Beauty," that made old wrinkled faces look young, smooth, and blooming again, was the special merchandise of the Countess, and was, of course, in great request among the faded beaux and dowagers of the day, who were easily persuaded of their own restored loveliness. The transmutation of baser metals into gold usually terminated in the transmigration of all the gold his victims had into the Count's own purse.

In 1776, the Count and Countess came to London. Here, funnily enough, they fell into the hands of a gambler, a shyster, and a female scamp, who together tormented them almost to death, because the Count would not pick them out lucky numbers to gamble by. They persecuted him fairly into jail, and plagued and outswindled him so awfully, that, after a time, the poor Count sneaked back to the Continent with only fifty pounds left out of three thousand which he had brought with him.

One incident of Cagliostro's English experience was the affair of the "Arsenical Pigs"—a notice of which may be found in the "Public Advertiser," of London of September 3, 1786. A Frenchman named Morande, was at that time editing there a paper in his own language, entitled *Le Courrier de l'Europe*, and lost no opportunity to denounce the Count as a humbug. Cagliostro, at length, irritated by these repeated attacks, published in the *Advertiser* an open challenge, offering to forfeit five thousand guineas if Morande should not be found dead in his bed on the morning after partaking of the flesh of a pig, to be selected by himself from among a drove fattened by the Count—the cooking, etc., all to be done at Morande's own house, and under his own eye. The time was fixed for this singular repast, but when it came round, the French Editor "backed down" completely, to the great delight of his opponent and his credulous followers.

Cagliostro and his spouse now resumed their travels upon the Continent, and, by their usual arts and trades, in a great measure renewed their fallen fortunes. Among other new dodges, he now assumed so supernatural a piety that (he said) he could distinguish an unbeliever by the smell! which, of course, was just the opposite of the "odor of sanctity." The Count's claim to have lived for hundreds of years was, by some, thoroughly believed. He ascribed his immortality to his own Elixir, and his comparatively youthful appearance to his "Water of Beauty," his Countess readily assisting him by speaking of her son, a Colonel in the Dutch service, fifty years old, while she appeared scarcely more than twenty.

At length, in Rome, he and the Countess fell into the clutches of the Holy Office; and both having been tried for their manifold offenses against the Church, were found guilty, and, in spite of their contrition and eager confessions, immured for life; the Count within the walls of the Castle of Sante Leone, in the Duchy of Urbino, where, after eight years' imprisonment, he died in 1795, and the Countess in a suburban convent, where she died some time after.

The portraits of Cagliostro, of which a number are extant, are pictures of a strong-built, bull-necked, fat, gross man, with a snub nose, a vulgar face, a look of sensuality and low hypocritical cunning.

The celebrated story of "The Diamond Necklace," in which Cagliostro, Marie Antoinette, the Cardinal de Rohan, and others were mixed in such a hodgepodge of rascality and folly, must form a narrative by itself.

Chapter 41

The diamond necklace.

In my sketch of Joseph Balsamo, alias the Count Alessandro de Cagliostro, I referred to the affair of the diamond necklace, known in French history as the *Collier de la Reine*, or Queen's necklace, from the manner in which the name and reputation of Marie Antoinette, the consort of Louis XVI, became entangled in it. I shall now give a brief account of this celebrated imposition—perhaps the boldest and shrewdest ever known, and almost wholly the work of a woman.

On the Quai de la Ferraille, not far from the Pont Neuf, stood the establishment, part shop, part manufactory, of Messrs. Boehmer & Bassange, the most celebrated jewelers of their day. After triumphs which had given them worldwide fame during the reign of Louis XV, and made them fabulously rich, they determined, with the advent of Louis XVI, to eclipse all their former efforts and crown the professional glory of their lives. Their correspondents in every chief jewel market of the world were summoned to aid their enterprise, and in the course of some two or three years they succeeded in collecting the finest and most remarkable diamonds that could be procured in the whole world of commerce.

The next idea was to combine all these superb fragments in

one grand ornament to grace the form of beauty. A necklace was the article fixed upon, and the best experience and most delicate taste that Europe could boast were expended on the design. Each and every diamond was specially set and faced in such manner as to reveal its excellence to the utmost advantage, and all were arranged together in the style best calculated to harmonize their united effect. Form, shape, and the minutest shades of color were studied, and the result, after many attempts and many failures, and the anxious labor of many months, was the most exquisite triumph that the genius of the lapidary and the goldsmith could conceive.

The whole necklace consisted of three triple rows of diamonds, or nine rows in all, containing eight hundred faultless gems. The triple rows fell away from each in the most graceful and flexible curves over each side of the breast and each shoulder of the wearer, the curves starting from the throat, whence a magnificent pendant, depending from a single knot of diamonds, each as large as a hazelnut, hung down halfway upon the bosom in the design of a cross and crown, surrounded by the lilies of the royal house—the lilies themselves dangling on stems which were strung with smaller jewels. Rich clusters and festoons spread from the loop over each shoulder, and the central loop on the back of the neck was joined in a pattern of emblematic magnificence corresponding with that in front.

It was in 1782 that this grand work was finally completed, and the happy owners gloated with delight over a monument of skill as matchless in its way as the Pyramids themselves. But, alas! the necklace might as well have been constructed of the common boulders piled in those same pyramids as of the finest jewels of the mine, for all the good it seemed destined to bring the poor jewelers, beyond the rapture of beholding it and calling it theirs.

The necklace was worth 1,500,000 francs, equivalent to more than $300,000 in gold, as money then went, or nearly $500,000 in gold, nowadays. Rather too large a sum to keep locked up in a casket, the reader will confess! And then it seems that Messrs. Boehmer & Bassange had not entirely paid for it yet. They had ten creditors on the diamonds in different countries, and an immense capital still locked up in their other jewelry.

Of course, then, after their first delight had subsided, they were most anxious to sell an article that had to be constantly and painfully watched, and that might so easily disappear. How many a nimble-fingered and stouthearted rogue would not, in those days, have imperiled a dozen lives to clutch that blazing handful of dross, convertible into an Elysium of pomp and pleasure! It would hardly have been a safe noonday plaything in moral Gotham, let alone the dissolute Paris of eighty years ago!

The first thought, of course, that kindled in the breasts of Boehmer and Bassange was, that the only proper resting-place for their matchless bauble was the snowy neck of the Queen Marie Antoinette, then the admired and beloved of all! Her peerless beauty alone could live in the glow of such supernal splendor, and the French throne was the only one in Christendom that could sustain such glittering weight. Moreover, the Queen had already once been a good customer to the court jewelers, for in 1774 she bought four diamonds of them for $75,000.

Louis XV would not have hesitated to fling it on the shoulders of the Du Barry, and Louis XVI, in spite of his odd notions upon economy and just administration, easily listened to the delicate insinuations of his court-jewelers; and, one fine morning, laid the necklace in its casket on the table of his Queen. Her Majesty, for a moment, yielded to the promptings of feminine weakness, and danced and laughed with the glee of an overjoyed child in the new sunshine of those burning, sparkling, dazzling gems. Once and once only she placed it on her neck and breast, and probably the world has never before or since seen such a countenance in such a setting. It was almost the head of an angel shining in the glory of the spheres. But a better thought prevailed, and quickly removing it, she, with a wave of her beautiful hand, declined the gift and besought the King to apply the sum to any other purpose that would be useful or honorable to France, whose finances were sadly straitened. "We want ships of war more than we do necklaces," said she. The King was really delighted at this act of the Queen's, and the incident soon becoming widely known, gave the latter immense popularity for at least twenty-four hours after it occurred. In fact, the amount was really applied to the construction of a grand line-of-battle ship called the Suffren, after the great Admiral of that name.

Boehmer, who seems to have been the business manager of the jeweler firm, found his necklace as troublesome as the cobbler did the elephant he won in a raffle, and tried so perseveringly to induce the Queen to buy it, that he became a real torment. She seems to have thought him a little cracked on the subject; and one day, when he obtained a private audience, he besought her either to buy the necklace or to let him go and drown himself in the Seine. Out of all patience, the Queen intimated that he would have been wiser to secure a customer to begin with; that she would not buy; that if he chose to throw himself into the Seine it would be entirely on his own responsibility; and that as for the necklace, he had better pick it to pieces and sell it. The poor German (for Boehmer was a native of Saxony) departed in deep distress, but accepted neither his own suggestion nor the Queen's.

For some months after this, the court jewelers busied themselves in peddling their necklace about among the courts of Europe. But none of these concerns found it convenient just then to pay out three hundred and sixty thousand dollars for a concatenation of eight hundred diamonds; and still the sparkling elephant remained on the jewelers' hands.

Time passed on. Madame Campan, one of the Queen's confidential ladies, happened to meet Boehmer one day, and the necklace was alluded to.

"What is the state of affairs about the necklace," asked the lady.

"Highly satisfactory," replied Boehmer, whose serenity of countenance Madame Campan had already remarked. "I have sold it to the Sultan at Constantinople, for his favorite Sultana."

This the lady thought rather curious, but she was glad the thing was disposed of, and said no more.

Time passed on again. In the beginning of August 1785, Boehmer took the trouble to call on Madame Campan at her country-house, somewhat to her surprise.

"Has the Queen given you no message for me?" he inquired.

"No!" said the lady; "What message should she give?"

"An answer to my note," said the jeweler.

Madame remembered a note which the Queen had received from Boehmer a little while before, along with some ornaments sent by his hands to her as a present from the King. It congratulated her on having the finest diamonds in Europe, and hoped she would remember him. The Queen could make nothing of it, and destroyed it. Madame Campan therefore replied,

"There is no answer, the Queen burned the note. She does not even understand what you meant by writing that note."

This statement very quickly elicited from the now startled German a story which astounded the lady. He said the Queen owed him the first installment of the money for the diamond necklace; that she had bought it after all; that the story about the Sultana was a lie told by her directions to hide the fact; since the Queen meant to pay by installments, and did not wish the purchase known. And Boehmer said, she had employed the Cardinal de Rohan to buy the necklace for her, and it had been delivered to him for her, and by him to her.

Now the Queen, as Madame Campan knew very well, had always strongly disliked this Cardinal; he had even been kept from attending at Court in consequence, and she had not so much as spoken to him for years. And so Madame Campan told Boehmer, and further she told him he had been imposed upon.

"No," said the man of sparklers decisively, "It is you who are deceived. She is decidedly friendly to the cardinal. I have myself the documents with her own signature authorizing the transaction, for I have had to let the bankers see them in order to get a little time on my own payments."

Here was a monstrous mystification for the lady of honor, who told Boehmer to instantly go and see his official superior, the chief of the king's household. She herself being very soon afterwards summoned to the Queen's presence, the affair came up, and she told the Queen all she knew about it. Marie Antoinette was profoundly distressed by the evident existence of a great scandal and swindle, with which she was plainly to be mixed up through the forged signatures to the documents which Boehmer had been relying on.

Now for the Cardinal.

Louis de Rohan, a scion of the great house of Rohan, one of the proudest of France, was descended of the blood royal of Brittany; was a handsome, proud, dissolute, foolish, credulous, unprincipled noble, now almost fifty years old, a thorough rake, of large revenues, but deeply in debt. He was Peer of France, Archbishop of Strasburg, Grand Almoner of France, Commander of the Order of the Holy Ghost, Commendator of the benefice of St. Wast d'Arras, said to be the mostwealthy in Europe, and a Cardinal. He had been ambassador at Vienna a little after Marie Antoinette was married to the Dauphin, and while there had taken advantage of his official station to do a tremendous quantity of smuggling. He had also further and most deeply offended the Empress Maria Theresa, by outrageous debaucheries, by gross irreligion, and above all by a rather flat but in effect stingingly satirical description of her conduct about the partition of Poland. This she never forgave him, neither did her daughter Marie Antoinette; and accordingly, when he presented himself at Paris soon after she became Queen, he received a curt repulse, and an intimation that he had better go to—Strasburg.

Now in those days a sentence of exclusion from Court was to a French noble but just this side of a banishment to Tophet; and de Rohan was just silly enough to feel this infliction most intensely. He went however, and from that time onward, for year after year, lived the life of a persevering Adam thrust out of his paradise, hanging about the gate and trying all possible ways to sneak in again. Once, for instance, he had induced the porter at the palace of the Trianon to let him get inside the grounds during an illumination, and was recognized by the glow of his cardinal's red stockings from under his cloak. But he was only laughed at for his pains; the porter was turned off, and the poor silly miserable cardinal remained "out in the cold," breaking his heart over his exclusion from the most tedious mess of conventionalities that ever was contrived—except those of the court of Spain.

About 1783, this great fool fell in with an equally great knave, who must be spoken of here, where he begins to converge along with the rest, towards the explosion of the necklace swindle. This was Cagliostro, who at that time came to Strasburg and created a tremendous excitement with his fascinating Countess, his Egyptian masonry, his Spagiric Food (a kind of Brandreth's pill of the period,) which he fed out to poor sick people, his elixir of life, and other humbugs.

The Cardinal sent an intimation that he would like to see the quack. The quack, whose impudence was far greater than the Cardinal's pride, sent back this sublime reply: "If he is sick let him come to me, and I will cure him. If he is well, he does not need to see me, nor I him."

This piece of impudence made the fool of a cardinal more eager than ever. After some more affected shyness, Cagliostro allowed himself to be seen. He was just the man to captivate the Cardinal, and they were quickly intimate personal friends, practising transmutation, alchemy, masonry, and still more particularly conducting a great many experiments on the Cardinal's remarkably fine stock of Tokay wine. Whatever poor de Rohan had to do, he consulted Cagliostro about it, and when the latter went to Switzerland, his dupe maintained a constant communication with him in cipher.

Lastly is to be mentioned Jeanne de St. Remi, Countess de Lamotte de Valois de France, the chief scoundrel, if the term may be used of a woman—of the necklace affair. She seems to have been really a descendant of the royal house of Valois, to which Francis I belonged; through an illegitimate son of Henry II created Count de St. Remi. The family had run down and become poor and rascally, one of Jeanne's immediate ancestors having practiced counterfeiting for a living. She herself had been protected by a certain kind hearted Countess de Boulainvilliers; was receiving a small pension from the Court of about $325 a year; had married a certain tall soldier named Lamotte; had come to Paris, and was living in poverty in a garret, hovering about as it were for a chance to better her circumstances. She was a quick-witted, bright-eyed, brazen-faced hussy, not beautiful, but with lively pretty ways, and indeed somewhat fascinating.

Her protectress, the countess de Boulainvilliers, was now dead; while she was alive Jeanne had once visited her at de Rohan's palace of Saverne, and had thus scraped a slight acquaintance with the gay Cardinal, which she resumed during her abode at Paris.

Everybody at Paris knew about the Diamond Necklace, and about de Rohan's desire to get into court favor. This sharp-witted female swindler now came in among the elements I have thus far been describing, to frame necklace, jeweller, cardinal, queen, and swindler, all together into her plot, just as the keystone drops into an arch and locks it up tight.

No mortal knows where ideas come from. Suddenly a conception is in the mind, whence, or how, we do not know, any more than we know Life. The devil himself might have furnished that which now popped into the cunning, wicked mind of this adventuress. This is what she saw all at once:

Boehmer is crazy to sell his necklace. De Rohan is crazy after the Queen's favor. I am crazy after money. Now if I can make De Rohan think that the Queen wants the necklace, and will become his friend in return for his helping her to it; if I can make him think I am her agent to him, then I can steal the diamonds in their transit.

A wonderfully cunning and hardy scheme! And most wonderful was the cool, keen promptitude with which it was executed.

The countess began to hint to the cardinal that she was fast getting into the Queen's good graces, by virtue of being a capital gossip and storyteller; and that she had frequent private audiences. Soon she added intimations that the Queen was far from being really so displeased with the cardinal, as he supposed. At this the old fool bit instantly, and showed the keenest emotions of hope and delight. On a further suggestion, he presently drew up a letter or memoir humbly and plaintively stating his case, which the countess undertook to put into the Queen's hands. It was the first of over *two hundred* notes from him, notes of abasement, beseeching argument, expostulation, and so on, all entrusted to Jeanne. She burnt them, I suppose.

In order to make her dupe sure that she told the truth about her access to the Queen, Jeanne more than once made him go and watch her enter a side gate into the grounds of the Trianon palace, to which she had somehow obtained a key; and after waiting he saw her come out again, sometimes under the escort of a man, who was, she said one Desclos, a confidential valet of the Queen. This was Villette de Rétaux, a "pal" of Jeanne's and of her husband Lamotte, who had, by the way, become a low-class gambler and swindler by occupation.

Next Jeanne talked about the Queen's charities; and on one occasion, told how much the amiable Marie Antoinette longed to expend certain sums for benevolent purposes if she only had them—but she was out of funds, and the King was so close about money!

The poor cardinal bit again—If the Queen would only allow him the honor to furnish the little amount!"

The countess evidently hadn't thought of that. She reflected—hesitated. The cardinal urged. She consented—it was not much—and was so kind as to carry the cash herself. At their next meeting she reported that the Queen was delighted, telling a very nice story about it. The cardinal would only be too happy to do so again. And sure enough he did, and quite a number of times too; contributing in all to the funds of the countess in this manner, about $25,000.

Well: after a time the cardinal is at Strasburg, when he receives a note from the countess that brings him back again as quick as post-horses can carry him. It says that there is something very important, very secret, very delicate, that the queen wants his help about. He is overflowing with zeal. What is it? Only let him know—his life, his purse, his soul, are at the service of his liege lady.

His purse is all that is needed. With infinite shyness and circumspection, the countess gradually, half unwillingly, lets him find out that it is the diamond necklace that the Queen wants. By diabolical ingenuities of talk she leads de Rohan to the full conviction that if he secures the Queen that necklace, he will thenceforward bask in all the sunshine of court favor that she can show or control.

And at proper times sundry notes from the Queen are bestowed upon the enraptured noodle. These are written in imitation of the Queen's handwriting, by that Villette de Rétaux who personated the Queen's valet, and who was an expert at counterfeiting.

A last and sublime summit of impudent pretension is reached by a secret interview which the Queen, says the countess, desires to grant to her beloved servant the cardinal. This suggestion was rendered practicable by one of those mere coincidences which are found though rarely in history, and which are too improbable to put into a novel— the casual discovery of a young woman of loose character who looked much like the Queen. Whether her name was d'Essigny or Gay d'Oliva, is uncertain; she is usually called by the latter. She was hired and taught; and with immense precautions, this ostrich of a cardinal was one night introduced into the gardens of the Trianon, and shown a little nook among the thickets where a stately female in the similitude of the Queen received him with soft spoken words of kindly greeting, allowed him to kneel and kiss a fair and shapely hand, and showed no particular timidity of any kind. Yet the interview had scarcely more than begun before steps were heard. "Someone is coming," exclaimed the lady, "it is Monsieur and Madame d'Artois—Wemust part. There"—she gave him a red rose—You know what that means! Farewell!" And away they went—Mademoiselle d'Oliva to report to her employers, and the cardinal, in a seventh heaven of ineffable tomfoolery, to his hotel.

But the interview, and the lovely little notes that came sometimes, "fixed" the necklace business! And if further encouragement had been needed, Cagliostro gave it. For the cardinal now consulted him about the future of the affair, having indeed kept him fully informed about it for a long time, as he did of all matters of interest. So the quack set up his tabernacles of mummery in a parlor of the cardinal's hotel, and conducted an Egyptian Invocation there all night long in solitude and pomp; and in the morning he decreed (in substance) "go ahead." And the cardinal did so. Boehmer and Bassange were only too happy to bargain with the great and wealthy church and state dignitary. A memorandum of terms and time of payment was drawn up, and was submitted to the Queen. That is, swindling Jeanne carried it off, and brought it back, with an entry made by Villette de Rétaux in the margin, thus: *"Bon, bon—Approuvé, Marie Antoinette de France."* That is, "Good, good—I approve. Marie Antoinette de France." The payment was to be by installments, at six months, and quarterly afterwards; the Queen to furnish the money to the cardinal, while he remained ostensibly holden to the jewellers, she thus keeping out of sight.

So the jewels were handed over to the cardinal de Rohan; he took them one evening in great state to the lodgings of the countess, where with all imaginable formality there came a knock at the door, and when it was open a tall valet entered who said solemnly "On the part of the Queen!" De Rohan *knew* it was the Queen's confidential valet, for he saw with his own eyes that it was the same man who had escorted the countess from the side gate at the Trianon! And so it was;

to wit, Villette de Rétaux, who, calmly receiving the fifteen hundred thousand franc treasure, marched but as solemnly as he had come in.

As that counterfeiting rascal goes out of the door, the diamond necklace itself disappears from our knowledge. The swindle was consummated, but there is no whisper of the disposition of the spoils. Villette, and Jeanne's husband Lamotte, went to London and Amsterdam, and had some money there; but seemingly no more than the previous pillages upon the cardinal might have supplied; nor did the countess' subsequent expenditures show that she had any of the proceeds.

But that is not the last of the rest of the parties to the affair, by any means. Between this scene and the time when the anxious Boehmer, having a little bill to meet, beset Madame Campan about his letter and the money the Queen was to pay him, there intervened six months. During that time countess Jeanne was smoothing as well as she could, with endless lies and contrivances, the troubles of the perplexed cardinal, who "couldn't seem to see" that he was much better off in spite of his loyal performance of his part of the bargain.

But this application by Boehmer, and the enormous swindle which it was instantly evident had been perpetrated on somebody or other, of course waked up a commotion at once. The Baron de Breteuil, a deadly enemy of de Rohan, got hold of it all, and in his overpowering eagerness to ruin his foe, quickly rendered the matter so public that it was out of the question to hush it up. It seems probable that Jeanne de Lamotte expected that the business would be kept quiet for the sake of the Queen, and that thus any very severe or public punishments would be avoided and perhaps no inquiries made. It is clear that this would have been the best plan, but de Breteuil's officiousness prevented it, and there was nothing for it but legal measures. De Rohan was arrested and put in the Bastile, having barely been able to send a message in German to his hotel to a trusty secretary, who instantly destroyed all the papers relating to the affair. Jeanne was also imprisoned, and Miss Gay d'Oliva and Villette de Rétaux, being caught at Brussels and Amsterdam, were in like manner secured. As for Cagliostro, he was also imprisoned, some accounts saying that he ostentatiously gave himself up for trial.

This was a public trial before the Parliament of Paris, with much form.

The result was that the cardinal, appearing to be only fool, not knave, was acquitted. Gay d'Oliva appeared to have known nothing except that she was to play a part, and she had been told that the Queen wanted her to do so, so she was let go. Villette was banished for life. Lamotte, the countess' husband, had escaped to England, and was condemned to the galleys in his absence, which didn't hurt him much. Cagliostro was acquitted. But Jeanne was sentenced to be whipped, branded on the shoulder with the letter *V* for *Voleuse* (thief), and banished.

This sentence was executed in full, but with great difficulty; for the woman turned perfectly furious on the public scaffold, flew at the hangman like a tiger, bit pieces out of his hands, shrieked, cursed, rolled on the floor, kicked, squirmed and jumped, until they held her by brute force, tore down her dress, and the red hot iron going aside as she struggled, plunged full into her snowy white breast, planting there indelibly the horrible black *V*, while she yelled like a fiend under the torment of the smoking brand. She fled away to England, lived there some time in dissolute courses, and is said to have died in consequence of falling out of a window when drunk, or as another account states, of being flung out by the companions of her orgy, whom she had stung to fury by her frightful scolding. Before her death she put forth one or two memoirs—false, scandalous things.

The unfortunate Queen never entirely escaped some shadow of disrepute from the necklace business. For to the very last, both on the trial and afterwards, Jeanne de Lamotte impudently stuck to it that at least the Queen had known about the trick played on the Cardinal at the Trianon, and had in fact been hidden close by and saw and laughed heartily at the whole interview. So sore and morbid was the condition of the public mind in France in those days, when symptoms of the coming Revolution were breaking out one very side, that this odious story found many and willing believers.

Chapter 42

The Count de St. Germain, sage, prophet, and magician.

Superior to Cagliostro, even in accomplishments, and second to him in notoriety only, was that human nondescript, the so-called Count de St. Germain, whom Fredrick the Great called, "a man no one has ever been able to make out."

The Marquis de Crequy declares that St. Germain was an Alsatian Jew, Simon Wolff by name, and born at Strasburg about the close of the seventeenth or the beginning of the eighteenth century; others insist that he was a Spanish Jesuit named Aymar; and others again intimate that his true title was the Marquis de Betmar, and that he was a native of Portugal. The most plausible theory, however, makes him the natural son of an Italian princess, and fixes his birth at San Germano, in Savoy, about the year 1710; his ostensible father being one Rotondo, a tax-collector of that district.

This supposition is borne out by the fact that he spoke all his many languages with an Italian accent. It was about the year 1750 that he first began to be heard of in Europe as the Count St. Germain, and put forth the astounding pretensions that soon gave him celebrity over the whole continent. The celebrated Marquis de Belleisle made his acquaintance about that time in Germany, and brought him to Paris, where he was introduced to Madame de Pompadour, whose favor he very quickly gained. The influence of that famous beauty was just then paramount with Louis XV, and the Count was soon one of the most eminent men at court. He was remarkably handsome—as an old portrait at Friersdorf, in Saxony, in the rooms he once occupied, sufficiently indicated; and his musical accomplishments, added to the ineffable charm of his manners and conversation, and the miracles he performed, rendered him an irresistible attraction, especially to the ladies, who appear to have almost idolized him. Endowed with an enchanting voice, he could also play every instrument then in vogue, but especially excelled upon the violin, which he could handle in such a manner as to give it the effect of a small orchestra. Cotemporary writers declare that, in his more ordinary performances, a connoisseur could distinctly hear the separate tones of a full quartet when the count was extemporizing on his favorite Cremona. His little work, entitled *La Musique Raisonnée*, published in England, for private circulation only, bears testimony to his musical genius, and to the wondrous eccentricity, as well as beauty, of his conceptions. But it was in alectromancy, or divination by signs and circles; hydromancy, or divination by water; cleidomancy, or divination by the key, and dactylomancy, or divination by the fingers, that the count chiefly excelled, although he, at the same time, professed alchemy, astrology, and prophecy in the higher branches.

The fortunes of the Count St. Germain rose so rapidly in France, that in 1760 he was sent by Louis XV, to the Court of England, to assist in negotiations for a peace. M. de Choiseul, then Prime Minister of France, however, greatly feared and detested the Count; and secretly wrote to Pitt,

begging the latter to have that personage arrested, as he
was certainly a Russian spy. But St. Germain, through his
attendant sprites, of course, received timely warning, and
escaped to the Continent. In England, he was the inseparable
friend of Prince Lobkowitz—a circumstance that gave some
color to his alleged connection with the Russians. His sojourn
there was equally distinguished by his devotion to the ladies,
and his unwavering success at the gaming-table, where he
won fabulous sums, which were afterward dispensed with
imperial munificence. It was there, too, that he put forward
his claims to the highest rank in Masonry; and, of course,
added, thereby, immensely to the éclat of his position. He
spoke English, French, Spanish, Portuguese, Italian, German,
Russian, Polish, the Scandinavian, and many of the Oriental
tongues, with equal fluency; and pretended to have traveled
over the whole Earth, and even to have visited the most
distant starry orbs frequently, in the course of a lifetime
which, with continual transmigrations, he declared to have
lasted for thousands of years. His birth, he said, had been
in Chaldea, in the dawn of time; and that he was the sole
inheritor of the lost sciences and mysteries of his own and
the Egyptian race. He spoke of his personal intimacy with
all the twelve Apostles—and even the august presence of
the Savior; and one of his pretensions would have been
most singularly amusing, had it not bordered upon profanity.
This was no less an assertion than that he had upon several
occasions remonstrated with the Apostle Peter upon the
irritability of his temperament! In regard to later periods
of history, he spoke with the careless ease of an everyday
looker on; and told anecdotes that the researches of scholars
afterwards fully verified. His predictions were, indeed, most

startling; and the cotemporaneous evidence is very strong and explicit, that he did foretell the time, place, and manner of the death of Louis XV, several years before it occurred. His gift of memory was perfectly amazing. Having once read a journal of the day, he could repeat its contents accurately, from beginning to end; and to this endowment he united the faculty of writing with both hands, in characters like copperplate. Thus, he could indite a love-letter with his right while he composed a verse with his left hand, and, apparently, with the utmost facility—a splendid acquisition for the Treasury Department or a literary newspaper! He would, however, have been ineligible for any faithful Post Office, since he read the contents of sealed letters at a glance; and, by his clairvoyant powers, detected crime, or, in fact, the movements of men and the phenomena of nature, at any distance. Like all the great Magi, and Brothers of the Rosy Cross, of whom he claimed to be a shining light, he most excelled in medicine; and along with remedies for "every ill that flesh is heir to," boasted his *Aqua Benedetta* as the genuine elixir of life, capable of restoring youth to age, beauty and strength to decay, and brilliant intellect to the exhausted brain; and, if properly applied, protracting human existence through countless centuries. As a proof of its virtues, he pointed to his own youthful appearance, and the testimony of old men who had seen him sixty or seventy years earlier, and who declared that time had made no impression on him. Strangely enough, the Margrave of Anspach, of whom I shall presently speak, purchased what purported to be the recipe of the *Aqua Benedetta*, from John Dyke, the English Consul at Leghorn, towards the close of the last century; and copies of it are still preserved with religious care and the utmost secrecy by certain noble families in Berlin and Vienna, where the preparation has been used (as they believe) with perfect success against a host of diseases.

Still another peculiarity of the Count would be highly advantageous to any of us, particularly at this period of high prices and culinary scarcity. He never ate nor drank; or, at least, he was never seen to do so! It is said that boarding house regime in these days is rapidly accustoming a considerable class of our fellow-citizens to a similar condition, but I can scarcely believe it.

Again, the Count would fall into cataleptic swoons, which continued often for hours, and even days; and, during these periods, he declared that he visited, in spirit, the most remote regions of the Earth, and even the farthest stars, and would relate, with astonishing power, the scenes he there had witnessed!

He, of course, laid claim to the transmutation of baser metals into gold, and stated that, in 1755, while on a visit to India, to consult the erudition of the Hindu Brahmins, he solved, by their assistance, the problem of the artificial crystallization of pure carbon—or, in other words, the production of diamonds! One thing is certain, viz.: that upon a visit to the French ambassador to the Hague, in 1780, he, in the presence of that functionary, induced him to believe and testify that he broke to pieces, with a hammer, a superb diamond, of his own manufacture, the exact counterpart of another, of similar origin, which he had just sold for 5,500 louis d'or.

His career and transformations on the Continent were multiform. In 1762, he was mixed up with the dynastic conspiracies and changes at St. Petersburg; and his importance there was indicated ten years later, by the reception given to him at Vienna by the Russian Count Orloff, who accosted him joyously as "caro padre" (dear father,) and gave him twenty thousand golden Venetian sequins.

From Petersburg he went to Berlin, where he at once attracted the attention of Frederick the Great, who questioned Voltaire about him; the latter replying, as it is said, that he was a man who knew all things, and would live to the end of the world—a fair statement, in brief, of the position assumed by more than one of our ward politicians!

In 1774, he took up his abode at Schwabach, in Germany, under the name of Count Tzarogy, which is a transposition of Ragotzy, a well-known noble name. The Margrave of Anspach met him at the house of his favorite Clairon, the actress, and became so fond of him, that he insisted upon his company to Italy. On his return, he went to Dresden, Leipzig, and Hamburg, and finally to Eckernfiorde, in Schleswig, where he took up his residence with the Landgrave Karl of Hesse; and at length, in 1783, tired, as he said, of life, and disdaining any longer immortality, he gave up the ghost.

It was during St. Germain's residence in Schleswig that he was visited by the renowned Cagliostro, who openly acknowledged him as master, and learned many of his most precious secrets from him—among others, the faculty of discriminating the character by the handwriting, and of fascinating birds, animals, and reptiles.

To trace the wanderings of St. Germain is a difficult task, as he had innumerable aliases, and often totally disappeared for months together. In Venice, he was known as the Count de Bellamare; at Pisa, as the Chevalier de Schoening; at

Milan, as the Chevalier Welldone; at Genoa, as the Count Soltikow, etc.

In all these journeys, his own personal tastes were quiet and simple, and he manifested more attachment for a pocket-copy of Guarini's *Pastor Fido*—his only library—than for any other object in his possession.

On the whole, the Count de St. Germain was a man of magnificent attainments, but the use he made of his talents proved him to be also a most magnificent humbug.

Chapter 43

Riza Bey, the Persian envoy to Louis XIV.

The most gorgeous, and with one sole exception the most glorious reign that France has known, so far as military success is concerned, was that of Louis XIV, the Grand Monarque. His was the age of lavish expenditure, of magnificent structures, grand festivals, superb dress and equipage, aristocratic arrogance, brilliant campaigns, and great victories. It was, moreover, particularly distinguished for the number and high character of the various special embassies sent to the court of France by foreign powers. Among these, Spain, the Netherlands, Great Britain, and Venice rivaled each other in extravagant display and pomp. The singular and really tangible imposture I am about to describe, practiced at such a period and on such a man as Louis of France, was indeed a bold and dashing affair.

L'etat c'est moi—I am the State," was Louis' celebrated and very significant motto; for in his own hands he had really concentrated all the powers of the realm, and woe to him who trifled with a majesty so real and so imperial!

However, notwithstanding all this imposing strength, this mighty domineering will, and this keen intelligence, a man was found bold enough to brave them all in the arena of pure humbug. It was toward the close of the year 1667, when Louis, in the plenitude of military success, returned from his campaign in Flanders, where his invincible troops had proven too much for the broad breeched but gallant Dutchmen. In the short space of three months he had added whole provinces, including some forty or fifty cities and towns, to his dominions; and his fame was ringing throughout Christendom. It had even penetrated to the farthest East; and the King of Siam sent a costly embassy from his remote kingdom, to offer his congratulations and fraternal greeting to the most eminent potentate of Europe.

Louis had already removed the pageantries of his royal household to his magnificent new palace of Versailles, on which the wealth of conquered kingdoms had been lavished, and there, in the Great Hall of Mirrors, received the homage of his own nobles and the ambassadors of foreign powers. The utmost splendor of which human life was susceptible seemed so common and familiar in those days, that the train was dazzling indeed that could excite any very particular attention. What would have seemed stupendous elsewhere was only in conformity with all the rest of the scene at Versailles. But, at length, there came something that made even the pampered courtiers of the new Babylon stare—a Persian embassy. Yes, a genuine, actual, living envoy from that wonderful Empire in the East, which in her time had ruled the whole Oriental world, and still retained almost fabulous wealth and splendor.

It was announced formally, one morning, to Louis, that His Most Serene Excellency, Riza Bey, with an interminable tail of titles, hangers-on and equipages, had reached the port of Marseilles, having journeyed by way of Trebizond and Constantinople, to lay before the great "King of the Franks" brotherly congratulations and gorgeous presents from his own illustrious master, the Shah of Persia. This was something entirely to the taste of the vain French ruler, whom unlimited good fortune had inflated beyond all reasonable proportions. He firmly believed that he was by far the greatest man who had ever lived; and had an embassy from the moon or the planet Jupiter been announced to him, would have deemed it not only natural enough, but absolutely due to his preeminence above all other human beings. Nevertheless, he was, secretly, immensely pleased with the Persian demonstration, and gave orders that no expense should be spared in giving the strangers a reception worthy of himself and France.

It would be needless for me to detail the events of the progress of Riza Bey from Marseilles to Paris, by way of Avignon and Lyons. It was certainly in keeping with the pretensions of the Ambassador. From town to town the progress was a continued ovation. Triumphal arches, bonfires, chimes of bells, and hurrahing crowds in their best bibs and tuckers, military parades and civic ceremonies, everywhere awaited the children of the farthest East, who were stared at, shouted at—and by some wretched cynics sneered and laughed at— to their hearts' content. All modern glory very largely consists in being nearly stunned with every species of noise, choked with dust, and dragged about through the streets, until you are well nigh dead. Witness the Japanese Embassy and their visit to this country, where, in some cases, the poor creatures, after hours of unmitigated boring with all sorts of mummery, actually had their pigtails pulled by Young America in the rear, and—as at the windows of Willard's Hotel in

Washington—were stirred up with long canes, like the Polar Bear or the Learned Seal.

Still Riza Bey and his dozen or two of dusky companions did not, by any means, cut so splendid a figure as had been expected. They had with them some camels, antelopes, bulbuls, and monkeys—like any travelling caravan, and were dressed in the most outrageous and outlandish attire. They jabbered, too, a gibberish utterly incomprehensible to the crowd, and did everything that had never been seen or done before. All this, however, delighted the populace. Had they been similarly transmogrified, or played such queer pranks themselves, it would only have been food for mockery; but the foreign air and fame of the thing made it all wonderful, and, as the chief rogue in the plot had foreseen, blinded the popular eye and made his "embassy" a complete success.

At length, after some four weeks of slow progress, the "Persians" arrived at Paris, where they were received, as had been expected, with tremendous éclat. They entered by Barriére du Trône, so styled because it was there that Louis Quatorze himself had been received upon a temporary throne, set up, with splendid decorations and triumphal arches, in the open air, when he returned from his Flanders campaign. Riza Bey was upon this occasion a little more splendid than he had been on his way from the seacoast, and really loomed up in startling style in his tall, black, rimless hat of wool, shaped precisely like an elongated flowerpot, and his silk robes dangling to his heels and covered with huge painted figures and bright metal decorations of every shape and size unknown, to European man-millinery. A circlet or collar, apparently of gold, set with precious stones (California diamonds!) surrounded his neck, and monstrous glittering rings covered all the fingers, and even the thumbs of both his hands. His train, consisting of sword, cup, and pipe bearers, doctors, chief cooks, and bottle-washers, cork extractors and chiropodists (literally so, for it seems that sharing the common lot of humanity, great men have corns even in Persia,) were similarly arrayed as to fashion, but less stupendously in jewelry.

Well, after the throng had scampered, crowded, and shouted themselves hoarse, and had straggled to their homes, sufficiently tired and pocket-picked, the Ambassador and his suite were lodged in sumptuous apartments in the old royal residence of the Tuileries, under the care and charge of King Louis' own assistant Majordomo and a guard of courtiers and regiments of Royal Swiss. Banqueting and music filled up the first evening; and upon the ensuing day His Majesty, who thus did his visitors especial honor, sent the Duc de Richelieu, the most polished courtier and diplomatist in France, to announce that he would graciously receive them on the third evening at Versailles.

Meanwhile the most extensive preparations were made for the grand audience thus accorded; and when the appointed occasion had arrived, the entire Gallery of Mirrors with all the adjacent spaces and corridors, were crowded with the beauty, the chivalry, the wit, taste, and intellect of France at that dazzling period. The gallery, which is three hundred and eighty feet in length by fifty in height, derives its name from the priceless mirrors which adorn its walls, reaching from floor to ceiling, opposite the long row of equally tall and richly mullioned windows that look into the great court and gardens. These windows, hung with the costliest silk curtains and adorned with superb historical statuary, give to the hall a light and aerial appearance indescribably enchanting; while the mirrors reflect in ten thousand variations the hall itself and its moving pageantry, rendering both apparently interminable. Huge marble vases filled with odorous exotics lined the stairways, and twelve thousand wax lights in gilded brackets, and chandeliers of the richest workmanship, shone upon three thousand titled heads.

Louis the Great himself never appeared to finer advantage. His truly royal countenance was lighted up with pride and satisfaction as the Envoy of the haughty Oriental king approached the splendid throne on which he sat, and as he descended a step to meet him and stood there in his magnificent robes of state, the Persian envoy bent the knee, and with uncovered head presented the credentials of his mission. Of the crowd that immediately surrounded the throne, it is something to say that the Grand Colbert, the famous Minister, and the Admiral Duquesne were by no means the most eminent, nor the lovely Duchess of Orleans and her companion, the bewitching Mademoiselle de Kerouaille, who afterward changed the policy of Charles II, of England, by no means the most beautiful personages in the galaxy.

A grand ball and supper concluded this night of splendor, and Riza Bey was fairly launched at the French court; every member of which, to please the King, tried to outvie his compeers in the assiduity of his attentions, and the value of the books, pictures, gems, equipages, arms, etc., which they heaped upon the illustrious Persian. The latter gentleman very quietly smoked his pipe and lounged on his divan before company, and diligently packed up the goods when he and his "jolly companions" were left alone. The presents of the Shah had not yet arrived, but were daily expected via

Marseilles, and from time to time the olive-colored suite was diminished by the departure of one of the number with his chest on a special mission (so stated) to England, Austria, Portugal, Spain, and other European powers.

In the meantime, the Bey was fêted in all directions, with every species of entertainment, and it was whispered that the fair ones of that dissolute court were, from the first, eager in the bestowal of their smiles. The King favored his Persian pet with numerous personal interviews, at which, in broken French, the Envoy unfolded the most imposing schemes of Oriental conquest and commerce that his master was cordially willing to share with his great brother of France. At one of these chatty tête-á-têtes, the munificent Riza Bey, upon whom the King had already conferred his own portrait set in diamonds, and other gifts worth several millions of francs, placed in the Royal hand several superb fragments of opal and turquoise said to have been found in a district of country bordering on the Caspian sea, which teemed with limitless treasures of the same kind, and which the Shah of Persia proposed to divide with France for the honor of her alliance. The king was enchanted; for these mere specimens, as they were deemed, must, if genuine, be worth in themselves a mint of money; and a province full of such— why, the thought was charming!

Thus the great Kingfish was fairly hooked, and Riza Bey could take his time. The golden tide that flowed in to him did not slacken, and his own expenses were all provided for at the Tuileries. The only thing remaining to be done was a grand foray on the tradesmen of Paris, and this was splen-didly executed. The most exquisite wares of all descriptions were gathered in, without mention of payment; and one by one the Persian phalanx distributed itself through Europe until only two or three were left with the Ambassador.

At length, word was sent to Versailles that the gifts from the Shah had come, and a day was appointed for their presentation. The day arrived, and the Hall of Audience was again thrown open. All was jubilee; the King and the court waited, but no Persian—no Riza Bey—no presents from the Shah!

That morning three men, without either caftans or robes, but very much resembling the blacklegs of the day in their attire and deportment, had left the Tuileries at daylight with a bag and a bundle, and returned no more. They were Riza Bey and his last bodyguard; the bag and the bundle were the smallest in bulk but the most precious in value of a month's successful plunder. The turquoises and opals left with the King turned out, upon close inspection, to be a new and very ingenious variety of colored glass, now common enough, and then worth, if anything, about thirty cents in cash.

Of course, a hue and cry was raised in all directions, but totally in vain. Riza Bey, the Persian Shah, and the gentlemen in flowerpots, had "gone glimmering through the dream of things that were." *L'etat c'est moi* had been sold for thirty cents! It was afterward believed that a noted barber and suspected bandit at Leghorn, who had once really traveled in Persia, and there picked up the knowledge and the ready money that served his turn, was the perpetrator of this pretty joke and speculation, as he disappeared from his native city about the time of the embassy in France, and did not return.

All Europe laughed heartily at the Grand Monarque and his fair court-dames, and "An Embassy from Persia" was for many years thereafter an expression similar to "Walker!" in English, or "Buncombe!" in American conversation, when the party using it seeks to intimate that the color of his optics is not a distinct pea-green!

Part IX

RELIGIOUS HUMBUGS

Chapter 44

*Diamond cut diamond; or, yankee
superstitions—Matthias the impostor—New York follies
thirty years ago.*

There is a story that on a great and solemn public occasion
of the Romish Church, a Pope and a Cardinal were, with
long faces, performing some of the gyrations of the occasion,
when, instead of a pious ejaculation and reply, which were
down in the program, one said to the other gravely, in Latin
"mundus vult decipi;" and the other replied, with equal gravity
and learning, *"decipiatur ergo:"* that is, "All the world chooses
to be fooled."—Let it be fooled then."

This seems, perhaps, a reasonable way for priests to talk
about ignorant Italians. It may seem inapplicable to cool,
sharp, school-trained Protestant Yankees. It is not, however—
at least, not entirely. Intelligent Northerners have, sometimes,
superstition enough in them to make a first-class Popish
saint. If it had not been so, I should not have such an absurd
religious humbug to tell of as Robert Matthews, notorious
in our goodly city some thirty years ago as "Matthias, the
Impostor."

In the summer of 1832, there was often seen riding in
Broadway, in a handsome barouche, or promenading on the

Battery (usually attended by a sort of friend or servant,) a tall man, of some forty years of age, quite thin, with sunken, sharp gray eyes, with long, coarse, brown and gray hair, parted in the middle and curling on his shoulders, and a long and coarse but well-tended beard and mustache. These Esau-like adornments attracted much attention in those close-shaving days. He was commonly dressed in a fine green frock-coat, lined with white or pink satin, black or green pantaloons, with polished Wellington boots drawn on outside, fine cambric ruffles and frill, and a crimson silk sash worked with gold and with twelve tassels, for the twelve tribes of Israel. On his head was a steeple-crowned patent-leather shining black cap with a shade.

Thus bedizened, this fantastic-looking personage marched gravely up and down, or rode in pomp in the streets. Sometimes he lounged in a bookstore or other place of semi-public resort; and in such places he often preached or exhorted. His preachments were sufficiently horrible. He claimed to be God the Father; and his doctrine was, in substance, this:— The true kingdom of God on Earth began in Albany in June 1830, and will be completed in twenty-one years, or by 1851. During this time, wars are to stop, and I, Matthias, am to execute the divine judgments and destroy the wicked. The day of grace is to close on December 1, 1836; and all who do not begin to reform by that time, I shall kill." The discourses by which this blasphemous humbug supported his pretensions were a hodgepodge of impiety and utter nonsense, with rants, curses and cries, and frightful threats against all objectors. Here is a passage from one;—All who eat swine's flesh are of the devil; and just as certain as he eats it he will tell a lie in less than half an hour. If you eat a piece of pork, it will go crooked through you, and the Holy Ghost will not stay in you; but one or the other must leave the house pretty soon. The pork will be as crooked in you as rams' horns." Again, he made these pleasant points about the ladies: "They who teach women are of the wicked. All females who lecture their husbands their sentence is: 'Depart, ye wicked, I know you not.' Everything that has the smell of woman will be destroyed. Woman is the cap-sheaf of the abomination of desolation, full of all deviltry." There, ladies! Is anything further necessary to convince you what a peculiarly wicked and horrible humbug this fellow was?

If we had followed this impostor home, we should have found him lodged, during most of his stay in New-York city, with one or the other of his three chief disciples. These were Pierson, who commonly attended him abroad, Folger, and—for a time only—Mills. All three of these men were wealthy merchants. In their handsome and luxuriously-furnished homes, this noxious humbug occupied the best rooms, and controlled the whole establishment, directing the marketing, meal times, and all other household-matters. Master, mistress (in Mr. Folger's home,) and domestics were disciples, and obeyed the scamp with an implicitness and prostrate humility even more melancholy than absurd, both as to housekeeping and as to the ceremonies, washing of feet, etc., which he enjoined. When he was angry with his female disciples, he frequently whipped them; but, being a monstrous coward, he never tried it on a man. The least opposition or contradiction threw him into a great rage, and set him screaming, and cursing, and gesticulating like any street drab. When he wished more clothes, which was pretty often, one of his dupes furnished the money. When he wanted cash for any purpose indeed, they gave it him.

This half-crazy knave and abominable humbug was Robert Matthews, who called himself Matthias. He was of Scotch descent, and born about 1790, in Washington county, New York; and his blood was tainted with insanity, for a brother of his died a lunatic. He was a carpenter and joiner of uncommon skill, and up to nearly his fortieth year lived, on the whole, a useful and respectable life, being industrious, a professing Christian of good standing, and (having married in 1813) a steady family-man. In 1828 and 1829, while living at Albany, he gradually became excited about religious subjects; his first morbid symptoms appearing after hearing some sermons by Rev. E. N. Kirk, and Mr. Finney the revivalist. He soon began to exhort his fellow-journeymen instead of minding his work, so uproariously that his employer turned him away.

He discovered a text in the Bible that forbid Christians to shave. He let his hair and beard grow; began street-preaching in a noisy, brawling style; announced that he was going to set about converting the whole city of Albany—which needed it badly enough, if we may believe the political gentlemen. Finding however, that the Lobby, or the Regency, or something or other about the peculiar wickedness of Albany, was altogether too much for him, he began, like Jonah at Nineveh, to announce the destruction of the obstinate town; and at midnight, one night in June, 1826, he waked up his household, and saying that Albany was to be destroyed next day, took his three little boys—two, four, and six years old—his wife and oldest child (a daughter refusing to go,) and "fled to the mountains." He actually walked the poor little fellows forty miles in twenty-four hours, to his sister's in Washington county. Here he was reckoned raving crazy; was forcibly turned out of church for one of his brawling interruptions of service, and sent back to Albany, where he resumed his street-preaching more noisily than ever. He now began to call himself Matthias, and claimed to be a Jew. Then he went on a long journey to the Western and Southern States, preaching his doctrines, getting into jail, and sometimes fairly cursing his way out; and, returning to New York city, preached up and down the streets in his crazy, bawling fashion, sometimes on foot and sometimes on an old bony horse.

His New York city dupes, Elijah Pierson and Benjamin H. Folger and their families, together with a Mr. Mills and a few more, figured prominently in the chief chapter of Matthews' career, during two years and a half, from May, 1832, to the fall of 1834.

Pierson and Folger were the leaders in the folly. These men, merchants of wealth and successful in business, were of that sensitive and impressible religious nature which is peculiarly credulous and liable to enthusiasms and delusions. They had been, with a number of other persons, eagerly engaged in some extravagant religious performances, including excessive fasts and asceticisms, and a plan, formed by one of their lady friends, to convert all New York by a system of female visitations and preachings—a plan not so very foolish, I may just remark, if the she apostles are only pretty enough!

Pierson, the craziest of the crew, besides other wretched delusions, had already fancied himself Elijah the Tishbite; and when his wife fell ill and died a little while before this time, had first tried to cure her, and then to raise her from the dead, by anointing with oil and by the prayer of faith, as mentioned in the Epistle of Saint James.

Curiously enough, a sort of lair or nest, very soft and comfortable, was thus made ready for our religious humbug, just as he wanted it worst; for in these days he was but seedy. He heard something of Pierson, I don't know how; and on the 5th of May, 1832, he called on him. Very quickly the poor fellow recognized the long-bearded prophetical humbug as all that he claimed to be—a possessor and teacher of all truth, and as God himself.

Mills and Folger easily fell into the same pitiable foolery, on Pierson's introduction. And the lucky humbug was very soon living in clover in Mills' house, which he chose first; had admitted the happy fools, Pierson and Folger, as the first two members of his true church; Pierson, believing that from Elijah the Tishbite he had become John the Baptist, devoted himself as a kind of servant to his new Messiah; and the deluded men began to supply all the temporal wants of the impostor, believing their estates set apart as the beginning of the material Kingdom of God!

After three months, some of Mills' friends, on charges of lunacy, caused Mills to be sent to Bloomingdale Asylum, and Matthias to be thrust into the insane poor's ward at Bellevue, where his beard was forcibly cut off, to his extreme disgust. His brother, however, got him out by a habeas corpus, and he went to live with Folger. Mills now disappears from the story.

Matthias remained in the full enjoyment of his luxurious establishment, until September, 1834, it is true, with a few uncomfortable interruptions. He was always both insolent and cowardly, and thus often irritated some strong-minded auditor, and got himself into some pickle where he had to sneak out, which he did with much ease. In his seedy days the landlord of a hotel in whose barroom he used to preach and curse, put him down when he grew too abusive, by coolly and sternly telling him to go to bed. Mr. Folger himself had one or two brief intervals of sense, in one of which, angered at some insolence of Matthias, he seized him by the throat, shook him well, and flung him down upon a sofa. The humbug knowing that his living was in danger, took this very mildly, and readily accepted the renewed assurances of belief which poor Folger soon gave him. In the village of Sing Sing where Folger had a country-seat which he called Mount Zion, Matthias was exceedingly obnoxious. His daughter had married a Mr. Laisdell; and the humbug, who claimed that all Christian marriages were void and wicked, by some means induced the young wife to come to Sing Sing, where he whipped her more than once quite cruelly. Her husband came and took her away after encountering all the difficulty which Matthias dared make; and, at a hearing in the matter before a magistrate, he was very near getting tarred and feathered, if not something worse, and the danger frightened him very much.

He barely escaped being shaved by violence, and being thrown overboard to test his asserted miraculous powers, at the hands of a stout and incredulous farmer on the steam-boat between Sing Sing and New York. While imprisoned at Bellevue before his trial, he was tossed in a blanket by the prisoners, to make him give them some money. The unlucky prophet dealt out damnation to them in great quantities; but they told him it wouldn't work, and the poor humbug finally, instead of casting them into hell, paid them a quarter of a dollar apiece to let him off. When he was about to leave

Folger's house, some roguish young men of Sing Sing forged a warrant, and with a counterfeit officer seized the humbug, and a second time shaved him by force. He was one day terribly "set back" as the phrase is, by a sharpish answer. He gravely asserted to a certain man that he had been on the Earth eighteen hundred years. His hearer, startled and irreverent, exclaimed:

"The devil you have! Do you tell me so?"

"I do," said the prophet.

"Then," rejoined the other, "all I have to say is, you are a remarkably good-looking fellow for one of your age."

The confounded prophet grinned, scowled, and exclaimed indignantly:

"You are a devil, Sir!" and marched off.

In the beginning of August, 1834, the unhappy Pierson died in Folger's house, under circumstances amounting to strong circumstantial evidence that Matthias, with the help of the colored cook, an enthusiastic disciple, had poisoned him with arsenic. The rascal pretended that his own curse had slain Pierson. There was a post mortem, an indictment, and a trial, but the evidence was not strong enough for conviction. Being acquitted, he was at once tried again for an assault and battery on his daughter by the aforesaid whippings; and on this charge he was found guilty and sent to the county jail for three months, in April, 1835. The trial for murder was just before—the prophet having lain in prison since his apprehension for murder in the preceding autumn. Mr. Folger's delusion had pretty much disappeared by the end of the summer of 1834. He had now become ruined, partly in consequence of foolish speculations jointly with Pierson, believed to be conducted under Divine guidance, and partly because his strange conduct destroyed his business reputation and standing. The death of Pierson, and some very queer matters about another apparent poisoning-trick, awakened the suspicions of the Folgers; and after a good deal of scolding and trouble with the impostor, who hung on to his comfortable home like a good fellow, Folger finally turned him out, and then had him taken up for swindling. He had been too foolish himself, however, to maintain this charge; but, shortly after, the others, for murder and assault, followed, with a little better success.

This imprisonment seems to have put a sudden and final period to the prophetical and religious operations of Master Matthias, and to the follies of his victims, too. I know of no subsequent developments of either kind. Matthias disappears from public life, and died, it is said, in Arkansas; but when, or after what further career, I don't know. He was a shallow knave, and undoubtedly also partly crazy and partly the dupe of his own nonsense. If he had not so opportunely found victims of good standing, he would not have been remembered at all, except as George Munday, the "hatless prophet," and "Angel Gabriel Orr," are remembered—as one more obscure, crazy street-preacher. And as soon as his accidental supports of other people's money and enthusiasm failed him, he disappeared at once. Many of my readers will remember distinctly, as I do, the remarkable career of this man, and the humiliating position in which his victims were placed. In the face of such an exposition as this of the weakness and credulity of poor human nature in this enlightened country of common schools and colleges, in the boasted wide-awake nineteenth century, who shall deny that we can study with interest and profit the history of impositions which have been practiced upon mankind in every possible phase throughout every age of the world, including the age in which we live? There is literally no end to these humbugs; and the reader of these pages, weak as may be my attempts to do the subject justice, will learn that there is no country, no period, and no sphere in life which has not been impiously invaded by the genius of humbug, under more disguises and in more shapes than it has entered into the heart of man to conceive.

Chapter 45

*A religious humbug on John Bull—Joanna
Southcott—The second Shiloh.*

Joanna Southcott was born at St. Mary's Ottery in Devonshire, about the year 1750. She was a plain, stout-limbed, hard-fisted farmer lass, whose toils in the field—for her father was in but very moderate circumstances—had tawned her complexion and hardened her muscles, at an early age. As she grew toward woman's estate, necessity compelled her to leave her home and seek service in the city of Exeter, where for many years, she plodded on very quietly in her obscure path, first, as a domestic hireling, and subsequently as a washer woman.

I have an old and esteemed friend on Staten Island whose father, still living, recollects Joanna well, as she used to come regularly to his house of a Monday morning, to her task of cleansing the family linen. He was then but a little lad, yet he remembers her quite well, with her stout, robust frame, and buxom and rather attractive countenance, and her queer ways. Even then she was beginning to invite attention by her singular manners and discourse, which led many to believe her demented.

It was at Exeter that Joanna became religiously impressed,

and joined the Wesleyan Methodists, as a strict and extreme believer in the doctrines of that sect. During her attendance upon the Wesleyan rites, she became intimate with one Sanderson, who, whether a designing rogue, or only a very fanatical believer, pretended that he had discovered in the good washerwoman a Bible prodigy; and it was not long before the poor creature began literally, to "see sights" and dream dreams of the most preternatural description, for which Sanderson always had ready some very telling interpretation. Her visions were of the most thoroughly "mixed" character withal, sometimes transporting her to the courts of heaven, and sometimes to a very opposite region, celebrated for its latent and active caloric. When she ranged into the lower world, she had a very unpleasant habit of seeing sundry scoffers and unbelievers (in herself) belonging to the congregation, in very close but disadvantageous intercourse with the Evil One, who was represented as having a particular eye to others around her, even while they laid claim to special piety. Of course, such revelations as these could not be tolerated in any well regulated community, and when some most astounding religious gymnastics performed by Joanna in the midst of prayers and sermons, occurred to heap up the measure of her offenses, it became full time to take the matter in hand, and the prophetess was expelled. Now, those whom she had not served up openly with brimstone, agreeing with her about those whom she had thus "cooked," and delighted in their own exemption from that sort of dressing, seceded inconsiderable numbers, and became Joanna's followers. This gave her a nucleus to work upon, and between 1790 and 1800, she managed to make herself known throughout Britain, proclaiming that she was to be the destined Mother of the Second Messiah, and although originally quite illiterate, picking up enough general information and Bible lore, to facilitate her publication of several very curious, though sometimes incoherent works. One of the earliest and most startling of these was her "Warning to the whole World, from the Sealed Prophecies of Joanna Southcott, and other communications given since the writings were opened on the 12th of January, 1803." This foretold the close approach of the great red dragon of the Revelations, "with seven heads and ten horns, and seven crowns upon his heads," and the birth of the "man-child who was to rule all nations with a rod of iron."

In 1805, a shoemaker named Tozer built her a chapel in Exeter at his own expense, and it was, from the first, constantly filled on service-days with eager worshipers. Here she gave exhortations, and prophesied in a species of religious frenzy or convulsion, sometimes uttering very heavy prose, and sometimes the most fearful doggerel rhyme resembling— well—perhaps our album effusions here at home! Indeed, I can think of nothing else equally fearful. In these paroxysms, Joanna raved like an ancient Pythoness whirling on her tripod, and to just about the same purpose. Yet, it was astonishing to see how the thing went down. Crowds of intelligent people came from all parts of the United Kingdom to listen, be converted, and to receive the "seals" (as they were called) that secured their fortunate possessor unimpeded and immediate admission to heaven. Of course, tickets so precious could not be given away for nothing, and the seal trade in this new form proved very lucrative.

The most remarkable of all these conversions was that of the celebrated engraver, William Sharp, who, notwithstanding his eminent position as an artist, by no means bore out his name in other things. He had previously become thoroughly imbued with the notions of Swedenborg, Mesmer, and the famous Richard Brothers, and was quite ripe for anything fantastic. Such a convert was a perfect godsend to Joanna, and she was easily persuaded to accompany him to London, where her congregations rapidly increased to enormous proportions, even rivaling those now summoned by the "drum ecclesiastical" and orthodox of the Rev. Mr. Spurgeon.

The whole sect extended until, in 1813, it numbered no less than one hundred thousand members, signed and "sealed"—Mr. Sharp occupying a most conspicuous position at the very footstool of the Prophetess. Late in 1813, appeared the *Book of Wonders*, "in five parts," and it was a clincher. Poor Sharp came in largely for the expenses, but valiantly stood his ground against it all. At length, in 1814, the great Joanna dazzled the eyes of her adherents and the world at large with her *Prophecies Concerning the Prince of Peace*. This delectable manifesto flatly announced to mankind that the second Shiloh, so long expected, would be born of the Prophetess at midnight, on October 19, in that same year, i.e. 1814. The inspired writer was then *enceinte*, although a virgin, as she expressly and solemnly declared, and in the sixty-fourth year of her age. Among the other preternatural concomitants of this anticipated eventful birth, was the fact that the period of her pregnancy had lasted for several years.

Of course, this stupendous announcement threw the whole sect into ecstasies of religious exultation; while, on the other hand, it afforded a fruitful subject of ridicule for the utterly irreverent London pamphleteers. Poor Sharp, who had caused a magnificent cradle and baby-wardrobe to be got ready at his own expense, was most unmercifully scored. The infant was caricatured with a long gray beard and spectacles, with Sharp in a duster carefully rocking him to sleep, while Joanna the Prophetess treated the engraver to some "cuts" in her own style, with a bunch of twigs.

On the appointed night, the street in which Joanna lived was thronged with the faithful, who, undeterred by sarcasm, fully credited her prediction. They bivouacked on the sidewalks in motley crowds of men, women, and children; and as the hours wore on, and their interest increased, burst forth into spontaneous psalmody. The adjacent thoroughfares were as densely jammed with curious and incredulous spectators, and the mutton pie and ballad businesses flourished extensively. The interior of the house, with the exception of the sick chamber, was illuminated in all directions, and the dignitaries of the sect held the anterooms and corridors, "in full fig," to receive the expected guest. But the evening passed, then midnight came, then morning, but—alas! no Shiloh; and, little by little, the disappointed throngs dispersed! Poor Joanna, however, kept her bed, and finally, after many fresh paroxysms and prophecies, on the 27th of December, 1814, gave up the ghost—the indefatigable Sharp still declaring that she had gone to heaven for a season, only to legitimatize the unborn infant, and would re-arise again from death, after four days, with the Shiloh in her arms. So firm was this faith in him and many other respectable persons, that the body of the Prophetess was retained in her house until the very last moment. When the dissection demanded by the majority of the sect could no longer be delayed, that operation was performed, and it was found that the subject had died of ovarian dropsy; but was—as she had always maintained herself to be—a virgin. Dr. Reece, who had been a devout believer, but was now undeceived, published a full account of this and all the other circumstances of her death, and another equally earnest disciple bore the expenses of her burial at St. John's Wood, and placed over her a tombstone with appropriate inscriptions.

As late as 1863, there were many families of believers still existing near Chatham, in Kent; and even in this country can here and there be found admirers of the creed of Joanna Southcott, who are firmly convinced that she will reappear some fine morning, with Sanderson on one side of her and Sharp on the other.

Chapter 46

*The first humbug in the world—Advantages of studying
the impositions of former ages—Heathen humbugs—The
ancient mysteries—The cabiri—Eleusis—Isis.*

The domain of humbug reaches back to the Garden of Eden,
where the Father of lies practised it upon our poor, innocent
first grandmother, Eve. This was the first and worst of all
humbugs. But from that eventful day to the present moment,
falsehood, hypocrisy, deception, imposition, cant, bigotry,
false appearances and false pretences, superstitions, and all
conceivable sorts of humbugs, have had a full swing, and he
or she who watches these things most closely, and reflects
most deeply upon these various peculiarities, bearings, and
results, will be best qualified to detect and to avoid them.
For this reason, I should look upon myself as somewhat of a
public benefactor, in exposing the humbugs of the world, if
I felt competent to do the subject full justice.

Next to the fearful humbug practiced upon our first parents, came heathen humbugs generally. All heathenism and
idolatry are one grand complex humbug to begin with. All
the heathen religions always were, and are still, audacious,
colossal, yet shallow and foolish, humbugs. The heathen
humbugs were played off by the priests, the shrewdest men

then alive. It is a curious fact that the heathen humbugs were all solemn. This was because they were intended to maintain the existing religions, which, like all false religions, could not endure ridicule. They always appealed to the pious terrors of the public, as well as to its ignorance and appetite for marvels. They offered nothing pleasant, nothing to love, nothing to gladden the heart and lift it up in joyful gratitude, true adoration, and childlike confidence, prayer, and thanksgiving. On the contrary, awful noises, fearful sights, frightful threats, foaming at the mouth, dark sayings, secret processions, bloody sacrifices, grim priests, costly offerings, sleeps in darksome caverns to wait for a dream from the god—these were the machineries of the ancient heathen. They were as crude and as ferocious as those of the King of Dahomey, or of the barbarous negroes of the Guinea coast. But they often show a cunning as keen and effective as that of any quack, or Philadelphia lawyer, or Davenport Brother, or Jackson Davis of today.

The most prominent of the heathen humbugs were the mysteries, the oracles, the sibyls (N.B., the word is often misspelled sybils,) and augury. Every respectable Pagan religion had some mysteries, just as every respectable Christian family has a bible—and, as an ill-natured proverb has it, a skeleton. It was considered a poor religion—a one horse religion, so to speak—that had no mysteries.

The chief mysteries were those of the Cabiri, of Eleusis, and of Isis. These mysteries used exactly the same kind of machinery which proves so effective every day in modern mysteries, viz., shows, processions, voices, lights, dark rooms, frightful sights, solemn mummeries, striking costumes, big talks and preachments, threats, gabbles of nonsense, etc., etc.

The mysteries of the Cabiri are the most ancient of which anything is known. These Cabiri were a sort of "Original old Dr. Jacob Townsends" of divinities. They were considered senior and superior to Jupiter, Neptune, Plato, and the gods of Olympus. They were Pelasgic, that is, they belonged to that unknown ancient people from whom both the Greek and the Latin nations are thought to have come. The Cabiri afterward figured as the "elder gods" of Greece, the inventors of religion, and of the human race in fact, and were kept so very dark that it is not even known, with any certainty, who they were. The ancient heathen gods, like modern thieves, very usually objected to pass by their real names. The Cabiri were particularly at home in Lemnos, and afterward in Samothrace.

Their mysteries were of a somewhat unpleasant character, as far as we know them. The candidate had to pass a long time almost starved, and without any enjoyment whatever; was then let into a dark temple, crowned with olive, tied round with a purple girdle, and frightened almost to death with horrid noises, terrible sights of some kind, great flashes of light and deep darkness between, etc., etc. There was a ceremony of absolution from past sin, and a formal beginning of a new life. It is a curious fact, that this performance seems to have been a kind of pious marine insurance company; as the initiated, it was believed, could not be drowned. Perhaps they were put in a way to obtain a drier strangulation. The reason why these ceremonies were kept so successfully secret, is plain. Each man, as he was let in, and found what nonsense it was, was sure to hold his tongue and help the next man in, as in the modern case of the celebrated "Sons of Malta." It is to be admitted, however, to the credit of the

Cabiri, that a doctrine of reformation, or of living a better practical life, seems to have been part of their religion. This is an interesting recognition, by heathen consciences, of one of the greatest moral truths which Christianity has enforced. Something of the same kind can be traced in other heathen mysteries. But these heathen attempts at virtue invariably rotted out into aggravations of vice. No religion except Christianity ever contained the principle of improvement in it. Bugaboos and hobgoblins may serve for a time to frighten the ignorant into obedience; but if they get a chance to cheat the devil, they will be sure to do it. Nothing but the great doctrine of Christian love and brotherhood, and of a kind and paternal Divine government, has ever proved to be permanently reformatory, and tending to lift the heart above the vices and passions to which poor human nature is prone.

The mysteries of Eleusis were celebrated every year at Eleusis, near Athens, in honor of Ceres, and were a regular "May Anniversary," so to speak, for the pious heathens of the period. It took just nine days to complete them; long enough for a puppy to get its eyes open. The candidates were very handsomely put through. On the first day, they got together; on the second, they took a wash in the sea; on the third, they had some ceremonies about Proserpine; on the fourth, no mortal knows what they did; on the fifth, they marched round a temple, two and two, with torches, like a Wide-Awake procession; on the sixth, seventh, and eighth, there were more processions, and the initiation proper, said to have been something like that of Freemasonry; so that we may suppose the victims rode the goat and were broiled on the gridiron. On the ninth day, the ceremony, they say, consisted in overturning two vessels of wine. I fear by this means that they all got drunk; and the more so, because the coins of Eleusis have a hog on one side, as much as to say, We make hogs of ourselves.

There was a set of mysteries at Athens, called Thesmophoria, and one at Rome, called the mysteries of the *Bona Dea*, which were celebrated by married women only. Various notions prevailed as to what they did. But can there be any reasonable doubt about it? They were, I fear, systematic conspirators' meetings, in which the more experienced matrons instructed the junior ones how to manage their husbands. If this was not their object, then it was to maintain the influence of the heathen clergy over the heathen ladies. Women have always been the constituents of priests where false religions prevailed, as they have, for better purposes, of the ministers of the Gospel among Christians.

The mysteries of the goddess Isis, which originated in Egypt, were, in general, like those of Ceres at Eleusis. The Persian mysteries of Mithra, which were very popular during part of the latter days of the Roman empire, were of the same sort. So were those of Bacchus, Juno, Jupiter, and various other heathen gods. All of them were celebrated with great solemnity and secrecy; all included much that was terrifying; and all of their secrets have been so faithfully kept that we have only guesses and general statements about the details of the performances. Their principal object seems to have been to secure the initiated against misfortunes, and to gain prosperity in the future. Some have imagined that very wonderful and glorious truths were revealed in the midst of these heathen humbugs. But I guess that the more we find out about them, the bigger humbugs they will appear, as happened to the travelers who held a post mortem on the great heathen god in the story. This was a certain very terrible and powerful divinity among some savage tribes, of whom dreadful stories were told—very authentic, of course! Some unbelieving scamps of travelers, by unlawful ways, managed to get into the innermost sacred place of the temple one night. They found the god to be done up in a very large and suspicious looking bundle. Having sacrilegiously cut the string, they unrolled one envelop of mats and cloths after another, until they had taken off more than a hundred wrappers. The god grew smaller, and smaller, and smaller; and the wonder of the travelers what he could be, larger and larger. At last, the very innermost of all the coverings fell off, and the great heathen god was revealed in all his native majesty. It was a cracked soda-water bottle! This indicates—what is beyond all question the fact—that the heathen mysteries had their foundation in gas. Indeed, the whole composition of these impositions was, gammon, deception, hypocrisy— Humbug! Truly, the science of Humbug is entitled to some consideration, simply for its antiquity, if for nothing else.

Chapter 47

*Heathen humbugs No. 2—Heathen stated
services—Oracles—Sibyls—Auguries.*

Something must be said about the Oracles, the Sibyls, and
the Auguries; which, besides the mysteries elsewhere spoken
of, were the chief assistant humbugs or side shows used for
keeping up the great humbug heathen religion.

One word about the regular worship of heathenism; what
maybe called their stated services. They had no weekly day
of worship, indeed no week, and no preaching such as ours
is; that is, no regular instruction by the ministers of religion,
intended for all the people. They had singing and praying
after their fashion; the singing being a sort of chant of praise
to whatever idol was under treatment at the time, and the
praying being in part vain repetitions of the name of their
god, and for the rest a request that the god would do or give
whatever was asked of him as a fair business transaction,
in return for the agreeable smell of the fine beef they had
just roasted under his nose, or for whatever else they had
given him; as, a sum of money, a pair of pantaloons (or
whatever they wore instead,) a handsome golden cup. This
made the temple a regular shop, where the priests traded
off promised benefits for real beef; coining blessings into

cash on the nail; a very thorough humbug. Such public religious ceremonies as the heathen had were mostly annual, sometimes monthly. There were also daily ones, which were, however, the daily business of the priests, and none of the business of the laymen. To return to the subject.

All the heathen oracles, old and new (for abundance of them are still agoing,) sibyls, auguries and all, show how universally and naturally, and humbly and helplessly too, poor human nature longs to see into the future, and longs for help and guidance from some power, higher than itself.

Thus considered, these shallow humbugs teach a useful lesson, for they constitute a strong proof of man's inborn natural recognition of some God, of some obligation to a higher power, of some disembodied existence; and so they show a natural human want of exactly what the Christian revelation supplies, and constitute a powerful evidence for Christianity.

All the heathen religions, I believe, had oracles of some kind. But the Greek and Latin ones tell the whole story. Of these there were over a hundred; more than twenty of Apollo, who was the god of soothsaying, divination, prophecy, and of the supernatural side of heathen humbug generally; thirty or forty collectively of Jupiter, Ceres, Mercury, Pluto, Juno, Ino (a very good name for a goddess that gave oracles, though she didn't know!), Faunus, Fortune, Mars, etc., and nearly as many of demigods, heroes, giants, etc., such as Amphiaraus, Amphilochus, Trophonius, Geryon, Ulysses, Calchas, Aesculapius, Hercules, Pasiphae, Phryxus, etc. The most celebrated and most patronized of them all was the great oracle of Apollo, at Delphi. The "little fee" appears to have been the only universal characteristic of the proceedings for obtaining an answer from the god. Whether you got your reply in words spoken by the rattling of an old pot, by observing an ox's appetite, throwing dice, or sleeping for a dream, your own proceedings were essentially the same. "Terms invariably net cash in advance or its equivalent." A fine ox or sheep sacrificed was cash; for after the god had had his smell (those ladies and gentlemen appear to have eaten as they say the Yankees talk—through their noses,) all the rest was put carefully away by the reverend clergy for dinner, and saved so much on the butcher's bill. If your credit was good, you might receive your oracle and afterward send in any little acknowledgment in the form of a golden goblet, or statue, or vase, or even of a remittance in specie. Such gifts accumulated in the oracle at Delphi and to an immense amount, and to the great emolument of Brennus, a matter of fact Gaulish commander, who, at his invasion of Greece, coolly carried off all the bullion, without any regard to the screeches of the Pythoness, and with no more scruples than any burglar.

The Delphian oracle worked through a woman, who, on certain days, went and sat on a three-legged stool over a hole in the ground in Apollo's temple. This hole sent out gas; which, instead of being used like that afforded by holes in the ground at Fredonia, N.Y., to illuminate the village, was much more shrewdly employed by the clerical gentlemen to shine up the knowledge-boxes of their customers, and introduce the glitter of gold into their own pockets. I merely throw out the hint to any speculating Fredonian who owns a hole in the ground. Well, the Pythia, as this female was termed, warmed up her understanding over this hole, as you have seen ladies do over the register of a hot-air furnace, and becoming excited, she presently began to be drunk or crazy, and in her fit she gabbled forth some words or noises. These the priests took down, and then told the customer that the noises meant so-and-so! When business was brisk they worked two Pythias, turn and turn about (or, as they say at sea, watch and watch), and kept a third all cocked and primed in case of accident, besides; for this gas sometimes gave the priestess (literally) fits, which killed her in a few days.

Other oracles gave answers in many various ways. The priest quietly wrote down whatever answer he chose; or inspected the insides of a slaughtered beast, and said that the bowels meant this and that. At Telmessus the inquirer peeped into a well, where he must see a picture in the water which was his answer; at any rate, if this wouldn't do he got none. This plan was evidently based on the idea that "truth is at the bottom of a well." At Dodona, they hung brass pots on the trees and translated the banging these made when the wind blew them together. At Pherae, you whispered your question in the ear of the image of Mercury, and then shutting your ears until you got out of the marketplace, the first remark you heard from anybody was the answer, and you might make the best of it. At Pluto's oracle at Charae, the priest took a dream, and in the morning told you what he chose. In the cave of Trophonius, after various terrifying performances, they pulled you through a hole the wrong way of the feathers, and then back again, and then stuck you upon a seat, and made you write down your own oracle, being what you had seen, which would, I imagine, usually be "the elephant."

And so-forth, and so on. Humbug ad libitum!

Like some of the more celebrated modern fortune-tellers,

the managers of the oracles were frequently shrewd fellows, and could often pick up the materials of a very smart and judicious answer from the appearance of the customer and his question. Very often the answer was sheer nonsense. It was, in fact, believed by many that as a rule you couldn't tell what the response meant until after it was fulfilled, when you were expected to see it. In many cases the answers were ingeniously arranged, so as to mean either a good or evil result, one of which was pretty likely.

Thus, one of the oracles answered a general who asked after the fate of his campaign as follows: (the ancients, remember, using no punctuation marks) "Thou shalt go thou shalt return never in war shalt thou perish." The point becomes visible when you first make a pause before "never," and then after it.

On a similar occasion, the Delphic oracle told Croesus that if he crossed the River Halys he would overthrow a great empire. This empire he chose to understand as that of Cyrus, whom he was going to fight. It came out the other way, and it was his own empire that was overthrown. The immense wisdom of the oracle, however, was tremendously respected in consequence!

Pyrrhus, of Epirus, on setting off against the Romans, received equal satisfaction, the Pythia telling him (in Latin) what amounted to this:

"I say that you Pyrrhus the Romans are able to conquer!"

Pyrrhus took it as he wished it, but found himself sadly thimble-rigged, the little joker being under the wrong cup. The Romans beat him, and most woefully too.

Trajan was advised to consult the oracle at Heliopolis, about his intended expedition against the Parthians. The custom was to send your query in a letter; so Trajan sent a blank note in an envelope. The god (very naturally) sent back a blank note in reply, which was thought wonderfully smart; and so the imperial dupe sent again, a square question:

"Shall I finish this war and get safe back to Rome?"

The Heliopolitan humbug replied by sending a piece of an old grapevine cut into pieces, which meant either: "You will cut them up," or "They will cut you up;" and Trajan, like the little boy at the peepshow who asked: "which is Lord Wellington and which is the Emperor Napoleon?" had paid his penny and might take his choice.

Sometimes the oracles were quite jocular. A man asked one of them how to get rich? The oracle said: "Own all there is between Sicyon and Corinth." Which places are some fifteen miles apart.

Another fellow asked how he should cure his gout? The oracle coolly said: "Drink nothing but cold water!"

The Delphic oracle, and some of the others, used for a long time to give their answers in verses. At last, however, irreverent critics of the period made so much fun of the peculiarly miserable style of this poetry, that the poor oracle gave it up and came down to plain prose. Every once in a while some energetic and cunning man, of skeptical character, insisted on having just such an answer as he wanted. It was well known that Philip of Macedon bought what responses he wished at Delphi. Anybody with plenty of money, who would quietly "see" the priests, could have such a response as he chose. Or, if he was a bullheaded, hard-fisted, fighting-man, of irreligious but energetic mind, the priests gave him what he wished, out of fear. When Themistocles wanted to encourage the Greeks against the Persians, he "fixed" Delphi by bribes. When Alexander the Great came to consult the same oracle, the Pythia was disinclined to perform. But Alexander rather roughly gave her to understand that she must, and she did. The Greek and Roman oracles finally all gave out not far from the time of Christ's coming, having gradually become more or less disreputable for many years.

All the heathen nations, as I have said, had their oracles too. The heathen Scandinavians had a famous one at Upsal. The Getae, in Scythia, had one. The Druids had them; so did the Mexican priests. The Egyptian and Syrian divinities had them; in short, oracles were quite as necessary as mysteries, and continue so in heathen religions. The only exception, I believe, is in Mohammedanism, whose votaries save themselves any trouble about the future by their thorough fatalism. They believe so fully and vividly that everything is immovably predestinated, being at the same time perfectly sure of heaven at last, that they quietly receive everything as it comes, and don't take the least trouble to find out how it is coming.

The Sibyls were women, supposed to be inspired by some divinity, who prophesied of the future. Some say there was but one; some two, three, four, or ten. All sorts of obscure stories are told about the time and place of their activity. There was the Persian or Chaldean, who is said to have foretold with many details the coming and career of Christ; the Lybian, the Delphic, the Cumaean, much honored by the Romans, and half a dozen more. Then there was Mantho, the daughter of Tiresias, who was sent from Thebes to Delphi in a bag, seven hundred and twenty years before the destruction of Troy. These ladies lived in caves, and among them are said to have composed the Sibylline books, which contained the mysteries of religion, were carefully kept out of sight at Rome, and finally came into the hands of the Emperor Constantine. They were burned, one story has it, about fifty years after his death. But there are some Sibylline books extant, which, however, are among the most transparent of humbugs, for they are full of all sorts of extracts and statements from the Old and New Testaments. I do not believe there ever were any Sibyls. If there were any, they were probably ill-natured and desperate oldmaids, who turned so sour-tempered that their friends had to drive them off to live by themselves, and who, under these circumstances, went to work and wrote books.

I must crowd in here a word or two about the Auguries and the Augurs. These gentlemen were a sort of Roman priests, who were accustomed to foretell future events, decide on coming good or bad fortune, whether it would do to go on with the elections, to begin any enterprise or not, etc., by means of various signs. These were thunder; the way any birds happened to fly; the way that the sacred chickens ate; the appearance of the entrails of beasts sacrificed, etc., etc. These augurs were, for a long time, much respected in Rome, but, at last, the more thoughtful people lost their belief in them, and they became so ridiculous that Cicero, who was himself one of them, said he could not see how one augur could look another in the face without laughing.

It is humiliating to reflect how long and how extensively such barefaced and monstrous humbugs as these have maintained unquestioned authority over almost the whole race of man. Nor has humanity, by any means, escaped from such debasing slavery now; for millions and millions of men still believe and practice forms and ceremonies even more absurd, if possible, than the Mysteries, Oracles, and Auguries.

Chapter 48

Modern heathen humbugs—Fetishism—Obi—Vaudoux—Indian powwows—Lamaism—Revolving prayers—Praying to death.

A scale of superstition and religious beliefs of today, arranged from the lowest to the highest, would show many curious coincidences with another scale, which should trace the history of superstitions and religious beliefs backward in time toward the origin of man. Thus, for instance, the heathen humbugs, whether revolting or ridiculous, which I am to speak of in this chapter, are in full blast today; and they furnish perfect specimens of the beliefs which prevailed among the heathen of four thousand and of eighteen hundred years ago; of the Chaldee and Canaanite superstitions, and equally of those of the Romans under Augustus Caesar.

The most dirty, vulgar, low, silly and absurd of all the superstitions in the world are, as is natural, those of the darkest minded of all the heathen, who have any superstition at all. For, as if for the humiliation of our proud human nature, there are really some human beings who seem to have too little intellect even to rise to the height of a superstition. Such are the Andaman Islanders, who crawl on all fours, wear nothing but a plaster of mud to keep the mosquitoes off, eat bugs, and grubs, and ants, and turn their children out to shift for themselves as soon as the little wretches can learn to crawl and eat bugs.

These lowest of superstitions are Fetishism and Obi, believed and practiced by negro tribes, and, remember this, even by their ignorant white mistresses in the West Indies and in the United States, today. Yes, I know where Southern refugee secessionist women are living in and about New York city at this moment, who really believe in the negro witchcraft called Obi, practiced by the slaves.

A Fetish is anything not a living being, worshiped because supposed to be inhabited by some god. In some parts of Africa the Fetishes are a sort of guardian divinity, and there is one for each district like a town constable; and sometimes one for each family. The Fetish is any stone picked up in the street—a tree, a chip, a rag. It may be some stone or wooden image—an old pot, a knife, a feather. Before this precious divinity the poor darkeys bow down and worship, and sometimes, sacrifice a sheep or a rooster. Each more important Fetish has a priest, and here is where the humbug comes in. This gentleman lives on the offerings made to the Fetish, and he "exploits" his god, as a Frenchman would say, with great profit.

Obi or Obeah, is the name of the witchcraft of the negro tribes; and the practitioner is termed an Obi-man or Obi-woman. They practice it at home in Africa, and carry it with them to continue it when they are made slaves in other lands. Obi is now practiced, as I have already hinted, in Cuba and in the Southern States, and is believed in by the more ignorant and foolish white people, as much as by their barbarous slaves. Obi is used only to injure, and the way to perform it upon your enemy is, to hire the Obi man or woman to concoct a charm, and then to hide this, or cause it to be hidden, in some place about the person or abode of the victim where he will find it. He is expected thereupon to fall ill, to wither and waste away, and so to die.

Absurd as it may seem, this cursing business operates with a good deal of certainty on the poor negroes, who fall sick instantly on finding the ball of Obi, two or three inches in diameter, hidden in their bed, or in the roof, or under the threshold, or in the earthen floor of their huts. The poor wretches become dejected, lose appetite, strength, and spirits, grow thin and ill, and really wither away and die. It is a curious fact, however, that if under these circumstances you can cause one of them to become converted to Christianity, or to become a Christian by profession, he becomes at once free from the witches' dominion and quickly recovers.

The ball of Obi—or, as it is called among the Brazilian negroes, Mandinga—may be made of various materials, always, I believe, including some which are disgusting or horrible. Leaves of trees and scraps of rag may be used; ashes, usually from bones or flesh of some kind; pieces of cats' bones and skulls, feathers, hair, earth, or clay, which ought to be from a grave; teeth of men and of snakes, alligators or other beasts; vegetable gum, or other sticky stuff; human blood, pieces of eggshell, etc., etc. This mixture is curiously like that in the witches' cauldron in Macbeth, which, among other equally toothsome matters, contained frogs' toes, bats' wool, lizards' legs, owlets' wings, wolfs' teeth, witches' mummy, Jew's liver, tigers' bowels, and lastly, as a sort of thickening to the gravy, baboon's blood.

A creole lady, now at the North, recently told a friend of mine that "the negroes can put some pieces of paper, or powder, or something or other in your shoes, that will make you sick, or make you do anything they want!" The poor foolish woman told this with a face full of awe and eyes wide open. Another lady known to me, long resident at the South, tells me that the belief in this sort of devilism is often found among the white people.

The practices called Vaudoux or Voudoux, are a sort of Obi; being, like that, an invoking of the aid of some god to do what the worshipers wish. The Vaudoux humbug is quite prevalent in Cuba, Haiti, and other West India islands, where there are wild negroes, or where they are still imported from Africa. There is also a good deal of this sort of humbug among the slaves in New Orleans, and cases arising from it have recently quite often appeared in the police reports in the newspapers of that city.

The Vaudoux worshipers assemble secretly, with a kind of chief witch or mistress of ceremonies; there is a boiling cauldron of hell-broth, à la Macbeth; the votaries dance naked around their soup; amulets and charms are made and distributed. During a quarter of a century last past, some hundreds of these orgies have been broken up by the New Orleans police, and probably as many more have come off as per program. The Vaudoux processes are most frequently appealed to for the purposes of some unsuccessful or jealous lover; and the Creole ladies believe in Vaudouxism as much as in Obi.

In the West Indies, the Vaudoux orgies are more savage than in this country. It is but a little while since in Haiti, under the energetic and sensible administration of President

Geffrard, eight Vaudoux worshipers were regularly tried and executed for having murdered a young girl, the niece of two of them, by way of human sacrifice to the god. They tied the poor child tight, put her in a box called a humfort, fed her with some kind of stuff for four days, and then deliberately strangled her, beheaded her, flayed her, cooked the head with yams, ate of the soup, and then performed a solemn dance and chant around an altar with the skull on it.

The Caffres in Southern Africa have a kind of humbug somewhat like the Obi-men, who are known as rainmakers. These gentlemen furnish what blessing and cursing may be required for other purposes; but as that country is liable to tremendous droughts, their best business is to make rain. This they do by various prayers and ceremonies, of which the most important part is, receiving a large fee in advance from the customer. The rainmaking business, though very lucrative, is not without its disadvantages; for whenever Moselekatse, or Dingaan, or any other chief sets his rain-maker at work, and the rain was not forthcoming as per application, the indignant ruler caused an assegai or two to be stuck through the wizard, for the encouragement of the other wizards. This was not so unreasonable as it may seem; for if the man could not make rain when it was wanted, what was he good for?

The ceremonies of the powwows or medicine-men of the North American Indians, are less brutal than the African ones. These soothsayers, like the Obi-men, prepared charms for their customers, usually, however, not so much to destroy others as to protect the wearer. These charms consist of some trifling matters tied up in a small bag, the "medicine-bag," which is to be worn round the neck, and will, it is supposed, insure the wearer the special help and protection of the Great Spirit. The powwows sometimes do a little in the cursing line.

There is a funny story of a Puritan minister in the early times of New England, who coolly defied one of the most famous Indian magicians to play off his infernal artillery. A formal meeting was had, and the powwow rattled his traps, howled, danced, blew feathers, and vociferated jargon until he was perfectly exhausted, the old minister quietly looking at him all the time. The savage humbug was dumb-founded, but quickly recovering his presence of mind, saved his home-reputation by explaining to the red gentlemen in breechcloths and nose-rings, that the Yankee ate so much salt that curses wouldn't take hold on him at all.

The Shamans (or Schamans) of Siberia, follow a very similar business, but are not so much priestly humbugs as mere conjurors. The Lamas, or Buddhist leaders of Central and Southern Asia are, however, regular priests, again, and may be said, with singular propriety, to "run their machine" on principles of thorough religious humbug, for they do really pray by a machine. They set up a little mill to go by water or wind, which turns a cylinder. On this cylinder is written a prayer, and every time the barrel goes round once, it counts, they say, for one prayer. It may be imagined how piety intensifies in a freshet, or in a heavy gale of wind! And there is a ludicrous notion of economy, as well as a pitiable folly in the conception of profiting by such windy supplications, and of saving all one's time and thoughts for business, while the prayers rattle out by the hundred at home. Only imagine the pious fervor of one of these priests in a first-class Lowell mill, of say a hundred thousand spindles. Print a large edition of some good prayer and paste a copy on each spindle, and the place would seem to him the very gate of a Buddhist heaven. He would feel sure of taking heaven by storm, with a sustained fire of one hundred thousand prayers every second. His first requisite for a prosperous church would be a good waterpower for prayer-mills. And yet, absurd as these prayer-mills of the heathen really are, it may not be safe to bring them under unqualified condemnation: for who among us has not sometimes heard windy prayers even in our Christian churches? Young clergymen are especially liable and, I might say, prone to this mockery. These, however, are but exceptions to the general Christian rule, viz.: that the Omniscient careth only for heart-service; and that, before Him, all mere lip-service or machine-service, is simply an abomination.

A less innocent kind of praying is one of the religious humbugs of the bloody and cruel Sandwich Islands form of heathenism. Here a practice prevailed, and does yet, of paying money to a priest to pray your enemy to death. For cash in advance, this bargain could always be made, and so groveling was the spiritual cowardice of these poor savages, that, like the negro victim of Obi, the man prayed at seldom failed to sicken as soon as he found out what was going on, and to waste away and die.

This bit of heathen humbug now in operation, from so many distant portions of the Earth, shows how radically similar is all heathenism. It shows, too, how mean, vulgar, filthy, and altogether vile, is such religion as man, unassisted, contrives for himself. It shows, again, how sadly great is the proportion of the human race still remaining in this brutal darkness. And, by contrast, it affords us great reason for thankfulness that we live in a land of better culture, and happier hopes and practices.

Chapter 49

*Ordeals—Duels—Wager of battle—Abraham
Thornton—Red hot iron—Boiling
water—Swimming—Swearing—Corsned—Pagan
ordeals.*

Ordeals belong to times and communities of rudeness, violence, materialism, ignorance, gross superstition and blind faith. The theory of ordeals is, that God will miraculously decide in the case of any accused person referred to Him. He will cause the accused to be victorious or defeated in a duel, will punish him on the spot for perjury, and if the innocent be exposed to certain physical dangers, will preserve him harmless.

The duel, for instance, used to be called the "ordeal by battle," and was simply the commitment of the decision of a cause to God. Duels were regularly prefaced by the solemn prayer "God show the right." Nowadays nobody believes that skill with a pistol is going to be specially bestowed by the Almighty, without diligent practice at a mark. Accordingly, the idea of a divine interposition has long ago dropped out of the question, and duelling is exclusively in the hands of the devil and his human votaries—is a purely brutal absurdity. But in England, so long was this bloody, superstitious humbug kept up, that any hardened scoundrel who was a good hand at his weapon might, down to the year 1819, absolutely have committed murder under the protection of English law. Two years before that date, a country "rough" named Abraham Thornton, murdered his sweetheart, Mary Ashford, but by deficiency of proof was acquitted on trial. There was however a moral conviction that Thornton had killed the girl, and her brother, a mere lad, caused an appeal to be entered according to the English statute, and Thornton was again arraigned before the King's Bench. In the meantime his counsel had looked up the obsolete proceedings about "assize of battle," and when Thornton was placed at the bar he threw down his glove upon the floor according to the ancient forms, and challenged his accuser to mortal combat. In reply, the appellant, Ashford, set forth facts so clearly showingThornton's guilt as to constitute (as he alleged,) cause for exemption from the combat, and for condemnation of the prisoner. The court, taken by surprise, spent five months in studying on the matter. At last it decided that the fighting man had the law of England on his side, admitted his demand, and further, found that the matters alleged for exemption from combat were not sufficient. On this, poor William Ashford, who was but a boy, declined the combat by reason of his youth, and the prisoner was discharged, and walked in triumph out of court, the innocent blood still unavenged upon his hands. The old fogies of Parliament were startled at finding themselves actually permitting the practice of barbarisms abolished by the Greek emperor, Michael Palaeologus, in 1259, and by the good King Louis IX of France in 1270; and two years afterwards, in 1819, the legal duel or "assize of battle" was by law abolished in

England. It had been legal there for five centuries and a half, having been introduced by statute in 1261.

Before that time, the ordeals by fire and by water were the regular legal ones in England. These were known even to the Anglo Saxon law, being mentioned in the code of Ina, AD, about 700. It appears that fire was thought the most aristocratic element, for the ordeal by fire was used for nobles, and that by water for vulgarians and serfs. The operations were as follows: When one was accused of a crime, murder for instance, he had his choice whether to be tried "by God and his country," or "by God." If he chose the former he went before a jury. If the latter, he underwent the ordeal. Nine red hot ploughshares were laid on the ground in a row. The accused was blindfolded, and sent to walk over them. If he burnt himself he was guilty; if not, not. Sometimes, instead of this, the accused carried a piece of red hot iron of from one to three pounds' weight in his hand for a certain distance.

The ordeal by water was, in one form at least, the same wise alternative in after years so often offered to witches. The accused was tied up in a heap, each arm to the other leg, and flung into water. If he floated he was guilty, and must be killed. If he sank and drowned, he was innocent—but killed. Trial was therefore synonymous with execution. The nature of such alternatives shows how important it was to have a character above suspicion! Another mode was, for the accused to plunge his bare arm into boiling water to the elbow. The arm was then instantly sealed up in bandages under charge of the clergy for three days. If it was then found perfectly well, the accused was acquitted; if not, he was found guilty.

Another ordeal was expurgation or compurgation. It was a simple business—as easy as swearing;" very much like a "custom house oath." It was only this: the accused made solemn oath that he was not guilty, and all the respectable men he could muster came and made their solemn oath that they believed so too. This is much like the jurisprudence of the Dutch justice of the peace in the old story, before whom two men swore that they saw the prisoner steal chickens. The thief however, getting a little time to collect testimony, brought in twelve men who swore that they did not see him take the chickens. "Balance of evidence overwhelmingly in favor of the prisoner," said the sapient justice (in Dutch I suppose,) and finding him innocent in a ratio of six to one, he discharged him at once.

This ordeal by oath was reserved for people of eminence, whose word went for something, and who had a good many thoroughgoing friends.

Another sort of ordeal was reserved for priests. It was called "corsned." The priest who took the ordeal by corsned received a bit of bread or a bit of cheese which was loaded heavily, by way of sauce, with curses upon whomsoever should eat it falsely. This he ate, together with the bread of the Lord's supper. Everybody knew that if he were guilty, the sacred mouthful would choke him to death on the spot. History records no instance of the choking of any priest in this ordeal, but there is a story that the Saxon Earl Godwin of Kent took the corsned to clear himself of a charge of murder, and (being a layman) was choked. I fully believe that Earl Godwin is dead, for he was born about the year 1000. But I have not the least idea that corsned killed him.

The priests had the management of ordeals, which, being

appeals to God, were reckoned religious ceremonies. They of course much preferred the swearing and eating and hot iron and water ordeals, which could be kept under the regulation of clerical good sense. Not so with the ordeal by battle. No priests could do anything with the wrath of two great mad ugly brutes, hot to kill each other, and crazy to risk having their own throats cut or skulls cleft rather than not have the chance. In consequence, the whole influence of the Romish church went against the ordeal by battle, and in favor of the others. Thus the former soon lost its religious element and became the mere duel; a base indulgence of a beast's passion for murder and revenge. The progress of enlightenment gradually pushed ordeals out of court. Mobs have however always tried the ordeal by water on witches.

Almost all the heathen ordeals have depended on fire, water, or something to eat or drink. Even in the Bible we find an ordeal prescribed to the Jews (*Numbers 5*) for an unfaithful wife, who is there directed to drink some water with certain ceremonies, which drink God promises shall cause a fatal disease if she be guilty, and if not, not. It is worth noticing that Moses says not a word about any "water of jealousy," or any other ordeal, for unfaithful husbands!

This drinking or eating ordeal prevails quite extensively even now. In Hindustan, theft is often enquired into by causing the suspected party to chew some dry rice or rice flour, which has some very strong curses stirred into it, corsned fashion. After chewing, the accused spits out his mouthful, and if it is either dry or bloody, he is guilty. It is easy to see how a rascal, if as credulous as rascals often are, would be so frightened that his mouth would be dry, and would thus betray his own peccadillo. Another Hindu mode was, to give a certain quantity of poison in butter, and if it did no harm, to acquit. Here, the man who mixes the dose is evidently the important person. In Madagascar they give some tangena water. Now tangena is a fruit of which a little vomits the patient, and a good deal poisons or kills him; a quality which sufficiently explains how they manage that ordeal.

Ordeals by fire and water are still practiced, with some variations, in Hindustan, China, Pegu, Siberia, Congo, Guinea, Senegambia and other pagan nations. Some of those still in use are odd enough. A Malabar one is to swim across a certain river, which is full of crocodiles. A Hindu one is, for the two parties to an accusation to stand out doors, each with one bare leg in a hole, he to win who can longest endure the bites they are sure to get. This would be a famous method in some of the New Jersey and New York and Connecticut seashore lowlands I know of. The mosquitoes would decide cases both civil and criminal, at a speed that would make a Judge of the Supreme Court as dizzy as a humming-top. Another Hindu plan was for the accused to hold his head under water while a man walked a certain distance. If the walker chose to be lazy about it, or the prisoner had diseased lungs, this would be a rather severe method. The Wanakas in Eastern Africa, draw a red hot needle through the culprit's lips—a most judicious place to get hold of an African!—and if the wound bleeds, he is guilty. In Siam, accuser and accused are put into a pen and a tiger is let loose on them. He whom the tiger kills is guilty. If he kills both, both are guilty; if neither, they try another mode.

Blackstone says that an ordeal might always be tried by attorney. I should think this would give the legal profession a very lively time whenever the courts were chiefly using tigers, poison, drowning, fire and red hot iron, but not so much so when a little swearing or eating was the only thing required.

This whole business of ordeals is a singular superstition, and the extent of its employment shows how ready the human race is to believe that God is constantly influencing even their ordinary private affairs. In other words, it is in principle like the doctrine of "special providence." Looked at as a superstition however—considered as a humbug—the history of ordeals show how corrupt becomes the nuisance of religious ways of deciding secular business, and how proper is our great American principle of the separation of state and church.

Chapter 50

Apollonius of Tyana.

The annals of ancient history are peculiarly rich in narratives of pretension and imposition, and either owing to the greater ignorance and credulity of mankind, or the superior skill of gifted but unscrupulous men in those days, present a few examples that even surpass the most remarkable products of the modern science of humbug.

One of their most surprising instances—in fact, perhaps, absolutely the leading impostor—was the sage or charlatan (for it is difficult to determine which) known as Apollonius Tyanaeus so called from Tyana, in Cappadocia, Asia Minor, his birthplace, where he first saw the light about four years earlier than Christ, and consequently more than eighteen and a half centuries ago. His arrival upon this planet was attended with some very amazing demonstrations. With his first cry, a flash of lightning darted from the heavens to the Earth and back again, dogs howled, cats mewed, roosters crowed, and flocks of swans, so say the olden chroniclers— probably geese, every one of them—clapped their wings in the adjacent meadows with a supernatural clatter. Ushered into the world with such surprising omens as these, young Apollonius could not fail to make a noise himself, ere long.

Sent by his doting father to Tarsus, in Cilicia, to be educated, he found the dissipations of the place too much for him, and soon removed to Aegae, a smaller city, at no great distance from the other. There he adopted the doctrines of Pythagoras, and subjected himself to the regular discipline of that curious system whose first process was a sort of juvenile gag-law, the pupils being required to keep perfectly silent for a period of five years, during which time it was forbidden to utter a single word. Even in those days, few female scholars preferred this practice, and the boys had it all to themselves, nor were they by any means numerous. After this probation was over, they were enjoined to speak and argue with moderation.

At Aegae there stood a temple dedicated to Aesculapius, who figured on Earth as a great physician and compounder of simples, and after death was made a god. The edifice was much larger and more splendid than the Brandreth House on Broadway, although we have no record of Aesculapius having bestowed upon the world any such benefaction as the universal pills. However, unlike our modern M.D.s, the latter was in the habit of reappearing after death, in this temple, and there holding forth to the faithful on various topics of domestic medicine. Apollonius was allowed to take up his residence in the establishment, and, no doubt, the priests initiated him into all their dodges to impose upon the people. Another tenet of the Pythagorean faith was a total abstinence from beans, an arrangement which would be objectionable in New England and in Nassau Street eating houses.

Apollonius however, who knew nothing of Yankees or Nassau Street, manfully completed his novitiate. Restored at length to the use of beans and of his talking apparatus, he set forth upon a lecturing tour through Pamphylia and Cilicia.

His themes were temperance, economy, and good behavior, and for the very novelty of the thing, crowds of disciples soon gathered about him. At the town of Aspenda he made a great hit, when he "pitched into" the corn merchants who had bought up all the grain during a period of scarcity, and sold it to the people at exorbitant prices. Of course, such things are not permitted in our day! Apollonius moved by the sufferings of women and children, took his stand in the market place, and with his stylus wrote in large characters upon a tablet the following advice to the speculators in grain:

"The Earth, the common mother of all, is just. But, ye being unjust, would make her a bountiful mother to yourselves alone. Leave off your dishonest traffic, or ye shall be no longer permitted to live."

The grain-merchants, upon beholding this appeal, relented, for there was conscience in those days; and, moreover, the populace had prepared torches, and proposed to fry a few of the offenders, like oysters in breadcrumbs. So they yielded at once, and great was the fame of the prophet. Thus elevated in his own opinion, Apollonius, still preaching virtue by the wayside, set out for Babylon, after visiting the cities of Antioch, Ephesus, etc., always attracting immense crowds. As he penetrated further toward the remote East, his troops of followers fell off, until he was left with only three companions, who went with him to the end. One of these was a certain Damis, who wrote a description of the journey, and, by the way, tells us that his master spoke all languages, even those of the animals. We have men in our own country who can talk "horse-talk" at the races, but probably none so perfectly as this great Tyanean. The author of *The Ruined Cities of Africa*, a recent publication, informs us that at Lamba, an African village, there is a leopard who can "speak." This would go to show that the "animals," are aspiring in a direction directly the opposite of the acquirements of Apollonius, and I shall secure that leopard, if possible, for exhibition in the Museum, and for a fair consideration send him to any public meeting where someone is needed who will come up to the scratch!

But, to resume. On his way to Babylon, Apollonius saw by the roadside a lioness and eight whelps, where they had been killed by a party of hunters, and argued from the omen that he should remain in that city just one year and eight months, which of course turned out to be exactly the case. The Babylonish monarch was so delighted with the eloquence and skill of the noted stranger, that he promised him any twelve gifts that he might choose to ask for, but Apollonius declined accepting anything but food and raiment. However, the King gave him camels and escort to assist his journey over the northern mountains of Hindustan, which he crossed, and entered the ancient city of Taxilia. On the way, he had a high time in the gorges of the hills with a horrible hobgoblin of the species called empusa by the Greeks. This demon terrified his companions half out of their wits, but Apollonius bravely assailed him with all sorts of hard words, and, to literally translate the old Greek narrative, "blackguarded" him so effectually that the poor devil fled with his tail between his legs. At Taxilia, Phraortes, the King, a lineal descendant of the famous Porus—and truly a porous personage, since he was renowned for drinking—gave the philosopher a grand reception, and introduced him to the chief of the Brahmins, whose temples he explored. These Hindu gentlemen opened the eyes of Apollonius wider than they had ever been before, and taught him a few things he had never dreamed of, but which served him admirably during his latter career. He returned to Europe by way of the Red Sea, passing through Ephesus, where he vehemently denounced the speculators in gold and other improper persons. As they did not heed him, he predicted the plague, and left for Smyrna. Sure enough, the pestilence broke out just after his departure, and the Ephesians telegraphed to Smyrna, by the only means in their power, for his immediate return; gold, in the meanwhile, falling at least ten percent. Apollonius reappeared in the twinkling of an eye, suddenly, in the very midst of the wailing crowd, on the market place. Pointing to a beggar, he directed the people to stone that particular unfortunate, and they obeyed so effectually, that the hapless creature was in a few moments completely buried under a huge heap of brickbats. The next morning, the philosopher commanded the throng to remove the pile of stones, and as they did so, a dog was discovered instead of the beggar. The dog sprang up, wagged his tail, and made away at "two-forty" and with him the pestilence departed. For this feat, the Ephesians called Apollonius a god, and reared a statue to his honor. The appellation of divinity he willingly accepted, declaring that it was only justice to good men. In these degenerate days, we have accorded the term to only one person, "the divine Fanny Ellsler!" That, too, was a tribute to superior understanding!

Our hero next visited Pergamus, the site of ancient Troy, where he shut himself up all night in the tomb of Achilles; and having raised the great departed, held conversation with him on a variety of military topics. Among other things, Achilles told him that the theory of his having been killed by a wound in the heel was all nonsense, as he had really died from being bitten by a puppy, in the back. If the reader does not believe me, let him consult the original MS. of Damis. The same accident has disabled several great generals in modern times.

Apollonius next made a tour through Greece, visiting Athens, Sparta, Olympia, and other cities, and exhorting the dissolute Greeks to mend their evil courses. The Spartans, particularly, came in for a severe lecture on the advantages of soap and water; and, it is said, that the first clean face ever seen in that republic was the result of the great Tyanean's teachings. At Athens, he cured a man possessed of a demon; the latter bouncing out of his victim, at length, with such fury and velocity as to dash down a neighboring marble statue.

The Isle of Crete was the next point on the journey, and an earthquake occurring at the time, Apollonius suddenly exclaimed in the streets:

"The Earth is bringing forth land."

Folks looked as he pointed toward the sea, and there beheld a new island in the direction of Therae.

He arrived at Rome, whither his fame had preceded him, just as the Emperor Nero had issued an edict against all who dealt in magic; and, although he knew that he was included in the denunciation, he boldly went to the forum, where he restored to life the dead body of a beautiful lady, and predicted an eclipse of the sun, which shortly occurred. Nero caused him to be arrested, loaded with chains, and flung into an underground dungeon. When his jailers next made their rounds, they found the chains broken and the cell empty, but heard the chanting of invisible angels. This story would not be believed by the head jailer at Sing Sing.

Prolonging his trip as far as Spain, Apollonius there got up a sedition against the authority of Nero, and thence crossed over into Africa. This was the darkest period of his history. From Africa, he proceeded to the South of Italy and the island of Sicily, still discoursing as he went. About this time, he heard of Nero's death, and returned to Egypt, where Vespasian was endeavoring to establish his authority. While in Egypt, he explored the supposed sources of the Nile, and learned all the lore of the Ethiopean necromancers, who could do anything, even to making a black man white; thus greatly excelling the skill of after ages.

Vespasian had immense faith in the Tyanean sage, and consulted him upon the most important matters of State. Titus, the successor of that monarch, manifested equal confidence, and regarded him absolutely as an oracle. Apollonius, who really seems to have been a most sensible politician, wrote the following brief but pithy note to Titus, when the latter modestly refused the crown of victory, after having destroyed Jerusalem.

"Apollonius to Titus, Emperor of Rome, sendeth greeting. Since you have refused to be applauded for bloodshed and victory in war, I send you the crown of moderation. You know to what kind of merit crowns are due."

Yet Apollonius was by no means an ultra peace man, for he strongly advocated the shaving and clothing of the Ethiopians, and their thorough chastisement when they refused to be combed and purified.

When Domitian grasped at the imperial sceptre, the great Tyanean sided with his rival, Nerva, and having for this offense been seized and cast into prison, suddenly vanished from sight and reappeared on the instant at Puteoli, one hundred and fifty miles away. The distinguished Mr. Jewett, of Colorado, is the only instance of similar rapidity of locomotion known to us in this country and time.

After taking breath at Puteoli, the sage resumed his travels and revisited Greece, Asia Minor, etc. At Ephesus he established his celebrated school, and then, once more returning to Crete, happened to give his old friends, the Cretans, great offense, and was shut up in the temple Dictymna to be devoured by famished dogs; but the next morning was found perfectly unharmed in the midst of the docile animals, who had already made considerable progress in the Pythagorean philosophy, and were gathered around the philosopher, seated on their hind legs, with open mouths and lolling tongues, intently listening to him while he lectured them in the canine tongue. So devoted had they become to their eloquent instructor, and so enraged were they at the interruption when the Cretans reopened the temple, that they rushed out upon the latter and made a breakfast of a few of the leading men.

This is one of the last of the remarkable incidents that we find recorded of the mighty Apollonius. How he came to his end is quite uncertain, but some veracious chroniclers declare that he simply dried up and blew away. Others aver that he lived to the good old age of ninety-seven, and then quietly gave up the ghost at Tyana, where a temple was dedicated to his memory.

However that may be, he was subsequently worshiped with divine honors, and so highly esteemed by the greatest men of after days, that even Aurelian refused to sack Tyana, out of respect to the philosopher's ashes.

Dion Cassius, the historian, records one of the most remarkable instances of his clairvoyance or second sight. He states that Apollonius, in the midst of a discourse at Ephesus, suddenly paused, and then in a different voice, exclaimed, to the astonishment of all:—Have courage, good Stephanus! Strike! strike! Kill the tyrant!" On that same day, the hated Domitian was assassinated at Rome by a man named Stephanus. The humdrum interpretation of this "miracle" is simply that Apollonius had a foreknowledge of the intended attempt upon the tyrant's life.

Long afterwards, Cagliostro claimed that he had been a fellow-traveler with Apollonius, and that his mysterious companion, the sage Athlotas, was the very same personage, who, consequently, at that time, must have reached the ripe age of some 1784 years—a lapse of time beyond the memory of even "the oldest inhabitant," in these parts, at least!

www.ingramcontent.com/pod-product-compliance
Lightning Source LLC
Chambersburg PA
CBHW060235100426
42742CB00011B/1539